DISCARD

SAVING THE PLACES WE LOVE

Praise for Ned Tillman's *The Chesapeake Watershed*

". . . takes you on a fascinating journey through nature and time, illustrating the importance of experiencing nature and the urgency of preserving it."
— Richard Louv, author of "Last Child in the Woods"

"These essays touched my soul. A must read for family, friends, and neighbors."
— Bernd Heinrich, author of "Mind of the Raven"

"I recommend this book to every Maryland citizen who is willing to work toward a healthier Chesapeake Bay and a more sustainable future for our children. This book provides valuable insight and background on the biggest environmental problems facing Maryland today."
— Governor Martin O'Malley

"An enlightening book. It speaks to the soul of anyone who cares about the Bay and our environment."
— Maryland Delegate Liz Bobo

"This book provides much needed context in our collective struggle to save the Chesapeake Bay. Ned Tillman's historical knowledge, broad perspective, and unwavering commitment give warning and provide hope."
— Ken Ulman, Howard County Executive

Saving the Places We Love

Paths to Environmental Stewardship

NED TILLMAN

BALTIMORE

THE CHESAPEAKE BOOK COMPANY

Library of Congress Cataloging-in-Publication data to come.

ISBN: 978-0-9823049--7-6

Manufactured in the United States of America on paper containing
30 percent post-consumer waste. The paper used in this publication
meets the minimum requirements of the American National Standard
for Information Sciences Permanence of Paper for Printed Library
Materials ANSI Z39.48-1984.

Cover designed by James F. Brisson, Williamsville, Vermont.

Contents DISCARD

PREFACE   IX
ACKNOWLEDGMENTS   xi

PROLOGUE: First Loss   1

CHAPTER 1: Mountains   7

CHAPTER 2: Lakes   31

CHAPTER 3: Meadows and Grasslands   49

CHAPTER 4: Beaches   61

CHAPTER 5: Islands   72

CHAPTER 6: Forests   86

CHAPTER 7: Rivers   112

CHAPTER 8: Backyards   134

CHAPTER 9: Farmlands   147

CHAPTER 10: Cities   162

CHAPTER 11: Alaska   174

CHAPTER 12: Oceans   189

CHAPTER 13: Planet   202

CHAPTER 14: Last Thoughts   233

A TRIBUTE TO STEWARDS OF THE PAST   238
REFERENCES   245
GLOSSARY   249

Highlighted Stories

The National Trail System 10

Encounters with Wildlife 14

Lilliputian Forests 16

The Full Cost of Coal 20

Challenges of Man-made Lakes 36

Finding the Source 42

Fishing Lures 46

Meadowland Master Plans 54

Santa Barbara Channel Blowout 64

Smith and Tangier—The Vanishing Islands 76

A Day on the Isle of Shoals 80

Movements Across America 92

Violence Comes to Vail 102

Bringing Back the American Chestnut 106

Leading Conservation Non-profit Organizations 108

What Happened to Elkridge Landing? 116

Why Plastic Bottles? 118

The Future of the Klamath River 128

Community Organizing 130

The Waterkeeper Alliance 132

The History of Backyards 138

Love Canal 140

Non-natives and Invasives 144

Portland Maine, CSA 158

The Role of Disaster Volunteers 164

The Value of Nature in Cities 170

The Alyeska Pipeline 182

Farmers' Market in Anchorage 184

What Fish Should I Eat? 196

A Species to Be Feared 208

Push-back on Global Climate Change 224

Illustrations

(following page 132)

Maps and Figures

Figure 1: Places discussed in this book

Figure 2: The health risk due to coal power plants

Figure 3: Residential Rain Garden Design

Figure 4: Ogallala Aquifer Depletion Risk.

Figure 5: National Woodland Owner Survey Map

Figure 6: Average Water Flows in the Major Rivers of the Contiguous U.S.

Figure 7: Map of Pacific Ocean gyres showing where trash accumulates

Figure 8: Toxic Liquid Spills from Pipelines

Figure 9: Gas Production from Conventional Fields

Figure 10: Projection of Power Sources in the Year 2050

Photographs

Mt. Katahdin, Maine

Algal blooms in Lake Erie

Dust storm engulfing homes in 1935

Dust storm in 2011

Crop circles in the Great Plains

Aerial view of the Prairie Pothole Region

Barrier islands

BP's Deepwater Horizon fire, 2010

Mount McKinley and Denali National Park, Alaska

How the West once looked

Wildflowers at Sparks Meadow, Oregon, 2005

Federally preserved northern Cascade mountains

Preface

MORE THAN ANY OTHER SOCIETY in the history of the world, Americans have preserved their special places for future generations to enjoy. We have also preserved land to conserve natural resources. Without these historic and ongoing efforts, we would be a far poorer nation and know much less about nature and about ourselves.

As our population grows, our "footprint" grows as well, and our favorite places deteriorate. This will continue unless we act now to protect the places we love—the lakes, the rivers, the beaches— the places we go to for respite, rejuvenation, and inspiration.

The challenge is not a new one. Over the past 150 years our ancestors have fought long and hard to preserve, conserve, and restore beautiful parts of the country. Sometimes they succeeded, and today millions of us get to visit the incredible places they preserved: Denali, Yosemite, Yellowstone, Glacier, the Adirondacks, the Everglades, and the Great Smoky Mountains. Unfortunately, even these natural wonders are once again threatened by expanding human activity that degrades our land, water, and atmosphere.

In addition to our parks, we watch as stunning regions of our country change before our eyes. As the result of continued population growth, insufficient efforts at conservation, and our lack of planning, we are now spending $100 billion annually *reacting* to the damage being done. These monies are being used to restore a few important spots as they hit a crisis point—contamination of the Great Lakes, drought in the Great Plains, forest fires in the West, nutrient runoff into the Chesapeake Bay, and hurricanes on the Gulf and Atlantic coasts. These are major disasters that must be repaired. But have we asked, what would it have cost to prevent them in the first place?

Have you ever wondered who is taking care of the lakes, woods, and rivers that are important to you and your community? What happens when those local ecosystems fail and you lose one of your favorite places? What could you be doing today to prevent that from happening tomorrow?

I realize that most of us do not have the time, the money, or the bandwidth to "save the planet," a concept far too abstract and daunting. But our homes and neighborhoods, and the places where we go on vacation, are real to us. We don't like to see them lose their magic, for they are important in our lives. You and your family may like to visit a favorite creek, a meadow, or a forest. You may have a special place as small as your backyard or as big as an ocean. As we get to know these marvelous spots, we want to protect them so we can keep coming back and eventually pass them on to our children. We develop a bond with them, a bond worth fighting for—and therein lies the key to saving special places, our country, our planet, and, finally, ourselves.

In this book I share the magic of my encounters with nature in places I love all across the country. I hope these stories will motivate you to go outside, explore, and fall in love with nature and the outdoors. These reflections are interwoven with stories of past and current efforts at preservation, ideas that may be of value to you. Knowing about Thoreau, Muir, Pinchot, Teddy Roosevelt, and others can help us get through those days when we grow frustrated and angry over the current state of things. It is easy to give up when our efforts don't work as quickly as we would like. But it takes time, and over time we will see that they do add up. There are things we can do, and we are making progress. I hope I can move you to action. I hope you will go out and find people who share your concerns, and together restore and preserve the places you have grown to love.

Ned Tillman
Columbia, Maryland
March 2014

Acknowledgments

I would like to thank Kathy Tillman, Tom Fulda, Tim Lattimer, Roy Meyers, John McCoy, Marsha Lemley, Rod Lemley, Elaine Pardoe, Dick Case, Pat Heidel, Arthur Trush, Susan Branting, Karl Branting, Kim Nagy, Mina Hilsenrath, and Roger Williams for their comments on the text and the organization of the manuscript.

I would like to thank the following experts for their technical and topical input; Dr. Nancy Rabalais, Executive Director of Louisiana Universities Marine Consortium, Dr. Bruce Bauman, Senior Scientific Advisor of the American Petroleum Institute, Kim Coble, Vice President of the Chesapeake Bay Foundation, Christina Mudd, Exeter Associates, Economic Analyst, Dr. Mark Southerland, Director of Ecological Sciences at VERSAR, Fred Tutman, Patuxent Riverkeeper, Dr. John C. Marlin, Prairie Research Institute, University of Illinois, Olivia Dorothy, Izaak Walton League, James McGarry, Chief Policy Analyst at Chesapeake Climate Action Network, Wendy Velman, Botanist with the Bureau of Land Management, Kate Wing, Marine Conservation at Moore Foundation, and Dan Buchner of the World Wildlife Fund.

Thanks to Ric Cottom of the Chesapeake Book Company for all his insights, suggestions, and efforts in turning my text into this book.

I would also like to acknowledge the efforts of American Rivers, the Audubon Society, the Environmental Defense Fund (EDF), the Izaak Walton League of America (IWLA), the Land Trust Alliance, the Natural Resource Defense Council (NRDC), the Nature Conservancy, the Sierra Club, the Union of Concerned Scientists (UCS), and the Waterkeepers.

First Loss

The man who is angered by nothing cares about nothing.
— Edward Abbey

Good Endeavor Farm, 1962 — I woke up to rumbling; the walls were shaking. I jumped up and peered through the old, wavy, single-pane glass windows and stared wide-eyed at the woods behind our house. Giant yellow and green mammoths were coming out of the woods eating tall trees in their path. I shook my head to clear my vision and grabbed my horn-rimmed glasses. The wild beasts morphed into yellow metal earth movers that pushed over anything and everything in their path. They churned their way through the trees into the field, *my* field, into my backyard. We were being invaded, and I ran around the house shouting that the enemy was coming.

They kept coming, more and more of these loud machines relentlessly treating beautiful oak and hickory trees as if they were worthless. They scraped away the topsoil that grew the crops that fed us and our livestock. Massive piles of downed trees, shrubs, and topsoil were pushed out of the way. All the life of the forest was left in windrows of trash, discarded as progress tore through our once peaceful farm.

Men in yellow hard hats followed behind the Caterpillars, setting fire to the piles of downed trees and reducing an important piece of my life, our woodlot, to ashes. Smoke from the fires and fumes from the massive diesel engines blew through the windows of our farmhouse. For weeks, the smoke scented our sheets, clothes, and lives with the terrible smell of destruction.

It was not a good year to be on the farm. Our family life was shrouded with a sense of helplessness. Our world was changing, and there was nothing we could do about it. Dad had tried to fight this particular path for Interstate 95 for several years. He had not known or even suspected that this might happen in 1951 when he bought the land. He had lost his battle of eminent domain with the government, and now we had to deal with a monumental intrusion into our lives. Our woods, our fields, and our pastoral view to the north and west were gone. A 40-acre chunk out of a 110-acre farm was a serious wound.

The rumble of the machines went on for weeks as they dug deeper and deeper down into the earth, and stopped only when they reached the steep banks of the historic Little Gunpowder River. I didn't know what to do. I felt violated, and my gut told me I had to fight back. It was the timeless anger of the disenfranchised. If my parents weren't going to do anything, I was. So I applied as many guerilla tactics as a twelve-year-old boy could invent to push back at them and slow their progress. I felt a deep need to do what I could.

I slalomed around their orange and white barrel barricades on my bike, kicking them over as I went and watching them roll down steep dirt embankments. That was my meager attempt at throwing down the gauntlet, my challenge to this great evil. Come out and fight "like a man" I yelled. One day I was careless during my pre-slaloming sur-veillance, and a policeman caught sight of me during my rampage and chased me down in his cruiser, complete with flashing lights. I took off across the construction site onto the main road and then took a quick detour down an old farm road, all to no avail. The cop apprehended me when the farm road ended at a farmhouse. I wasn't about to abandon my bike, so I stood straddling it as he reprimanded me, trying to scare me enough to discourage me from doing it again.

I might have been scared by this encounter with the law, but my anger did not subside. I considered my options. As long as I felt I was on the side of good versus evil, I was going to fight.

One day while crossing the newly constructed bridge across the Gunpowder River, I started unbolting the hand rails that lined the sides of the bridge. My dog, Bert, was running along the river below me. One of the workmen started throwing rocks at him for no good reason. Who was he to do that? He was the intruder, this had been my backyard. I immediately reacted. I threw my recently pocketed, unbolted handrail nuts back at him. He yelled and started after me. I took off for the woods. I felt him gaining on me, so I headed for the cliffs that I knew so well. I knew my way through these woods and soon lost the man, but I had made an enemy. Now he and the policeman were on the lookout for the local problem.

Late one afternoon I approached six very large Euclid and Caterpillar earthmovers the workmen had lined up, front to back, in a row before they'd left for the day. These were big vehicles, the biggest machines I'd ever seen, larger than the tractors I'd driven. They had six-foot-high tires, a foot taller than me. I climbed up on them to see how it felt to be in command of so much destructive force and discovered that the operators had left the keys in the ignition of an earthmover in the middle of the line. I turned the key, pushed a button, and heard this gurgling sound way down in the belly of the beast. It rumbled to life, shaking every bone in my body. I almost fell out of the seat. I played with the gears and somehow figured out how to engage them. Then I drove the thing into the one in front of me and backed it into the vehicle behind me. I had mastered the beast! But after a few more collisions, I turned the key to off, the engine rumble stopped, and I sat there wondering what I was really trying to do. Why was I so angry? I climbed down and slowly walked home.

One day I broke open a large box that I found on the construction site. It contained hundreds of sticks of dynamite. I sat there looking at the huge destructive power in that box. I had seen my father set off charges before and knew firsthand the explosive force of this many sticks. I realized that I had much more power at my fingertips than ever before. I could create a much higher level of violence than any of my previous escapades. With dynamite I could slow them down, and I could slow down the nation's progress toward having a vast interstate network of superhighways. But it also dawned upon me that my actions would only amount to a minor skirmish. There was no way to win the war. The road was going through no matter what I did. Eisenhower's military and commercial plan to tie the country together was going to happen. It was time for this warrior to retreat and learn other ways to fight to preserve the things that I loved. My uncontrolled anger may have finally dissipated, but an important seed had also been planted.

I often wonder about those feelings of anger that were so intense in the twelve-year-old me. It seemed so clear who the bad guys were—the government and its contractors. Or maybe it was the *special interests* who pursued growth at any cost and who probably controlled the government. Even Eisenhower had spoken out, warning the nation about the power of the military-industrial complex and its controlling hand on government. Either way I felt like a powerless victim, and as a result I reacted like a victim. That is why so many who are disenfranchised, who are left out of the process, react with anger and often in violent ways.

My father never acted that way. He talked about due process. He had diligently pursued the opportunity, going through the proper channels, to appeal the decision to locate the road on our property. He was certainly not pleased, but he got on with his life and his goal to be a good steward of the farm, albeit a smaller one, but a place he still loved. He created a vision of how he could fix the damage. He got on with his life.

Dad loved his farm, so soon as the work on I-95 was completed he focused on healing the wounds and working with what was left of our way of life. The first thing we did was start a reforestation effort along the sixty-foot-wide right-of-way adjacent to the highway. This was his attempt to block the sounds, the smells, and the sight of millions of cars and trucks that would eventually invade our country life. The state forester provided us with some of the twelve-inch saplings that we planted. Over the years my father, mother, sister, and I planted more than 30,000 trees. Although this process took time to be effective, many of those trees are now sixty feet tall. Dad spent the next forty years working on improving the topsoil of the farm by rotating crops and letting some fields go fallow. He also spent time improving the water quality, reducing runoff problems, and putting in native buffers around fields, hedgerows, and streams. What he inherited when he bought the land was a spent dirt farm. Through his affection for the farm, he became a dedicated steward of the land and improved it during his ownership.

I still have an emotional connection with that period in my life. There is something powerful about a childhood loss—it stays with you. Whether it is the loss of a place, an opportunity, or a family member, it becomes part of who you are. It shapes you. I went on to study science, build an environmental services business, and volunteer time to the preservation of historical, agricultural, and natural places in the community where I live.

With time I have also come to appreciate our interstate highway system. There are now 46,876 miles of roadway in the Dwight D. Eisenhower National System of Interstate Highways that began way back in 1956. I have driven on it many times and have been on I-95 from Maine to Florida. It allows me to visit my family and friends and those special places that I love much more often than if it did not exist.

I have also come to realize that as long as our population grows, we will have to learn how to live closer together. We will have to change our behaviors to accommodate one another. We will have to make room for transportation corridors. At the same time, it will be even more important to take steps to preserve farms and natural habitats along these busy corridors. Our best minds will have to figure out our options and keep refining the process so that we make the best decisions for the present and the future.

Unfortunately, we cannot preserve everything. Until we learn how to stabilize our population we will have to meet the needs of more and more people. We also have to realize that the environmental laws and regulations on the books today don't stop commerce; they are not designed to. They are intended to provide a path for commerce to proceed in a more orderly and sustainable way than in the past. This isn't easy. There are many unintended and costly consequences to continued growth and development.

Ironically, I was recently asked to speak to a meeting of the *Interstate*

95 Corridor Commission. They were meeting at the Belmont Conference Center in Elkridge, Maryland, and the conveners thought the members would like to know more about the natural history of their corridor. I was happy to speak, believing that the more they knew about the wonders of nature, the more they would want to protect it. Based on their level of interest and their questions, I think that is indeed the case. They are thoughtful and knowledgeable people trying to manage a complex system in a sustainable manner. I did not tell them about my youthful escapades as a terrorist.

I wonder how many other twelve-year-old boys or girls have experienced similar things. Dramatic events often plant the seeds of defiance and action. Fortunately our democratic system provides us the opportunity to respond to what we perceive as injustices without resorting to violence. Over the past fifty years Americans have done a great deal to respond to the unsustainable exploitation practices of the past. We have made progress, we have changed our society's relationship with nature, and we also have learned that we have a long way to go.

Congressman Elijah Cummings once told me, "Your pain becomes your passion which leads to finding your purpose in life." I do believe my childhood experiences have driven me to fight for a healthy balance between growth and preservation. I have found my purpose. I want to inspire others to go outside and enjoy all that nature has to offer, and then dedicate themselves to restoring and sustaining the places that they have come to love.

CHAPTER 1

Mountains

The mountains are calling and I must go.
— John Muir

Mount Katahdin, 1972 — Every mountain has its own microclimate, its own ecosystem, and its own challenges. I like to take the time to get to know a mountain's personality, history, geology, and wildlife. Every trip up a mountain is a new chapter in its story and in mine.

I am attracted to both the physical and mental challenges of summiting a mountain. Every step is a decision to keep pushing oneself forward or turning around. I have debated this simple decision with myself many, many times. With each step toward mastering a mountain, however, the rewards are significant. I gain new perspectives about myself as well as the world around me. I often go to the mountains to answer important questions in my life.

I recall the challenge of ascending Mount Katahdin (5,269 feet), the pinnacle of Maine's mountainous backbone (Figure 1). During the summer of 1972, I was living in the woods with Tom, Dale, and Sandy, fellow graduate students mapping the geology of Maine. Katahdin is the northern terminus of the 2,175-mile Appalachian Trail and lies adjacent to the Hundred-Mile Wilderness. Forty-one people have died on this mountain, but it is the biggest mountain in Maine so we felt compelled to climb it.

We made it up to the base camp the night before and went to sleep without even starting a fire. At dawn we climbed out of our bedrolls, pulled on our pants and shirts, and downed hot coffee and cereal. We were a scrubby looking group, for none of us had shaved that summer.

We were fit and had broken-in our hiking boots over the last month on slightly smaller mountains in Maine (Sugarloaf and the Bigelows), so we were ready for Katahdin. Off we went with small backpacks for food, water, maps, raincoats, and cameras. Tom, the recently discharged Vietnam vet, led the way.

Any attempt to reach Katahdin's summit requires a long, steep, climb through beautiful "second growth" forests. None of the famously tall white pines of the old growth forest are left of course. Those two-hundred-foot monsters that once filled these valleys fell to the axe in the seventeenth and eighteenth centuries in order to rebuild the King's navy and fuel our country's growth. Now, after the cessation of lumbering, the flanks of Katahdin are again layered with trees. The forest has been growing back ever since Governor Baxter preserved a large swath of land as a state park in 1930. These woods are beautiful to walk through. The main drawback to hiking in the Maine woods today is not the underbrush. It is the hordes of black flies, mosquitoes, and no-see-ums (biting midges) that constantly swirl around one's head during the spring and summer. We sprayed, slapped, cursed, and laughed our way through the woods as we climbed Katahdin on that late July morning.

After hours of hiking up the mountain and through the woods, we finally broke out of the dense forest and found the views to be stunning. The hazy greens and blues of New England seemed to stretch on forever. Canada lay to the northwest and the Atlantic Ocean to the southeast. We felt the view was our reward for our morning of hiking. A strong breeze chased away the insects and cooled our sweaty brows.

Although we were out of breath and our leg muscles ached, we decided to keep moving, not wanting to cramp up on top of a mountain. We carefully worked our way in single file across the infamous Knife Edge ridgeline leading to the peak. This was a treacherous trail at best. We had to place each foot carefully, hoping for solid rock. Pebbles dislodged by our boots cascaded a thousand feet down the talus slide. We had to balance ourselves on the edge between two very steep valleys.

The view on the upwind side of the Knife Edge was crystal clear, and we could see a long way down the cliff face and talus pile to the tree line below. On the downwind side of the ridgeline, the strong wind immediately condensed because of the lower pressure behind the ridge. Vapor formed before my eyes. A cloud began at the soles of my boots, blocking the view I knew from my topographic map to be as steep as on the other side. We were trekking above the clouds. It was almost as though I could reach out and touch a soft cottony mat that you could bounce on. But I knew better. I don't know which I feared more, the side where I could see my fate if I slipped, or the side where it was hidden from view. I moved cautiously, knowing that there was no other choice but to keep going straight, following Tom and Dale.

Every so often, I turned around to see if Sandy was still there, thinking our colleague from the Bronx might have the hardest time on this serrated ridgeline. He goaded me just to keep moving and take care of myself. Trash talk had kept us moving and our spirits high all morning. But now, every time I looked down the steep valley walls I was reminded that this hike was not just the boys out for fun. We were testing ourselves, our fears, and our fitness. Mountains have a way of bringing you face-to-face with your mortality. They often test you, physically and mentally. On this stretch, we kept our heads down, kept our comments to ourselves, and kept moving. We all reached the summit that day and then had the equally challenging hike back down the mountain. Going down a steep trail is much harder on the knees, especially tired knees. Fortunately, no one fell that afternoon while climbing Katahdin. We relished the experience while sitting around the campfire that night. It was just another step on our individual treks through life, and we all came out of this one safely and inspired to climb more peaks. We had met this challenge and began planning the next one.

Two weeks later I did fall off a mountain. While doing field work on Owls Head, just west of the Carrabassett River in Maine, I jumped up on a boulder at the top of a steep talus slide; it started to roll. Without solid footing, I had no control. I fell in front of the boulder. The boulder and I created an avalanche that slid, rolled, and crunched its way downhill. When the avalanche came to a stop, I was pinned under a large boulder,

The National Trail System

Can you imagine exploring a mountainous region without a good trail system? It would take far longer to find your way through the mountains or to find the tallest peak. You might even wander around lost for weeks trying to find your way in and out.

Fortunately, today there is a great system of trails throughout the country, and in many cases good Apps for finding your way. For the most part, they are well marked and maintained, largely by volunteers. For example, the 2,175-mile Appalachian Trail is maintained by 6,000 volunteers in small clubs all along the way (http://www.appalachiantrail.org/). This is true for many of the trails that crisscross our country. Thank you all for your efforts.

A great resource for getting a sense of the vast trail network of America is the National Trail System Map and Guide. In 1968, Congress passed the National Trail System Act, which established the Appalachian and Pacific Crest national scenic trails and supported the development of many more trails. The map and guide showing the national scenic trails and the national historic trails is available from the National Park Service (www.nps.gov/nts).

The map not only shows these two trails but also the Iditarod trail in Alaska, the Continental Divide trail through the Rocky Mountains, the Pony Express trail from Missouri to California, the Lewis and Clark trail, the Trail of Tears from the Smoky Mountains to the Ozarks, the North Country trail from Vermont to North Dakota, and others. A lifetime of opportunities is all laid out and waiting for you. Go for the exercise, go for the beauty, go for the history. Take a friend, but leave no trace behind.

unable to move. Fortunately, Dale was hiking with me that day and managed to dig me out of the talus and scree. Even though I was badly beaten-up, he managed to get me down off the mountain and to medical care. It was a good day to have a partner on hand. It was a good day to be alive.

That experience never dampened my enthusiasm for hiking in, around, and over mountains, but with time I've developed a greater appreciation for the risks and the unforgiving side of nature. I lost one teenaged friend to a mountain climbing incident and don't plan to join him. I go a little slower now, often with a partner, and increasingly enjoy aspects of hiking other than just summiting. There is so much to experience in the mountains if one takes the time and pays attention.

Going to the Mountains — Mountains intrigue me, just as they have many others, past and present. They seem to call to me. When a trip to the mountains is suggested, something instantly captures my imagination. I smile and am ready to grab my backpack and go off to explore a new vista. I'm never disappointed; it is time spent in a parallel universe to my everyday life. There is so much to see. Upon my return home from the mountains, I feel like a different man, a person with a broader view of my world, a view that helps me put my life back into order. It helps to look at the problems of the world from the perspective of a mountain.

What causes this transformation? Is it the physical challenge of summiting, the beauty of the views, or all the unexpected sights along the way? I really can't say. It is probably all of these and something to do with being away from man-made surroundings and schedules. I think I also treasure the experience of moving through and feeling at home in the mountains of America. I like cavorting with wilderness wherever I find it. I hope that I pass this love of the mountains on to my children and grandchildren.

For me, any mountain will do. Whether the trip is to the Rockies, Sierras, or the Smokies, or some other range that makes up the backbones of this country (Figure 1), I like experiencing them all. Each of the mountain ranges that I've climbed, rising above its surroundings, standing tall, distinct, and wonderful in its own unique way, has etched a vivid memory in my soul. This is apparently true for many of us, since many of the national and state parks that we've gone to great lengths and costs to preserve are mountainous areas. Great battles were fought in state legislatures and Congress by competing commercial, preservation, and conservation interests to preserve these mountains. We will discuss these battles more in the chapter on forests. But the bottom line is that our ancestors preserved a lot of mountains for the enjoyment of current and future generations. Thank you to John Muir, Bob Marshall, John Wesley Powell, and all the rest of our forebears who explored these dramatic areas and lobbied for their preservation.

The mountains across America vary greatly in size and shape, and size matters to many climbers. Coloradans talk about how many 14,000 foot peaks they've climbed (there are fifty-three "fourteeners"). I get a thrill from viewing the planet from a ridgeline 3,000 feet above the surrounding countryside as well as a view from 14,000 feet. In either case, there is something primeval in many of us that makes us want to test our skill and ability to "conquer" a mountain. One experiences a strong sense of satisfaction when standing atop a tall peak. It may only be for a moment, but the memory will last for a lifetime.

All summits in the East are less than 7,000 feet. Many eastern mountains consist of long, narrow ridges that run in straight lines northeast to southwest for hundreds of miles. When observed from the air, these dramatic ridgelines reveal the magnitude of a complexly folded geologic history and tell the story of an ancient and tumultuous collision between continents. In geologic terms the mountains are old and worn down. The Appalachians, which run from Maine to Georgia, are in fact hundreds of millions of years old. Back in the Paleozoic Age, the Appalachians rose from the seas to form one of the great mountain systems of the planet. They sutured the African and American continents together for two hundred million years. They've been steadily eroding from that time when they were much taller, rocky peaks. Today, largely cloaked with vegetation, they live a much quieter existence and are home to a wide array of wildlife. As a boy, my father took me hunting for the elusive ruffed grouse whose favorite habitat was in the heavily wooded mountains of western Maryland, central Pennsylvania, and southern New York. I don't remember shooting many grouse, but I sure enjoyed hiking the mountains and watching the dogs exploring the underbrush.

Mount Mitchell, the tallest point east of the Mississippi, lies hidden in the Black Mountains of North Carolina (it tops out at 6,684 feet). Mount Washington, the gem of the White Mountains of New Hampshire, is the tallest peak in New England (topping out at 6,288 feet). Although heavily wooded, many of these eastern mountains have lightning-blasted, rocky summits with great views. I hope someday you will visit them to enjoy the view, go on a hike, and take in a deep breath of mountain air. They are calling you.

In stark contrast to eastern mountains, many mountains in the more arid West are bare of vegetation and twice as high as their eastern counterparts. The highest peak in the contiguous U.S. (the lower forty-eight states) is Mount Whitney, rising 14,505 feet in the Sierra Nevada range of California. Some of these younger western mountains may still be rising, being shoved around by active subterranean forces even while their peaks have begun to crumble. Although there is quite a contrast between eastern and western mountains I find them all intriguing. Some people have a lifetime list of birds they have seen—I have a lifetime list of mountains that I've climbed.

The highest peak in all of North America is Mount McKinley (Denali) which rises 20,237 feet in the Alaska Range and has a year-round mantle of snow and ice. Ascending this peak is no afternoon jaunt but a very challenging and technical climb, and it requires a lot of preparation. The magnitude of the Alaska Range is such that it creates its own microclimate and its storms often send temperatures way below zero. The North American record for wind chill of -118 degrees Fahrenheit has been set here. Many have lost their lives on the way up and even more on the way back down.

For those climbers to whom size matters, there is a controversy about the tallest mountains. If you were to measure a mountain's height from its topographic base, top billing goes to Mauna Kea, which only rises 13,796 feet above the sea but extends 33,476 feet above the ocean floor from which the Hawaiian chain of relatively young volcanic is-

Encounters with Wildlife

After I'd climbed to the top of a ridge in the Appalachians, I sat down on a log to catch my breath and heard the rustling of leaves. I was too tired to do anything so I just sat there.

Into my peripheral vision bounced two, long, wiry weasels chasing each other in circles. Paying no heed to me, they bounded right up to the ridge top to the log where I was sitting. They did a figure eight through my legs and then were gone. To this day I don't know if they knew I was there. It was spring and they may have been too blissed out to care. Hormones can drive you crazy.

Animals are not always benign and playful. The closest encounter I've had with another predator was hiking back from a four-day wilderness survey. I had been alert for danger, being pretty far from civilization and assistance, and with no communication device, but now that the trip was wrapping up, I was intent on getting back before dark and was not paying attention. I was also tired and not very agile because I was carrying a seventy-pound pack of camping equipment and rock samples.

As I entered a large meadow, I headed toward a single shrub-pine shade tree, thinking it would be a good respite from the sun. When I was barely five feet from the tree, a very large cat (bigger than a dog) jumped up out of the shade and bounded right at me. I froze and he kept coming. I had no time to react and was too tired to move out of the way. He brushed my leg as he swept past and disappeared into the brush behind me. When my heart stopped racing, I realized that I had just seen a full-grown lynx, a short-tailed, long-legged wildcat that stands two feet tall and weighs up to thirty-five pounds. Seeing this beautiful, elusive animal at a very close range left an indelible image in my mind. I had touched a lynx, or I should say a lynx touched me. The mountains are alive with wonders.

lands grew. Measuring it this way actually makes this one-million-year-old volcano the tallest mountain on earth, with a base-to-peak height even greater than that of Mount Everest (29,035 feet) on the border between Nepal and Tibet.

Mountains are a good tonic for our souls, but they are threatened with a full range of challenges so we need to take action to preserve them. As global temperatures rise from climate change, we are seeing an increase in the frequency and intensity of forest fires, and new disease and insect infestations. Mountains also face other challenges, including overuse by humans and range animals, and the impacts from mining and drilling. These challenges are all about how to find the right balance between preservation, conservation, restoration, and utilization. We will discuss climate change and drilling in a later chapter. The rest of this chapter will focus on mountaintop mining and the burning of coal, issues that affect numerous mountains and the health of large numbers of Americans in fairly dramatic ways.

Redesigning Mountaintops — In the summer of 1986, I convinced my wife and our two elementary school-aged daughters to vacation in the central Appalachian Mountains. They all like to ride horses, so I billed it as a "riding vacation." We stayed in a very low-end, rustic cabin where you could see through the walls and feel the breezes. We shared it with a mouse family that stayed up late at night. It was an adventure, especially the outhouse with the swinging door. It had the best view of all—down the hillside and across the valley to the next mountaintop. Each day the four of us hiked or rode horseback across wide-open fields of tall grass. We had views for miles in all directions.

Partway through the first day, I found myself wondering how tall grasses came to be growing on the top of a mountain and why was this ridge so flat? I was also perplexed at the very steep piles of rock rubble on the valley walls. Dismounting from my horse, I grabbed a handful of "soil" and let it slowly filter through my fingers. It wasn't soil, just a chaotic mix of rocks and sand that had not had time to become organic-rich topsoil. That was unusual. Then it dawned on me. We were camping and

Lilliputian Forests

In addition to the raw physical aspects of mountains, a wide spectrum of life plays a role in the health of the forest. For instance, when I walk through forested mountains, even in late winter at a time when everything appears dormant, the multi-hued, pistachio-to-forest green mats of mosses stand out. It is their time to shine. They may be just as plentiful in the summer, but at that time of year they are lost in the crowd, outdone by taller forest flora. There are hundreds of different kinds of mosses (bog, broom, cord, and fern moss, etc.) that often form mats by intertwining with one another. The dense, velvety mats are soft to walk on, to touch, and to sleep on. Moisture and sunlight are all they need. When they don't have enough moisture, they close up shop, turn brown, and just wait till drops of rain reawaken them. Mosses are pretty basic, not having changed much over the past 350 million years.

Man has used mosses for eons. Bog moss, better known as peat or Sphagnum moss, has been used for bandaging and contains an antibacterial element that makes it even better for healing wounds than clean cotton. Historically, moss was used extensively by our ancestors for fuel, chinking of log cabins, and absorption in papooses. The *Iceman* who melted out of a 5,300-year-old glacier in the Alps in 1991 had well-insulated, moss-lined boots.

Despite their small size, mosses are critical to life in the mountains. In addition to their role in healing human wounds, mosses are the first to show up to heal wounds in the woods as well. Whether after a forest fire burn, a mudslide, mining, road or pipeline construction, or deeply scoured gullies and streams, mosses along with fungi will move in and start the process of restoration by breaking down the rocks and soil into the minerals needed for plants to take root. They are essential for getting the process of reclamation going on mined mountaintops all across the country.

riding on new land, a reclaimed mountaintop mine! This grassy meadow had been a coal mine at one time, and probably not so long ago.

Looking around I realized why we had such great views; it was because none of the ridges in this area were forested. In fact, with no decent topsoil they probably could not sustain a forest. It made me stop and try to get my bearings. I was confused by the feeling of thinking I was in the "wilderness" when as it turned out, I was on a man-made stage where nothing was natural. The mountaintops, the steep slopes of the hills, and the vegetation had all been redesigned by man. Neither the landscape nor the grasses were familiar. Where were the squirrels, weasels, mosses so common to a mature forest? I wondered how long it would take this mountaintop to re-establish a healthy soil profile and a balanced, dynamic ecosystem once again. Planting grasses is a start toward reclamation, but it will take thousands of years to get this mountaintop ecosystem back in balance.

I tried to picture what this mountain must have looked like prior to mining. Mountaintop mining removes up to 1,000 feet of rock to get at a coal seam that may only be a few feet thick. Where did all of the non-coal, cover rock go? It would have been very expensive to truck it away, so it must have all gone down into the valley, which is why the slopes were steep and treacherous. They were not slopes that I would venture to hike or hunt on. To learn more, I started asking around about the history of the area. The family from whom we rented the horses said they had lived there for several generations. They owned the mountain but evidently not the coal. Some ancestor must have sold off the mineral rights. The coal company came through and took away the top of the mountain to get the coal. When they left, they planted the grasses and gave back the land, the land with a much shorter mountain on top of it. So the family was trying to remake their lives, and, in an attempt to earn a living, renting out horses and cabins.

It turns out that this mountaintop is not unique; five hundred mountaintops have been stripped in West Virginia alone, and 22,000 miles of streams have been buried by the rock debris removed from these mines. Similar damage has been done in Kentucky, Ohio, Maryland, Tennessee, and Pennsylvania. It is difficult to grasp the vast scale of mining in America. I kept pondering this process of mountaintop mining and the "success" of the subsequent reclamation as we rode our horses across that newly created but foreign-looking landscape.

Eight million acres of land have been mined in the U.S., of which one million involved mountaintop removal in the Central Appalachians. More than a *billion tons of coal* is removed each year from U.S. mines, and as recently as when I was growing up, mining companies did not have to reclaim any of the land they mined. Congress tried to put a stop to the practice of stripping coal and leaving a wasteland when it enacted the Surface Mining Control and Reclamation Act in 1977. Since then, more than two million acres of coal mine lands have been reclaimed. That is a huge step in the right direction. With continued vigilance by all of us and effective regulation and enforcement by government agencies, I am hopeful that someday all of the mined areas will be reclaimed and on a path, even if it is a slow path, toward ecosystem restoration.

Impacts on Human Health — In addition to re-establishing a healthy ecosystem, proper reclamation should help reduce *acid mine drainage*. Acidic waters leak from 500,000 abandoned and inactive mines as well as thousands of operating mines across the country. A primary goal of reclamation is to bury the tailings so that air and water don't react with the rocks and produce sulfuric acid. If the tailings are left exposed, then the acid that forms leaches a host of chemicals out of the soil, contaminating as well as acidifying local waters. This is not just a problem for the fish downstream but also for people who live in downstream communities. There is a real public health problem today in areas of historic as well as active coal mining.

The U.S. Environmental Protection Agency (EPA) has singled out acid mine drainage as the number one water-quality problem in Appalachia. Acid mine drainage has degraded more than eight thousand miles of streams in the Appalachians and has left some aquatic habitats virtually lifeless. That's a pretty sad legacy from a hundred years of coal mining. Estimates place the remaining cleanup costs in Pennsylvania alone at around $5 billion.

Current coal industry practices do not just cause damage to mountaintops, adjacent river valley ecosystems, and downstream communities during mining. Coal also pollutes the air when used for generating electricity. Furthermore, if the solid and liquid waste products from combustion (fly ash) are not safely stored and managed, they can also damage our streams for many years into the future. You might remember a few years back in 2008 when the coal-fired power plant in Kingston, Tennessee, owned and operated by the Tennessee Valley Authority (TVA), had a major fly ash spill. It occurred when a retaining wall failed at an eighty-four-acre containment pond, and 1.1 billion gallons of coal fly ash slurry was released. The slurry cascaded downhill, swiftly burying three hundred acres and filling the Emory and Clinch rivers with fly ash. With time these coal wastes will wash downstream into the Tennessee and Mississippi rivers, and eventually into the Gulf of Mexico.

This spill occurred at 1 A.M., when everyone was at home and in bed. It was a hundred times larger than the volume of the Exxon Valdez crude oil spill in Alaska and was the largest fly ash release in U.S. history. Houses, roads, and rivers were destroyed in its wake. I remember seeing pictures of the devastation. How do local and downstream communities ever clean up from that scale of devastation? How do people ever put their lives back in order or sleep well at night after that middle-of-the-night catastrophe?

The firms operating coal mines and electrical generating stations claim to be following prescribed health and safety, operational, disposal, and reclamation plans. However, investigations of the 2008 disaster at TVA and the 2010 explosion at Massey Energy's Big Branch Mine, where twenty-eight miners were killed, revealed that *numerous flagrant safety violations* contributed to these disasters. The independent reports targeted poor management within those firms. They also found that state and federal oversight was not adequately funded or enforced in either case. Unfortunately, it appears that the coal industry often pressures government officials not to enforce regulations. Consequently, oversight

The Full Cost of Coal

The phrase "the Appalachian Effect" refers to the poor health of people living in those mountains. Over the past decade, Dr. Michael Hendryx and others at West Virginia University's School of Public Health have been studying the impact of mining on people living in coal mining communities in West Virginia. Hendryx and his colleagues (Ahern, et al., 2011) have found that poor health outcomes are concentrated in the mining counties, which see a greater number of incidents of heart, cardiovascular, respiratory, and kidney disease as well as cancer, hypertension, and asthma. The epidemiological evidence that people living in the coal mining areas are less healthy than people in areas with no mining is overwhelming. In addition to the heavy metals in the water, ultrafine sulfate and nitrate particles that get into the air are small enough to penetrate deep into lungs and even reach the bloodstream. Dr. Hendryx recommends that West Virginia eliminate mountaintop removal mining to improve the health of its residents. Taking into account the impact on health, coal mining costs the state more money than it generates.

Harvard Medical School's Center for Health and the Global Environment has put a price tag on coal's hidden costs (Paul R. Epstein, et al., 2011). Epstein's most conservative estimate of these uncounted costs to society (what economists call externalities) *would double the average cost of coal-fired electricity.* Most arise from well-documented public health problems like lung and heart disease. Epstein maintains that the true costs of coal are probably much higher. "Part of the epidemic of cancer can be attributable to some of these carcinogens that we're pouring into the groundwater from extracting fossil fuels. We see the accidents and the deaths of some of the miners. We see some of the impacts of mountaintop removal. We don't see the benzene and lead and mercury and arsenic—the whole slew of carcinogenic materials affecting household waters."

agencies often have a limited number of inspectors, many inadequately trained, to thoroughly inspect large, complex operations. Some of the players in the coal industry evidently don't think it is necessary to follow the rules.

In these two recent cases, coal industry business practices and underfunded government oversight systems failed to protect our citizens. The cases may not be unique. Coal may be cheap relative to other fuel sources directly because the coal industry is circumventing safety, environmental, and health practices. Their practices have endangered their employees, downstream and downwind communities, and our environment. If coal is to have a future, all stages of the coal extraction, burning, and waste disposal process will have to be managed in a much more sustainable manner, balancing economics with social and environmental health impacts. There should be no room for rogue companies in this industry.

Blue Ridge Mountains, Virginia — Hundreds of miles east of the coal-bearing strata of the Appalachian Mountains is one of the most visited scenic highways in the country. The 469-mile-long Blue Ridge National Parkway runs between Shenandoah National Park, Virginia, and Great Smoky Mountains National Park in North Carolina. This is a beautiful part of the country, and its preservation is a real tribute to the foresight of our ancestors and the sweat of the Civilian Conservation Corps. Driving along the parkway today, though, you will see many sick, dead, or dying trees. I find this deeply disturbing. When I was a boy in the fifties and sixties, these mountains were healthy and green, so the devastation has occurred on our watch, in our lifetime. How is it that they were being damaged while we all thought that we were cleaning up our environment?

As it turns out, the widespread forest damage is due to acid rain deposition and other types of air pollution from the combustion of fossil fuels. The average rainfall in North Carolina's mountains is now five-to-ten times more acidic than normal rain, and the clouds over the mountains can be a hundred times more acidic. Part of the problem is exhaust from cars and trucks. Does this mean that the park managers will have to close the parkway? That actually would not help much because most of the pollution comes from outside the park—from all of us across the nation who drive cars upwind from the park. However, the efforts taken to make all of our cars cleaner and more efficient are important steps in the recovery of this park and our other forested areas.

The other major contributors to acid rain in the Smokies and Blue Ridge mountains are coal-fired power plants in West Virginia, Ohio, Tennessee, Kentucky, Indiana, and the surrounding states. We have reduced the amount of acid rain over the years by requiring the reduction of sulfur pollution generated by power plants. That has helped, and there is less acid rain today than thirty years ago. But electricity-generating power plants all across the U.S. have been polluting our country with acid rain for decades. As a result the land, trees, rivers, and lakes continue to suffer from acid-enriched soils and water. The negative impact of an energy industry dependent on coal affects not only areas where the coal was mined and burned but also areas downwind all across the country. It will take eons to repair the damage.

In addition to the effects of acid rain, there are a range of health issues affecting our citizens who live downwind or downstream of coal-burning facilities. Respiratory problems are exacerbated by breathing particulates in the air that got there from burning coal. Then there is mercury pollution, one of the most widespread and toxic airborne waste products from burning coal. Most of the fish across America have accumulated mercury in their fat tissue. Humans who eat fish also have concentrated levels of mercury in their bodies. Mercury and the other airborne toxins released from coal plants result in a health cost to society and originate in the avoidance of costs by the coal companies. This is a part of why our health costs are so high, while coal is so cheap.

Figure 2 illustrates the extent of the health risks in counties across the U.S. due to coal power plants. The Clean Air Task Force created this figure showing the national mortality rates for existing coal-fired power plants. The colors show the annual deaths per 100,000 for each of the counties in the country. The darkest brown color reveals that more than fourteen people died per year per 100,000 population. The lightest color of brown indicates three or more deaths per 100,000. Go to their website to learn more about your county (www.catf.us).

How did we allow the coal industry to get away not paying for the safe disposal of its wastes? Well let's first realize that we are fortunate, in many ways, to have such vast supplies of energy resources in this country. Coal deposits are widespread in the U.S., and currently coal is mined in twenty-seven states. Because it has been an easily accessible and inexpensive source of fuel, it is a significant part of our economy with widespread political support. During the late nineteenth and twentieth centuries, the country's period of rapid industrialization, we were more focused on the growth of our economy than on the health of our citizens. We needed cheap energy to meet the needs of a growing country, so we mined and burned coal without concern about the impact on our health. Today with greater knowledge of the effect of pollution on our health and a greater appreciation that a healthy workforce is also important to the growth of our economy, we are re-evaluating the use of coal. With multiple energy alternatives, we have the opportunity to find a better balance between cheap fuel and the health of our citizens.

Because coal was so important to our growth for such a long time, it has been subsidized for many years. Federal tax dollars built the roads in mining areas that are reinforced to withstand the super-heavy trucks needed to transport the coal. We have developed a vast railroad and water transportation system to help move coal to where it can be used. We also subsidize the coal industry's waste disposal costs by allowing them to dump mine tailings into stream valleys and their combustion pollution into the air, our air, for free.

Only recently have we begun to understand and care about the downstream effects and societal costs of burning coal. Allowing coal plants to discharge their wastes into the air may have made sense to society at one time when there were only a few coal fired plants and far fewer people. But with 589 plants causing such widespread damage to health, we must rethink this strategy, especially now that we have viable alternative sources of energy. Health and environmental costs have to be reduced and internalized into the price of coal.

The coal industry does not want that to happen, of course. If they had to cover all of the costs by following better disposal practices, coal would become a more expensive form of energy and would lose market share. At the same time, cleaner energy requirements across the board could incentivize the coal industry to step up and develop and deploy *higher efficiency and lower emission* technologies for using their abundant resources in a safer manner.

The Future of Coal — Over and over again we arrive at the conclusion that coal mining, coal use, and the disposal of coal's waste products is severely damaging our citizens, our air, our water, our economy, and our environment. Where is the anger? Where is the mass mobilization of citizens to stop these practices, to close at least the worst polluting coal-fired plants? There actually is a lot of anger on the issue of coal, and the anger is on both sides. There is anger over the destruction the coal company operational practices have wrought. They have closed down towns, contaminated water supplies, polluted the air, and created a plague of chronic disease, driving many people to move away from their homes. There is also anger and fear on the part of those who work for the coal companies and who are afraid of losing their jobs.

Coal companies will fight to maintain their subsidies and challenge scientific and medical studies that point out their impacts on human health and the environment. We must keep the pressure on coal companies to focus their efforts on dramatically improving their operations and/or expanding into cleaner forms of energy. As it was for the tobacco companies, the writing is plainly on the wall. It is time for coal companies to reorient their efforts into more sustainable technologies or new business areas. There is a major concern in financial markets about deserting coal completely and leaving their assets stranded in a state of purgatory, but this too can be managed. If they want a future, it has to be one that doesn't damage the rest of us. What we don't want is to see them use their wealth to push our elected representatives into turning back the clock, weakening our environmental laws, and continuing their century-old practice of polluting our country.

Fortunately, over the past few years the licensing of new coal-fired plants has slowed dramatically and may even stop, owing to these concerns, the enforcement of regulations, and the rise of energy alternatives. The Clean Air Act is finally being used to require plants to scrub their exhaust gas better, so less contamination is released into the air. As a result, there will be several hundred closings of older, highly polluting coal-fired plants this decade. That will be a very important step toward reducing our emissions. But that may not be enough unless the industry figures out how to lower toxic and carbon emissions from their remaining plants and those being built overseas.

Ironically, even as we reduce our dependence on coal in the U.S., we allow coal companies to continue to mine and ship coal abroad. Again they are getting away without facing any liability for the health costs and global warming associated with coal combustion in other countries. U.S. coal companies can sell and ship coal overseas because we have such large reserves. This makes our coal, especially western U.S. coal, cheap on the world marketplace. Of course it is cheap because we have already invested in the road, rail, and barge infrastructure of getting it to market. But it still pollutes the atmosphere, changes our climate, and causes health problems. This makes no sense. We need some way to include all these costs into the price of coal. We need a tax on carbon to help drive the move to lower emissions technologies.

The global demand for coal is still rising due to the construction of low efficiency coal-fired plants in China and India. It will be interesting to see what China will do. They now suffer from extreme air pollution in many of their cities, and it is becoming a huge political issue for them to resolve. Many hotels offer their visitors face masks to wear whenever they go outside. Visitors often return from a trip to China with respiratory ailments. China will have to deal with the problem sooner rather than later. Their current plan is to cut carbon emissions by up to 45 percent per unit of GDP by 2020. How they will do it is not clear.

A lot more work must be done on the national and international levels. We have to develop an energy solution that will meet everyone's needs and protect the health of people everywhere. That realization is starting to reach an increasing number of organizations. The World Bank has recently decided to sharply restrict funding of new coal-fired plants in developing countries. Furthermore, the U.S. Export-Import Bank has recently declined funding for a huge coal plant in Vietnam for environmental reasons. A movement in this country is also discussing how to boycott investments in fossil fuel firms. The tide is turning.

The coal industry is responding to the pressure. They believe they have developed a technology and operational fix for capturing carbon emissions and storing them or using them below ground. There are at least two such carbon storage (sequestration) power plants under construction today, one in Canada's Saskatchewan Province, and the other in Mississippi's Kemper County. The carbon dioxide will either be stored in deep rock formations or used to enhance oil recovery. Storage of wanted and unwanted liquids and gases below ground is not a new thing. In addition to nature having done this for eons in oil and gas fields, the steel industry has pumped their pickling liquors into geologic formations for decades. Our 700 million barrel strategic petroleum reserve is also stored safely in deep salt caverns. (The Department of Energy last used these reserves following Hurricane Katrina's damage to our oil supply system on the Gulf Coast). Enhancing oil recovery by injecting CO_2 into the ground is also not a new technology.

Mississippi Power plans to gasify locally abundant lignite coal and capture 65 percent of the carbon dioxide produced, emitting carbon levels comparable to a similarly sized natural gas plant. They project that the process will result in fewer sulfur dioxide, particulate, and mercury emissions than traditional coal plants, and they plan to sell the carbon dioxide, sulfuric acid, and ammonia byproducts of the gasification process. There are many skeptics, so we will see if these newer technologies are effective and can replace the old, more polluting plants.

What Can We Do? — What is the best approach for moving away from our reliance on electricity from highly polluting, coal-fired power plants? No one likes regulations. If the coal industry accepted the responsibility for balancing human health and environmental liabilities with short- and long-term economic results, we would not need any rules. Because they do not accept this responsibility for their actions, the EPA has proposed a new rule to cap greenhouse gas emissions from all new coal-fired power plants and soon will propose a rule for older plants. This is a very big deal. EPA Administrator Gina McCarthy says that we have a "moral obligation to the next generation" to protect human health and the environment.

EPA is proposing standards to create a "path forward" to limit CO_2 emissions. Coal companies claim these rules will kill the industry. That is a fairly standard response from any industry facing regulation. In fact, most environmental changes of the past fifty years have only strengthened our country. This has been extensively documented in the Office of Management and Budget's "2013 Draft Report to Congress on the Benefits and Costs of Federal Regulations." According to this assessment, the benefits of environmental regulations have far outweighed the costs. Of course there will be lawsuits and battles over any new rules. It is part of the process and it is important for us to get the regulations right, so we can efficiently reduce the negative impacts of coal on our society. It will be an expensive, multi-year battle, but then again most major changes take time, and it takes time to ramp up alternative energy sources.

You can follow progress on this rule via EPA's website. To get the coal mining company perspective on the future of coal, go to the websites of Peabody Energy or Arch Coal, the two largest firms in the business, or to the National Mining Association or the American Coal Council websites. There are also numerous non-governmental organizations (NGOs) supporting EPA's changes and tighter regulation of the coal industry: 350.org, Natural Resources Defense Council (NRDC), Sierra Club, or Environmental Defense Fund (EDF) among others.

Support sustainability initiatives – In addition to watching and supporting these major policy and technology trends, there is much we can do in our everyday lives. The bottom line is that we must all do what it takes to ensure that the best sustainable practices are followed by industry, government, and, in fact, all of us. This will have to be done here in the U.S., and we should be requiring it on all goods and services that we obtain from overseas. When our largest corporations require manufacturers in developing countries to follow good sustainability practices, it lifts the quality of products and the quality of life around the world. If industry does not set adequate standards to better balance health, environmental, and economic concerns, the marketplace (consumers) or governments will have to step in. We should be demanding that all businesses and governments implement sustainability plans worldwide for moving toward a cleaner energy future.

Reduce emissions and subsidies – In keeping with the focus of this book, let's discuss what you can do as an individual to reduce your country's continued reliance on coal. On a national level, we should support EPA's efforts to enforce cleaner operations, not just for new power plants but at all the operating plants. We can also urge our representatives to rewrite the tax codes to limit subsidies to coal and other highly polluting sources of energy. There will be a tremendous amount of lobbying on both sides over the next few years. We will all have to support the efforts of the national non-profits as they work to support EPA's new rules. There will be disagreements between some of these NGOs since some of them support the possibility of Clean Coal technology in the future while others don't think any coal should be used since there are cleaner alternatives. But they all support EPA setting standards that will better regulate the coal industry.

It would be ideal if we could write national legislation to charge fossil fuel power plants for the full costs of their waste disposal. That would include the harm they are doing to our health and the health of our lakes, streams, and forests. On our now crowded planet, we must realize that it is cheaper for society to deal with pollution at the source (the generating facility) than to deal with the health and environmental impacts downstream.

Support alternative energy options – We can each have a positive impact on reducing the demand for coal when we purchase electricity, much of which is still generated from coal fired plants. Today in most parts of the country, we can choose to buy our electricity from wind and solar energy sources. By switching to non-coal suppliers for our electricity at home and at the office, we are supporting the development of alternative energy. Many people have been doing this for the past several years, and the increased market demand has caused a boom in wind and solar industries across the country. As a result, over the past decade America has become one of the world's top producers of wind and solar energy. We need to keep this growth in alternative energy production going.

I have been buying my electricity from an alternative supplier who supports the growth of wind power. This supplier has been reliable and at the same time a *less expensive* supplier of electricity. My electricity has been delivered via the same utility company that in the past has distributed electricity (derived from their coal, gas, and nuclear plants) to me. I still get the same bill from my utility distribution company. It is just broken down to *supplier* and *distributor* (the utility) charges. Because I don't want to support the building of any more coal-fired plants, I don't buy electricity from my old supplier. *It is as simple as that,* and it sends a clear message to the marketplace. If you are interested in moving away from fossil fuel–generated electricity, just call up your state's energy agency or utility. Ask them about options for buying wind or solar energy from alternative vendors. It is a rational step toward a healthier future that is easy to take.

Reduce demand – We can further reduce demand for electricity (from coal-fired plants) by reducing the energy used in our homes. You can insulate your attic, replace your windows and doors, turn off or unplug all electronic systems such as phone and computer charging devices when you're not using them, and upgrade to more energy-efficient appliances. Most people can reduce their utility bills by 30 to 40 percent, which is a big deal. By doing these things we are:

- lowering our energy use and our costs,
- getting a strong return on our investment in these upgrades
- improving the comfort of our homes,

- increasing the values of our homes, and
- sending a signal to the marketplace that energy conservation is important and effective.

Reducing our energy use and reducing our dependency on coal should be our primary goals as a nation. These are simple steps. If we all followed them, there would be less need to build more coal power plants and, as a result, less damage done to our world. We could even, once again, walk the mountains and see healthy forests far into the distance and not worry about the health of our kids. Mountains allow us to see the beauty of the world. They let us reach out and touch raw nature. When healthy they harbor vast ecosystems that are important to life on this planet. They are also good places to see the truth. They provide us with a remote vantage point from which we can assess our impacts on the health of America, to see how we are destroying or restoring our forests, waters, and our air.

The current view from the mountaintop is not good—we are pumping too much pollution into the air and into our water. It is time to clean up the negative impacts of coal mining and coal-fired electrical power. It is time to restore our country from the damage that burning coal has done in the past. It is time to take significant steps to reduce our dependence on coal. This is not a question of individual winners and losers. Everyone wins if we clean the air. Everyone wins if we lower our health costs. Everyone wins if we save our favorite places. Everyone loses if we don't. It is time for each of us to take action.

CHAPTER 2

Lakes

All waters of the United States should be swimmable and fishable.
— 1972 Clean Water Act

Long Lake, Rhode Island, 1984 — My daughter Anna, age five, and I went on ahead of the others, dressed in bathing suits and sun visors. We carried a three-by-eight-foot seine net and a bait bucket. She had bet her grandmother that we could bring home dinner. Not having a great track record in the past, we were scoffed at, so now we were determined to catch something. This challenge called for a special strategy, so we invited everyone to meet us at the lake in twenty minutes.

As the advance guard of the fishing party, we walked barefoot down the sandy lane, across the marsh, and onto a sandbar. The sand reached out like a finger pointing into the center of the lake. I wondered if this was some sort of cosmic sign telling us where to fish. Near one shore was a narrow trough of water between the sand bar and the bank. It was shallow enough for minnows to live in, hiding among the grasses, but not deep enough for the larger fish to prey on them. Anna and I stretched the brown seine net across the deeper end of the inlet, allowing the lead weights to pull the bottom edge of the finely woven mesh to the sandy bottom. Cork floats kept the top of the net floating at the lake's surface. We each took an end of the net, submerging one arm to pull the bottom of the net forward and the other arm to keep the top moving in sync with it.

Anna and I moved slowly, seeing nothing at first, but as we approached the shallow end of the inlet a few tiny fish began jumping as we corralled them with the net. As the trough of water petered out, we left the water, dragging the seine net behind us onto shore. It was full of grass and who knows what else. We laid it out on the sand and carefully searched the grass for minnows. They were the key to our strategy—we had to have minnows. We saw a few snails and then Anna found one minnow and then another—dozens of two-to-three-inch *small fry* flapping in the net. We collected them and moved them to the bait bucket, which we had filled with lake water. Now we were ready for the others.

Just as we were finishing our secret task, the rest of the family showed up armed with an array of old fishing rods. We had found these dusty antiques in the basement of the rental cottage, and most of them worked just fine—at least they seemed to fit the quality of our fishing party. Granny was decked out in her floppy white sun hat and blue beach coat, and the others were in various styles of swimwear and sun protection. Each selected a rod and then asked what was in our bucket. Anna just smiled. Our troupe walked out on the sand bar to be as close to the deeper water as possible. We were a motley crew of foragers, with little experience in these waters, but everyone was chattering excitedly about the prospect of catching fish. I rigged the lines with red and white bobbers for the younger kids and spinning lures for the adults. When we opened the bait bucket we got everyone's attention—it was roiling with mini-fish, so I set about putting a minnow on all the hooks and lures. Now, we were set. I took half the minnows that were left and pitched them out into the deep water.

What happened next was one of those marvels of nature. There was an instant feeding frenzy with the slapping of tails and the chomping of fish. Large, twelve-to-fourteen-inch white perch, unused to having so much lunch handed to them in their deep water habitat, hit anything and everything that moved. We each landed a sizable fish within seconds. Anna brought in the biggest perch, dragging it up onto the sandbar. When I tried to take it off the hook, I noticed that it had been so greedy it missed the hook and swallowed the large, red and white bobber instead. The bobber was so big the fish could not spit it out once it had gobbled it down. I had never seen such a thing before. I re-baited the lines, and we fished for a few more minutes to get enough fish for dinner. Everyone cheered Anna for winning the bet. From that point on she was respected as a serious fisherman, at least by her grandmother.

This is what our ponds and lakes were like once and could be again, teeming with fish. I've read accounts of fishermen landing dozens of fish back in the eighteenth and nineteenth centuries, but as most fishermen will tell you, it's not that easy today, even when inducing a feeding frenzy by chumming with minnows. We were fortunate. The excitement of having so many fish on our lines all at the same time is a great memory for everyone who was there on that very lucky day.

Many of us have places in our hearts closely connected to a lake or pond. Whether it is a special vacation place, a swimming hole, a romantic retreat, or a fishing spot, lakes have etched themselves into our collective memory through personal experience, folklore, family stories, and songs. My wife claims she can still hear the gentle lapping of small waves at a lake house she visited in New England as a child. I have an image of my daughter mastering a fly rod while standing on a pier at dusk. Just her silhouette stands out against the glassy surface of the lake in the fading light. These memories, like the lakes themselves, are beautiful and fragile. I hope that you have your own special memories of visiting a lake, and I hope the lake is still a safe and healthy place for you and your family to enjoy. Today, unfortunately, many lakes are not.

Lakes across America — Lakes come in all sizes and shapes. The lakes along the northern tier of our country are nearly all *glacial lakes*. They were scoured out of the land by a two-mile-thick icecap slowly grinding up earth and rocks as it slid southward. Flowing ice and rock debris, and raging sub-ice rivers, carved out the Great Lakes, the Finger Lakes, and thousands of smaller lakes from Maine to Alaska. South of the line marking the limit of glacier scouring (which runs through Pennsylvania, Ohio, Illinois, Wisconsin, Montana, and Washington), there are far fewer natural lakes. Our river systems have created *oxbow* lakes resulting from the constantly changing channels of meandering streams. In limestone (karst) areas, slightly acidic, migrating ground waters dissolve the lime out of the rocks, causing *sinkholes* to form. These can grow into lakes, sometimes swallowing homes in the process.

Mixed in among these natural lakes are thousands, actually millions, of lakes created by the damming of streams, rivers, and wetlands by beavers and humans. The lakes created by man-made dams are used for water supplies, power generation, shipping, recreation, and community development. Before our country ran on fossil fuels, we ran on the energy created by water and watermills. Thousands of our ancestors across the country with access to a river or stream built dams to power grist, textile, and paper mills, and forges. We have built nearly two million small dams in the U.S. and 75,000 large ones (six feet or higher). This historic endeavor of building dams and creating lakes is coming to an end with the growing realization that damming a river can cause major ecologic, social, and economic disruption. Straightening a river and building levees that prevent flood waters from naturally dissipating into flood plains can cause even bigger floods than the ones they are trying to stop. Yes, there are benefits to some dams, but often they produce greater problems to the land and the people living downstream. In some parts of the country, dams are being removed in an attempt to re-establish healthy rivers, improve flood control, and rebuild our fish stocks since many fish need to run up streams to spawn.

I've visited lakes all across the country and enjoyed recreating on the Tennessee Valley Authority (TVA) lakes and Lake Okeechobee in the South; Powell, Mead, Pyramid, Flathead, and the Great Salt lakes in the West; Moosehead, Champlain, Winnipesaukee, and the Finger lakes in the Northeast; and many other lakes in between. I know them mainly from my short stays fishing, canoeing, sailing, or swimming. Each has its own amazing story to tell. Each also faces its own challenge in dealing with the growing human population in its watershed and the demands of an expanding society. Each lake is changing, some slowly and some quickly, and not always for the better.

The Threat to Our Lakes — When only a few of us live on a lake, we have little impact. But with time and increasing population, our human presence is felt, and it almost always becomes a problem. The Great Lakes, which alone store 84 percent of North America's surface fresh water, served as the "free" disposal site for many of the industrial plants, farmlands, and cities throughout the Upper Midwest. The lakes "handled" our wastes for a long time, diluting their concentration and toxicity as the wastes mixed with the vast waters of the lake. But by the 1960s during the post-war population boom, the amount of waste got way out of balance, resulting in widespread pollution, toxic algae, and fish kills. We were forced to place a moratorium on fishing and the consumption of fish from these degraded fresh water resources.

Fishermen working the lakes were not happy when they lost their livelihoods. Some of their families had been living off the lakes for generations. Harvesting resources from *the commons* was a way of life that had always been available to them. They groused about the moratorium and blamed the government. How were they supposed to make a living? At the same time they were the first to realize that there was a problem. They just wanted a fix they could live with. In retrospect, they should have organized earlier and fought for common-sense regulation of the industries that were causing the pollution before it got so bad.

I remember fishing in 1975 with a friend, Mike, at the mouths of rivers that fed into Lake Ontario, the easternmost Great Lake. Mike was a Southerner, born and bred, and knew a lot about how to make ultra-lite spinning rods and how to catch and cook fish. He typically fed his young family with the fish he caught in other lakes, but after reading the warnings about pollution, Mike wanted nothing to do with the fish caught in Lake Ontario. He was quite incensed that the lakes had gotten that contaminated and was rightly concerned about feeding their fish to his small kids. He didn't want to take the risk of eating DDT, PCBs, lead, and other chemicals at any concentration. We decided that any fishing in the lake would be strictly "catch and release."

The fishing bans proved to be a wake-up call for many of us. The country had courageously passed the federal Clean Water Act in 1972 (CWA), and now we had to figure out how to implement it. Passing laws is never enough, it is merely the start of a decades-long process

Challenges of Man-made Lakes

Flood waters are full of sediment. When they slow as they enter a lake or approach a dam, sediment falls to the bottom, and eventually lakes fill up with it. This affects recreation, shipping, power generation, and flood control and requires very expensive fixes. The question today is, "Should they be fixed?"

Many dams in the U.S. have outlived their usefulness and could be removed. Others would have continuing value if their lakes were dredged routinely, but dredging and disposal of dredge spoils can be expensive as well (see www.istc.illinois.edu).

The Army Corps of Engineers has been re-engineering some of the biggest rivers (e.g., the Mississippi) into lakes or navigational pools to provide reliable pathways for barge and boat traffic. Unfortunately, in constructing this vast transportation system, they have also significantly disrupted the rivers' natural hydrology and natural flood protection features. They have straightened and channeled once meandering rivers, and that has resulted in more damaging floods.

Many of those man-made structures have reached the end of their engineering design-life. It is time to renovate the existing dams and levees, replace them with something better, or restore the natural conditions An independent assessment is required to determine the fate of aging dams and the need for new ones (see Olivia Dorothy's "Restoring America's River").

It won't be easy. As water availability, cheap transportation, and flood control become more essential to our growing society, pressure to build more dams will increase. Yet dams often cause far more problems than they are worth. We should be restoring the natural hydrology of our rivers. It's too bad that China and India have not learned from our mistakes. The Three Gorges Dam has flooded China's most fertile farmlands, destroyed the natural ecological and hydrologic systems, and will, in time, fill up with sediment.

of writing regulations, educating the public, and creating the ability to enforce the laws. Over the past forty-plus years since the CWA was written, the law has been the single most important factor in restoring our lakes. As a country, we have collectively spent billions cleaning up many of the nation's lakes and re-establishing businesses dependent on the health of the lakes. Of course, the money would not have been needed had we managed our wastes responsibly in the first place.

Lake Erie was one of the most polluted of the Great Lakes in the 1960s. Some referred to it as the "Dead Sea of America." Amendments to the CWA in 1987 initiated comprehensive watershed programs to clean up the Great Lakes and the Chesapeake Bay. As part of this program, a major effort was undertaken to stop dumping wastes into Lake Erie, and it became an environmental success story. The lake responded, toxicity levels dropped, and fishermen returned to their favorite activity—catching five million walleyes per year.

That level of effort was sufficient for several decades, but in the past few years Lake Erie has seen the *return* of blue-green algae, now sprawling nearly 120 miles, from Toledo to beyond Cleveland. The algae are producing lake-water concentrations of *microcystin*, a liver toxin, that are 1,200 times the limit set by the World Health Organization. It is tainting the drinking water for 2.8 million consumers. The algae contributes to an expanding dead zone on the lake bottom, reducing fish populations, fouling beaches, and again crippling a tourism industry that had rebounded. Tourism was generating more than $10 billion per year prior to the reversal of conditions in the lake.

So here we are *again*. How did we let it happen *on our watch*? Didn't we learn anything from the past fifty years? We should be angry that we can't come to an agreement and respond more quickly to these problems. Yes, the current problem has a different cause. However, it is all related to the runoff of chemicals (fertilizer this time) that we continue to dump on our land and the flushing of these chemicals down our river systems and into our lakes.

Much of the phosphorus that feeds the blue-green algae in the Great Lakes today comes from farmland. The current problem is the result of the intersection of two major trends. The first is that many agricultural operations have turned to herbicide-based, no-till farming methods. This has reduced siltation into the streams and preserves topsoil, which are worthy goals. As part of this process, farmers spread tens of pounds of fertilizer per acre each spring on their land. This fertilizer is often in the form of pellets that sit on top of the untilled ground until it rains. If it is a gentle rain, the fertilizer dissolves and moves into the soil, but in a heavy rain some of the fertilizer washes off the land and flows downstream. The second trend is the increase in the number of larger storms as one of the side effects from global warming. This increases the likelihood of fertilizer washing off the soil and entering the lake.

Of course, current farming practices are not the sole cause of problems in lakes, which also serve as the waste disposal option of choice for all of the camps, homes, and developments built around them. As more and more people move into a lake's watershed (the area around it that drains into the lake), an increasing volume of waste turns once pristine lakes into waters not fit for human consumption or recreation. In most cases deterioration occurs slowly. People begin getting sick. Sometimes, children die from hepatitis and other diseases. That leads to fishing and swimming bans and eventually to onsite and then to community-wide sewage treatment. Sixty-four percent of the lakes in this country are still not clean enough for fishing and swimming (see the EPA's *National Water Quality Inventory: Report to Congress*).

It is not just human waste that is the problem. In addition to rain, everything else that we spread on our lawns, gardens, and driveways, flows downhill into these once clean bodies of water. Pollution from power plants and automobiles eventually settles onto our lawns and runs into our lakes. The EPA, in conjunction with many states, has conducted a National Lakes Assessment, and the results are available online (visit the EPA Office of Water website). In short they have found a wide range of chemicals in the waters and in the fish in most American lakes. Some came from air deposition (mercury and acid rain) emitted by fossil-fuel power plants and waste incinerators. Others are due to runoff from farms and homes.

It may not be apparent to everyone, but today we spend a great deal of effort and money trying to restore the health of lakes all across the country. It has become a real challenge to find the right balance. Nature is forgiving and has bounced back from a great deal of abuse in the past, but in so many areas today we are exceeding her capacity to respond.

The cheapest and easiest way to restore the lakes is to adjust our individual behavior and reduce our impact by polluting less. Unfortunately, as our population grows, there will be more and more stress on the lakes. Each of us will have to continuously monitor our lake's water quality and our community's health. Good monitoring is the best way to determine our impact and adjust our actions on a timely basis. The equation is pretty clear: *more people = more impact = more regulation.* Lake Erie is only one of many lakes going through a renewed period of being out of balance with man's activities. How we handle these challenges to our lakes and how soon we can adjust will make all the difference to their future and ours.

Lake Elkhorn, Columbia, Maryland, 2013 — Land records reveal that my community grew up out of a pasture fifty years ago. The age of the trees around our man-made lake validate these records. The trees are all the same size. A pasture and a stream were transformed into a thirty-seven-acre lake surrounded by a forested buffer up to 150 feet wide. It is now surrounded by dozens of houses overlooking the water.

The watershed that feeds our small lake, though, is far bigger. It hosts a dozen streams and stormwater ponds that drain the backyards of thousands of homes in the area, and they all directly impact the health of the lake. Now, after more than forty years of development and suburban activity, the lake is struggling. It is under duress from the everyday behavior of all those people and the polluted stormwater runoff from their roofs, lawns, and the common areas. The community association (Columbia Association) recognizes what has happened to the lake and has engaged in a long-term plan to restore it. They are installing rain gardens and infiltration trenches, along with wider buffers along the streams and around the lake. The solutions are not easy, and they are expensive. There is a lot of debate on how to do it well. It will take decades but we have to start now.

Fortunately, our community was built with a public sewer system, so we do not dump sewage from the homes into the lake. But we do have thousands of dogs, cats, and wildlife in the neighborhood and many of us still fertilize our lawns. All those excess nutrients wash downhill and find their way into the lake, where they produce algae and thick accumulations of aquatic plants such as coontail, Eurasian millfoil, duckweed, water meal, and aquatic primrose. To clear the waters, the association invested in an aquatic weed-harvesting boat—a time-consuming, noisy, and expensive process. It would be far easier, cheaper, and more effective if our homeowners would reduce or stop the use of fertilizer and control the water that flows off their lots.

Rather than stopping the pollution at its source, we have chosen in the past to spend money cleaning up the downstream effects of stormwater runoff. The most expensive step we've had to take is dredging. After all the years of uncontrolled runoff, a great volume of silt and sand has eroded off our properties and ended up in the lake, turning part of it into a marsh. Although filling in with sediment is a normal part of a lake's natural succession into a marsh, it is not what the community wanted for recreation or scenic value. To fix the lake, a dredging firm was hired to restore more lake-like conditions. That is not easily done. A summer and fall with the drone and smoke of diesel engines and pumps working to *save our lake* has kept the water turbid and the birds and kayakers at a distance. But if we don't slow the runoff, we'll probably have to dredge again and again.

These problems are exacerbated by the stormwater management system used in our development and in most developments across America. All the houses were built with the idea of shedding water offsite as quickly as possible. That was the engineering solution used in this country for many years and continues to be used in many places today. It is a very short-sighted solution that has caused extensive harm to our infrastructure and will be extremely expensive to fix. The end result has been flash flooding and a great deal of soil erosion off our lots and into our local bodies of water. Rapid stormwater runoff due to so many impervious surfaces (e.g., roads, driveways, and roofs) also limits water infiltration that normally would recharge the groundwater table. As a consequence, our streams are badly eroded during storms and then dry out quickly after a rain. This results in deeply scoured, stagnant streams and silted-in lakes.

What Can We Do? — There are a number of things we can do to help restore our lakes and many of them are being done in different parts of the country. We have to stop and think how we can reduce *all* sources of contamination on a local, regional, national, and international level. The biggest step we can take as a country is to clean up our fossil fuel power plants that are now dumping so much waste into the air. This is a state, national, and international challenge so we need to pursue it on those levels. Other steps we can take on a local basis.

Waste disposal – The EPA's Toxic Release Inventory documented that more than four billion pounds of toxic chemicals are dumped annually into our waterways from outdated municipal sewage systems and large-scale agricultural operations. Our sewage treatment plants and farming operations will be further stressed by our increasing population. Many of our sewage treatment systems should be upgraded to *enhanced nutrient removal* systems that will further reduce the nitrogen, phosphorus, and other chemicals in our waste waters. Each of us can help by *not dumping chemicals, medicines, or grease down our sinks, toilets, and other drains* and educating our families, friends, and business colleagues not to do it as well. Chemicals should be disposed of safely at landfills, re-cycling centers, or at the locations where you bought them. Always ask suppliers of medicines and chemicals if they will take back any extras you may have, and ask how they will dispose of them.

CVS, America's leading retail pharmacy with more than 7,200 stores, has made a commitment to support safe medication disposal solutions. They claim to participate in local medication take-back events through-out the U.S. and the Drug Enforcement Administration's (DEA) annual National Prescription Drug Take-Back Day. They also provide mailing

Finding the Source

Today, following last night's big storm, I noticed that a creek bed had overflowed its banks, spreading a large amount of sand and trash across its floodplain, the bike path, and into the lake. This surprised me since the creek is not large and, in fact, is dry throughout much of the year. This flooding of its banks is a clear indication of a stressed watershed. Yet here at the head of a small creek, is also the perfect place to restore the natural hydrology. If we can't do it here, it will only be harder to manage storm waters as they accumulate strength and move downstream.

I decided to investigate so I walked upstream a hundred yards on the sandy floodplain. The sources of many healthy streams are often wetland environments. Not this one. This little valley contains a deeply carved-out streambed. The stream banks are ten feet apart and have four-foot-high, nearly vertical walls. I wondered what scoured this trench-like creek out of the floodplain.

As I walked upstream, the stream bed changed from sand to rock. The small creek has experienced enough flow over just a few decades (since our neighborhood was built) that it has carved its way down through the soil horizons into bedrock. As I walked the banks were steeper, and trees on both banks had been undercut by repeated rushes of large volumes of water. Tree trunks were strewn in all directions like giant pick-up sticks. I climbed through, over, and under the trees and a lot of debris before coming face-to-face with the heart of the problem.

I found myself at a dead end in a box canyon with ten-foot walls on three sides. Facing me at head level were three culverts, all dry. On further inspection I found that they drained the streets of the adjacent housing development. All the rain falling on rooftops, driveways, paved paths, decks, roads, and parking spaces is directed to these storm drains, which then dump it all right here in this little creek. It appears to be one of those cases of "out of sight/

out of mind." The development design got rid of one potential problem, standing water, but created other, even bigger problems in the process: cascading water, flash floods, erosion, siltation, and pollution of downstream water bodies.

Before retracing my steps, I looked up from the bottom of the stream bed and saw houses on both sides barely ten feet back from the current banks. The homeowners had already attempted to shore up the banks, but I think nature is going to win this one. Whoever designed this development did not appreciate the power of water. I would not buy either of those houses, for they are going to have serious problems in the not-too-distant future. This is a case of development that lacked an understanding of natural processes.

envelopes for sending your extra medicine back to a safe disposal site. That is all to the good, but I have found that many of their sales clerks do not know about it and therefore do not always dispense good advice.

The steps taken by CVS are very important, even if not well known, and they will help our society deal with the 200 million pounds of unwanted medications being improperly disposed of every year. Check out the latest options at DEA, CVS, or other websites. It's surprising how many of us throw our waste chemicals down the drains and back into the environment, thinking that sewage treatment plants or backyards can somehow miraculously deal with all of the thousands of man-made chemicals in existence.

Stormwater runoff – The problem is more than just what goes into sewage treatment systems. A large part of the problem is what washes off lawns and farms. Lakes are suffering from polluted runoff from all types of properties. To fix problem we will have to find ways to capture stormwater on our properties and allow it to filter into the ground. Then clean, filtered water would recharge groundwater tables, which keep our streams and lakes healthy. These challenges can and need to be addressed at the local level.

In many parts of the country runoff of nitrogen, phosphorous, and silt from farms makes up the biggest part of the problem because farms cover so much of the watershed. Lakes in the heavily farmed Great Plains are under much more duress from over nitrification from fertilizers than lakes in the Northeast, where there are far more forests. The good news is that in most areas farmers are taking steps to reduce their impacts. For example the U.S. Department of Agriculture (USDA) Conservation Reserve Enhancement Program (CREP) program has resulted in many more acres of buffers being planted around lakes, wetlands, and streams. In fact, the pollution from farms has been decreasing in areas that are implementing best management practices. Farmers can do more, so the story is not over, but the efforts of the agricultural sector have begun to be effective. In contrast, the pollution from suburban and urban sources has increased, due in part to the fact that the population in these areas is growing, but also because of the general lack of knowledge about how our everyday actions are causing such significant damage. Let's focus on some of those behaviors.

Many of us use far more fertilizer and pesticide than we need. I have heard that as much as half of what we apply ends up washing off our yards. We must be far more careful how and when we apply chemical fertilizers, if at all. In addition to the nutrients we add to our lawns, nitrogen also settles on our land from upwind power plants, car exhaust, and from natural causes. All those chemicals wash off our yards and flow into rivers and lakes—unless we design catchment areas on our property that encourage the water to filter into the ground.

Our biggest challenge is to find ways to encourage all landowners to step up and take responsibility for their stormwater runoff. This is very important for those of us who live on a lake but also for anyone whose runoff goes into a stream, which means all of us. In addition to rain gardens, buffers along streams and lakeshores are critical. The wider a tree and shrub buffer, the more runoff it will prevent from entering a body of water. The EPA promulgated Low Impact Development (LID) standards for new construction, which has helped to reduce the runoff from many recently built facilities.

Community action – Getting everyone involved is the challenge we face with Lake Elkhorn. Unless we take additional action, dredging will be needed again. Realizing this, our community came together and debated what to do. Some residents angrily complained about the cost of dredging; others complained that the community association and the county were not doing enough to save the lake. The irony, of course, is that the main problem is the management of stormwater as it flows off of each of our backyards.

After one of the meetings, several of us went for a walk around the neighborhood. Many of the homes had steep slopes and lawns. We noticed that many downspouts, that drained rooftop gutters, dumped that rainwater directly onto slopes or into streams. This channeling of water from a large roof or driveway directly into a narrow stream bed caused gullies to form and scoured sediment from the stream beds and banks. Most residents did not realize their landscaping was causing the problem, and some were not ready to accept the realization or the responsibility. It is the same challenge that Lake Erie and almost every other lake in America has—too many people lacking an understanding of their role in the problem. As a result too much water, sediment, and nutrient runs off into the lake. All of it can be fixed, but it will require everyone's commitment to individual action. We debated how to get that message out.

A conversation one day on the bridge across the lake resulted in the formation of a local watershed group called CLEER (Committee for Lake Elkhorn's Environmental Restoration). The group's concern was that all the focus and money were going into dredging, which was not fixing the real problem. They realized we needed money to reduce runoff from backyards, roofs, and parking lots.

CLEER lobbied for a watershed plan and for a watershed manager to lead the local efforts. Our homeowner association created a plan and hired a watershed manager who developed an extensive program to *slow the flow*. The association widened the tree and shrub buffer around the lake and streams feeding into it. It repaired the eroded banks and started to advocate for more permeable surfaces on driveways and park-

Fishing Lures

Everything we put into the air, on our lawns, or leave in our backyards may end up in a lake, a river, or the ocean. I regularly see clothes and soccer balls, sometimes hubcaps and bikes, on the banks or floating in the lake. Each spring I also notice hundreds of fishing lures caught in the branches around the lake and just picture them falling into the water as well. No one seems to care. But then again, life has its surprises. One day I came upon a man down by the water's edge. At first glance I took him for a fisherman. Then I saw he carried an aluminum extension pole with a small wire cage at its end.

I approached and asked him what he was after and he replied, "Fishing lures." I was pleased that someone was harvesting them. I've often wondered what happened to the hundreds of hooks and lures caught in trees, on stumps, and on submerged aquatic vegetation that filled the lake. I'm concerned that the hooks might snag birds, dogs, wild animals, or kids.

The man looked like he was in his sixties, give or take a decade. The palms of his hands were silvery gray from handling the slowly oxidizing aluminum pole. His weather-beaten face recorded a lifetime of outdoor work. I asked him what he did with the lures that he collected. He said that he kept them in tackle boxes. He had collected 12,420 lures. He also said that he had to repair many of them because the hooks were rusted. It doesn't take long for a lure to rust. I was "hooked" by his story and asked how long he had been collecting lures. He told me that he started in 1996 and had eighty-three locations he visited, many along the tidal stretches of the Potomac. His most valuable resource is the tide chart in the paper because he would walk along the banks an hour or two before and after low tide. His goal is to get to 15,000 lures, but he wasn't sure about stopping since he enjoyed it so much.

I thanked him for his work. He just nodded. It was heart-warming to meet a man with an unusual passion. His avocation is helping the wildlife—and all of us—by removing dangerous hooks from the environment. He is also fixing up lures that had been "thrown away" but now will be reused someday by his sons or by someone who may never know his story. You seldom know where help is coming from, but everyone's effort counts. We are all in this together, and each of us can play a role in repairing our world. We just have to find our niche.

ing lots. They made a great start. It will help slow the water and allow it to filter into the ground as opposed to running directly into the lake. One neighbor objected to losing some of his water view and cut down the buffer in front of his home. I hope as he learns more about the challenge of maintaining a lake, he will do his part to protect the buffer in the future.

The association also provides pet-waste disposal bags to reduce the volume of waste nutrient that flows into the water. Most people seem to follow the practice. Of course, geese contribute to this problem as well, so the association hired a man with a specially trained dog to chase unwanted, non-migratory geese away in the summer. That worked too. They put up signs encouraging people not to feed the geese or ducks, and began to repair stream banks and install rain gardens. We are seeing progress, but we have a long way to go. It helps to have a watershed committee and a home owner's association that is big enough to get things done.

Yet the bulk of the efforts will have to be made by individuals. It will be the responsibility of residents to take action on their own land. The challenge is how to get everyone involved. We have to take all the anger expressed at the town hall meeting and channel it into individual and collective action to fix the problem at its source—our backyards. This is being done with a series of talks, neighborhood walks, and the engagement of businesses, non-profits, and religious groups. In some areas there may be some financial incentives as well. The goal is to encourage each homeowner to build his own rain garden to capture the water flowing off impervious surfaces (see Figure 3). Further information about rain garden designs can be found on EPA and Master Gardener websites.

In addition to what we can do on our own properties, there is also a need to create a *stormwater utility to collect fees* that will fund managing the stormwater that falls on highways, schools, and other public areas. Fees are never welcomed, especially when people have gotten away without having to pay for stormwater management in the past. The problem we face is a direct result of increasing the density of developments and the increased area of impervious surfaces in our watershed over the past fifty years. I understand why folks are angry, but it's time to step up and fix the problem of our backyards. It took a lot of political leadership to pass our local stormwater utility fee. Fortunately, most people understand there is a need to fix the problem and clean up our waterways. The real debate today is how we do this in a fair and effective way. We just have to remember that when storm waters flow off our properties carrying our fertilizer and all of our trash downstream *we are the polluters*. We, the polluters, therefore have to manage our polluted stormwater better by capturing the rain that falls on our land and allowing it to filter into the ground.

If lakes are important to you and your family, it might be worth your time to understand your impact on the environment and what can be done to restore and preserve the lakes that you visit or the ones near your home. They all have unique challenges and they all are at risk as our society continues to grow. It will take all of us to ensure that they are healthy resources that play a positive role in our future.

CHAPTER 3

Meadows and Grasslands

We abuse land because we regard it as a commodity belonging to us. When we see land as a community to which we belong, we may begin to use it with love and respect. — Aldo Leopold

Good Endeavor Farm, 1959 — As a kid there are times when one just needs to escape. Escape from oversight, from chores, from siblings. Out behind the farmhouse where I grew up, there were always fallow fields, places we could run through, chasing butterflies, grasshoppers, and meadowlarks. Wildflowers bloomed throughout the spring, summer, and fall, bringing a host of colors to a late afternoon walk, and a sense of lazy abundance. Mother Nature showing off what she could do, if only we left her unattended. Meadows offer us a beautiful and vast cornucopia of life.

Often when I wanted to be alone on a sunny afternoon, I'd run through the meadows then collapse on the plant-cushioned ground. I'd lie there knowing I was safe, completely hidden in the tall grasses. I would lie still, slowly catching my breath, waiting for the dogs to find me or the dinner bell to ring. I would stare up at the blue sky and look for familiar shapes in the passing clouds. Planes were rare back then, so my attention was drawn to the less predictable flight of butterflies, grasshoppers, crickets, and bees all moving at their own pace. Invariably, I'd break off a stem of orchard grass and chew on one end, tasting the sourness of green grass. Then I'd roll over onto my belly and examine the clover thatch and all the plants and critters in the warm, moist, soil-supported jungle beneath me. The meadow was my refuge and my laboratory all mixed together in one place.

Where are the meadows today for our children to run through? Where do kids go to ponder, explore, and relax? As important as they've been in the past, meadowlands have become one of the most endangered habitats in my overbuilt neck of the woods. Very little land is left fallow here in suburbia. We have plans for protecting our forests, and we require reforestation when trees are cut down. We have plans for the preservation and construction of wetlands. We have plans for riparian buffers along streams. If there is open land it is farmed or planted in trees. But we have no plans for saving meadows. If land is available for sale, it is developed. No wonder some of the meadowland species of my youth—northern bobwhite and meadowlarks— are gone.

Dick Smith, our local expert on butterflies is also concerned. "We have definitely lost the regal fritillary over almost all of the eastern U.S. due to the loss of major expanses of prairie-like grassland. We have also seen declines in other butterflies such as the meadow fritillary and the Delaware skipper in the Piedmont because of losses of large grassland areas. More natural meadows and grasslands would certainly improve the status of almost all butterfly species." Most dramatically, Monarch butterfly numbers have drastically fallen throughout much of the country from the lack of meadows and the use of herbicides. This has caused a loss of milkweed plants, their primary host. This past year, I didn't see a single Monarch in our neighborhood.

What's more, local ornithological societies are very much concerned about the declining status of ground-nesting birds. Just a few decades ago one could hear quail and pheasant calling to their mates. As a kid, I routinely engaged a quail in conversation on my long walks through meadows on my way home from school. I haven't seen or even heard one here in years. I also wonder about the meadowlarks. Where have they gone? I was in Maine recently and saw a number of fallow fields and watched bob-o-links fly about. I wanted to run and join them, their flight like a child playing, a beautiful sight but a foreign one to me now. The Maryland Breeding Bird Survey, similar to other states' surveys, clearly documents large declines in all field nesting birds with the exception of bluebirds, which have adapted to lawns and bird boxes.

We are a poorer society for the lack of meadows. We must find ways to bring them back, to make room for them in our lives and in our neighborhoods.

Meadow Management — The closest habitat to meadowland in the Piedmont where I live are utility right-of-ways (ROWs). Sure we have to listen to the static of the high-tension power lines on humid days, but at least we get to observe bluebirds, indigo buntings, and foxes playing in the brush. Of course hawks patrol these parts too; it's open season on their prey when trees don't get in their way.

On the right-of-way near us are multiple red fox dens adjacent to the woods. I check them out in the spring when the kits are young. I can smell the dens that are inhabited as I approach them, for they have a strong odor. Last spring we had a batch of five kits out frolicking in the sun one day. I stopped a mere fifty feet from their den and watched four of them rough-housing and wrestling in their backyard, taking turns being the aggressor and rolling one another around. At the same time, a solitary kit was out a different exit to the den in the front yard, just slowly wandering about and sniffing the weeds, doing his or her own thing. I stood there and watched for ten minutes with no sign that they knew I was near. But the next day the foxes were gone; they had moved out and gone off to another den, probably one farther from the path. Maybe their mom had seen me after all.

On another evening my wife, Kathy, and I were outside as night was coming on and saw fox kits frolicking on the far side of a clearing. We stood motionless, and soon enough one came prancing in our direction. It was dusk and the fireflies were out in full force. We realized they were trying to catch fireflies by jumping up and snapping at them. At one point a kit, busily focused on the little lighted insects, came to within ten feet of us. Then he saw us, froze for a second, and bounded off back to his den. We walked home smiling, thinking of our magical evening by a meadow.

At first it may not seem like a lot of land, but our local utility manages about 550 miles of electric transmission right-of-ways across the state and a number of gas pipeline right-of-ways as well. The ROWs, some dating back more than a hundred years, have been maintained following the customary practice of mowing, cutting down trees, and general herbicide use. This has resulted in a heavy infestation of non-natives and invasives such as Tree of Heaven (ailanthus), black locust, black willow, wild Bradford pear, autumn olive, mile-a-minute weed, Japanese stilt grass, Japanese honeysuckle, and multi-flora rose. It was not an ideal strategy. The utility received a lot of calls from neighbors when it cut down trees or sprayed herbicide.

Our local watershed group, galvanized by a community outcry after an unprecedented and extensive clear-cutting one year, approached Baltimore Gas & Electric Company (BGE), our local utility, to discuss its ROW maintenance methods. BGE's forester, Bill Rees, agreed to do a pilot test in our area to see what other operational protocols they could follow that might improve stormwater management and preserve meadowland habitat. As it turns out, they were not pleased with their standard practices either. The annual cutting of vegetation on 550 miles of right-of-way is costly, both economically and in terms of public relations. Bill agreed to look into changing from a program of maintaining the existing vegetation to one of managing native vegetation *as long as it was compatible* with their primary responsibility of safe and reliable transmission of electricity. A consultant, IVM Partners, was hired to help develop and implement the plan and to provide ongoing maintenance expertise.

We were interested in a new approach because research has shown that a managed right-of-way could provide much-needed meadowland and early successional habitats that would benefit a wide variety of birds, pollinators, and other wildlife. It would also provide better stormwater management. One proven method of achieving these goals is called Integrated Vegetation Management (IVM). It involves selective spraying of invasive plants (in decreasing amounts as succession takes place) and the encouragement of the native seed bank already present in the soils in order to reclaim the area with native flora.

The utility company's goals were to see if IVM techniques could help them balance weed and tree control, costs, public health, environmental quality, and regulatory compliance. The pilot test also evaluated necessary changes to their corporate standards, contractor costs and capabilities, and training protocols for their foresters and contractors on proper maintenance procedures. They realized they would have to make the necessary process and cultural changes within the company to move to this more sustainable methodology.

The pilot test was implemented along a mile of right-of-way by Rick Johnstone of IVM Partners. He established a control site in one area that was managed according to BGE's standard practices. After two years Rick reports a dramatic difference between what is growing (*the plant community succession*) on the mowed control site versus the IVM-managed site. The aggressive nature of the invasive shrubs like autumn olive (Elaeagnus umbellata) allowed them to dominate the mowed control area, covering 50 percent of the ground cover just two years after mowing, and growing to a height of eight feet. Wild Bradford pear and Japanese honeysuckle also increased on the control site.

In contrast, the IVM-managed site released species such as yellow foxtail as the dominant grass in 2010, replaced in dominance by the native purple top grass in 2011. The predominant tree/shrub species of the IVM site is primarily blackberry. Combined with other herbaceous plants, the IVM site basically restored *prairie habitat*, which research has shown to have been present in this area for thousands of years.

The pilot test worked well and has increased the number of native species in this area. Our pilot area has now been converted from a routinely cut mixture of trees and invasive shrubs and vines to a selectively managed native prairie. "IVM has proven to be a successful approach for meeting the safety and reliability needs of the utility's electric transmission and pipeline right-of-way system, as well as the habitat and aesthetic needs of naturalists and the general public." BGE's Bill Rees is quite pleased with the results and has now scheduled work to transform transmission sites in three adjacent counties. We hope it will be expanded from the pilot stage to full implementation across their entire system and beyond to other states. Based on the pilot test results, it appears that IVM is also a more cost-effective approach to ROW maintenance.

Meadowland Master Plans

Our local land trust, the Howard County Conservancy, is very interested in maintaining meadowland habitat. They manage 232 acres of land on their flagship property, the Mt. Pleasant Farm. According to their master plan, one large area of the farm is planted in cold season grasses and another in warm season grasses. The meadows are cut on a rotating three-year schedule in which a third of each meadow is cut each year. This allows two-thirds of any habitat to remain undisturbed and at the same time prevents trees from growing up. The meadows are cut during the off-season so there is less damage to plants and animals living in them.

The conservancy manages the Mt. Pleasant Farm as a demonstration site. Trained naturalists lead hikes for groups of children and adults on a regular basis, stressing the importance of meadows and all habitats to a community. They try to make the point that everyone who maintains open lawns and fields should take at least the first step and leave part of the land fallow as meadows, mowing them only once every year or two. Many of us have grown up thinking that neatly mowed lawns look nice. We have to change that mindset and educate our neighbors that these places are not "weedy" or allergy promoting, but healthy ecosystems that benefit all of us and our environment. We should all go out and find a meadow to enjoy and then check to see what we can do to protect it.

One good way each of us can help is by joining a local land trust. There are over 900 land trusts in the country, protecting 2.7 million acres. Go encourage the ones near your home to restore and maintain their meadowlands. See how you can help them. Local environmental groups and government agencies should know where your land trusts are. If one is not close by, consider starting one by contacting the Land Trust Alliance in Washington, DC. You could make this happen, and it would have a significant impact on the area where you live that all of us could enjoy, literally forever.

This pilot study may indeed have national implications. Many local, county, state, and federal environmental officials, wildlife professionals, conservationists, and utility managers have been participants in both classroom education and field trips to the Columbia Pilot Study site. One audience included fifty EPA employees who chartered a bus from D.C. to learn the science of IVM. I have heard very favorable feedback from them. We hope they'll help spread awareness of the advantages of this approach to utilities and communities nationwide as one step toward rebuilding our meadows.

If this strategy would help bring meadowlands back to your neighborhood, I encourage you to talk to your utility and reference the IVM work that has already been done by BGE. Their forestry manager or corporate relations staff should be able to help. It should save your utility money and bring back to your neighborhood a diverse range of meadowland species as well. All it took in our area was a local group encouraging the local utility to try it.

Great Plains — Just as meadows and prairie lands are vanishing in other parts of the country, the Great Plains contain large areas of endangered grassland habitat. The once vast grasslands were devastated as Americans moved west, and many areas are at significant risk once again. We can learn a lot about the need to balance conservation and development just by looking at how our ancestors developed the West and the struggles taking place there today.

One of the biggest grassland habitat losses in the country started in the nineteenth century with the passage in 1862 of the first Homestead Act. It was a direct response to the rapid growth of our population and the increasing demand for land. Between 1862 and 1934, the government distributed 270,000,000 acres of federal land (10 percent of all land in the United States) to individuals. That was the beginning of the end of the Great Plains, grasslands that had existed for thousands of years—those vast areas where the buffalo once roamed. First, the buffalo were slaughtered and the Native Americans removed. In fact, the decimation of the buffalo was just part of the plan for destroying the

American Indians' way of life and removing them from the land. Then large sections of those tall grass prairies were burned, cultivated, and turned into farms. Much of the land presented significant challenges to farming because the soils dried out without the tall grasses to protect them. In many areas, converting prairie to farmland was only successful with the aid of extensive irrigation. There were no significant efforts to preserve grassland habitat or the wildlife it supported.

The Dust Bowl of the 1930s was a direct result of this unfortunate but intentional conversion of the Great Plains to farmland. There was a good reason why these areas had been grasslands and not forests. The region consisted of marginal soils in a dry climate. The deep-rooted grasses kept the soil in place and trapped moisture. When the grasses were burned off, the virgin soil dried out, especially in the dry, hot regions of Oklahoma and Texas. When the winds came up, there were no grasses or trees to stop them, and huge dust clouds, called "black blizzards," blew the topsoil across the country, often all the way to the East Coast and beyond. For a colorful account, see Timothy Egan, *The Worst Hard Time: The Untold Story of Those Who Survived the Great American Dust Bowl.*

During the extended dry spell of the 1930s, many farms in Oklahoma and Texas failed. People abandoned the land and moved farther west to find jobs. John Steinbeck captured the fear, the anger, and the desperation of this time of environmental debacle in *The Grapes of Wrath.* It was hard for me to read the book without wondering how I would have responded to such desperate conditions. I hope that our country does not have to face such challenging circumstances again. I wonder what we will do as the climate continues to warm. I hope we are proactive in ensuring this does not happen again.

In 1935, in response to the Dust Bowl, the Soil Conservation Service (SCS) was created to find ways to change agricultural practices in order to rebuild soil quality. The SCS, part of the USDA, wound up paying farmers in the Dust Bowl areas to keep their land uncultivated in order to rebuild the soil. Millions of trees were also planted in belts, or windbreaks, in an attempt to impede the wind. These efforts helped but were too late for people who had already abandoned their land to go search for jobs and food for their families.

Some areas of the Great Plains recovered with the extensive use of subsurface waters to irrigate the crops. But the region remains at risk today due to the overuse and withdrawal of water from depleting aquifers. The Ogallala Aquifer is the dominant formation of the High Plains Aquifer System, a vast underground water supply that underlies parts of eight states (Figure 4). It extends from South Dakota to Texas and is one of the world's largest shallow aquifers. To reach it, one must drill from 100 to 400 feet below the surface depending where you are. The Ogallala currently yields about a third of all ground water used for irrigation in the country. At present withdrawal rates, however, some parts of this aquifer will become depleted within the next several decades.

When you fly over the plains you see thousands of green or tan crop circles—areas where an irrigation pipe rotates around a central well. Crop circles are either a half mile or a full mile across, and each one uses hundreds and sometimes thousands of gallons of water *per minute*. These high rates of water withdrawal are unsustainable and have lowered water tables dramatically, in some areas by tens of feet. There are areas in Texas and Kansas where the aquifers have already gone dry. We are mining the water far faster than it is being recharged. That cannot continue forever.

Sure enough, dust clouds have appeared in the Great Plains once again. In 2012, the USDA declared natural disasters in more than 1,800 counties in thirty-five states, which is more than half of the country's counties. This was mostly because of the dry, hot weather we've been experiencing. The 2012 drought, more widespread than in any year since the 1930s, damaged a significant portion of the U.S. corn and soybean crops. This had deleterious impacts on all livestock sectors (cattle, hogs, poultry, and dairy) that depend on these crops for food. It also limited grazing opportunities and hay production for cattle ranchers in the affected regions and led to substantial herd liquidation. Total estimated damages exceeded $30 billion, and 123 people died. Are dust clouds a premonition of things to come?

What Can We Do? — There is concern today that climate change and dwindling aquifers will create conditions for another dust bowl. Because so much of this land requires irrigation, slight changes in annual temperature or rainfall will create an imbalance in the system. The higher temperatures and lower rainfall encountered over the past decade have already led to dryer conditions and a greater number of forest fires across much of the U.S. Unfortunately, the way we've been managing our land throughout the West has not helped. Forty percent of North America's crop and grasslands have already turned to desert. We must rethink how we manage our open range, utilize finite water supplies, and what steps to take to slow down global climate change and address these major challenges to our country.

What should we be doing today to prevent the economic ruin of a future dust bowl? Can we return the Great Plains to vast grasslands that would keep the soil intact and also serve as a carbon sink to help address global warming? The disaster of the 1930s was man-made—we had stripped the Great Plains of their natural protection. Are we going to act this time to prevent a similar outcome? The first step is to reduce global climate change by reducing carbon emissions. The second might be to bring back more bio-diverse grasslands and meadowlands. The Natural Resource Conservation Service (the successor to the Soil Conservation Service) continues to work with farmers on improving soil health. They are still the place to go to get the best insights on what to do to protect our soils.

The Farm Bill – One challenge to the health of the grasslands of the Great Plains has been a flaw in the crop insurance program part of the Farm Bill, which has inadvertently incentivized farmers to till ecologically sensitive and agriculturally marginal land. A good example of this are the prairie pothole areas of the northern Great Plains. This 276,000-square-mile area is critical to the breeding duck population. Over half the wild ducks in America hatch in these wetlands. Unfortunately, much of it is being drained for farming, which is wiping out this important habitat in exchange for marginal returns. Subsidized crop insurance has made these efforts economical where they would not be otherwise. It seems crazy that we are paying some farmers via the Natural Resource Conservation Service to keep their lands fallow while at the same time we encourage others to convert marginal lands to farmland. The battle has pitted sportsman against farmer in heated exchanges that extend all the way to the halls of Congress.

The new Farm Bill has attempted to fix this problem with crop insurance so that it includes conservation goals. It should also expand insurance to include all farm commodities. That could help local produce farmers and not just the big corn producers. It would be a big step toward protecting the family farms as climate change increases the risks of farming. Details like this can often be lost in such a large national program like the Farm Bill. The same is true of many aspects of farming, where a rule may be of value in one area while having a major negative impact in another. These anecdotes are disturbing, but how can they be fixed? One can certainly raise the issue with one's representative, but it deserves and requires more muscle than that. This is where national conservation organizations come in. They stay on top of these issues, and they need our support. For this particular conservation issue, I would contact the Izaak Walton League of America, Ducks Unlimited, or the Nature Conservancy and ask if they are tracking and lobbying on this issue. You might consider picking one or more of these national organizations that have your interests at heart, and support them to create change on the federal level.

Land preservation – There is much to do to maintain meadow and grassland habitats throughout the country and to preserve the diverse flora and fauna that they support. Start with encouraging your local jurisdictions to consider the importance of meadowlands as well as forests and wetlands in their land acquisition and green infrastructure mapping and restoration efforts. The next step is to locate the closest land trust and easement programs in your area. Many of these organizations have not placed as much value on open meadowland as they have on other habitats. Offer them your support and advice. One small group that has spearheaded its own projects to conserve or reclaim local grasslands in the Eastern U.S. is the Native Grassland Conservancy. Its goal is to preserve habitat, species, and genetic diversity. Their staff is concerned with the decline and disappearance of a wide range of flora and fauna and what this means for all essential pollinators that need a critical mass of a specific flora for their survival. It is a question of maintaining as complete and diverse a habitat as possible for us all. The staff may be able to advise you on approaches for preserving grasslands in your community. Another great resource is John Greenlee's, *The American Meadow Garden* (2009). *Suburban backyards will play a major role in preserving habitat and species in the future.*

The Nature Conservancy has been one of the biggest players in trying to acquire grasslands that help to connect critical habitat in the Northern Great Plains. They work closely with the U.S. Bureau of Land Management (BLM) to acquire and place conservation easements on key lands. The World Wildlife Fund (WWF) has also focused in on this area of the country as one that deserves a major conservation effort for saving a wide range of flora and fauna. Martha Kauffman, WWF's managing director for the Northern Great Plains, makes it clear by stating "Right here in America is one of the world's most threatened natural systems. The Northern Great Plains is as important as the Amazon or Arctic, and deserves our attention."

It is up to us to figure out where meadows fit in our future. Have we abandoned this habitat and all of its varied life forms completely, thus weakening our life support system? Or can we find ways to restore and preserve the meadows and grasslands of America? Work with your local utility and see if you can get them to convert to Integrated Vegetation Management on some or all of their lands. Collaborate with the local sportsmen's clubs to help bring quail back to your neighborhood. Go find the meadow or right-of-way closest to where you live and find out how you can help to restore and preserve it for generations to come.

CHAPTER 4

Beaches

*In every outthrust headland, in every curving beach, in every
grain of sand there is the story of the earth.*
— Rachel Carson

America's Silica Necklace — I've wandered barefoot for hours on the
beaches that encompass this continent. They are all different and beautiful in their own way. They beckon us to come and sit, walk, or surf, to
leave our busy offices and homes behind, relish the cool, salt breezes,
and soak up the sun or enjoy a cloudy day by the sea. They are national
treasures and tens of millions of us visit them each year. I think of these
crystalline beaches as America's silica necklace.

West Coast – I love the cool, foggy stretches of the young, turbu-
lent, and geologically evolving Pacific Coast. One moment you are all
socked-in, struggling to see a few feet ahead. The next moment the mist
rises and a beautiful cove with high banks dripping with vegetation
and dew appears right before your eyes. Northern California, Oregon,
and Washington beaches are perfect for a day of exploring. The steep
mudslide-prone escarpments are a jumble of loose rocks and soil rising
right out of the sea. The rocks appear to be precariously perched on the
steep banks, just waiting to crumble back down during the next storm
or crustal adjustment. I have climbed up and sat down on gigantic logs
that have accumulated on these beaches. Somehow they have traveled
down rivers from inland forests to end up in a pile of thousand-year-old
trunks here on the sandy shore. While ambling along, I have watched
black-suited surfers bobbing in the chilly waters of the Pacific. They sit
for hours, straddling their boards, waiting for just the right wave, a big

cascading wave, to bring them smoothly in to shore. I've also enjoyed exploring the crystal clear tidal pools in search of some exotic creature that I've not yet discovered.

Gulf Coast – I also love rambling along the flat, sleepy beaches and paddling mangrove-snarled stretches of the Gulf Coast. Here the land at first appears flat, not a bit of elevation in any direction except man-made steps to decks and houses that rise up, like pop tarts, out of the sand. Ascending these steps one can see miles of the same sandy landscape all the way to a curved horizon. These shores of quietly lapping Gulf water offer solitude to the weary traveler seeking escape from the bustle of city living. Here there is space to meander as far as you would like. The birds float by as if they had all the time in the world to find their next meal. They are right; with the wide expanse of wetlands, there is plenty for all to eat.

East Coast – In my youth I body-surfed the murky waters and moderate waves of the ancient Atlantic. I never tired of riding waves, counting them, and waiting for the biggest to roll into shore. There is plenty of activity along this coast, in or out of the water. Wave-borne sand-crabs scurry to dig deep into the wet sands before tiny hands dig them out. Fishing from jetty or shore brings in a day's catch without the need to charter a boat to chase the big fish out in the Gulf Stream. Then there are the bay sides of barrier island beaches, where the water is calm and the blue crabs will eat anything you put on a line. I tread slowly in these shallow waters, picking up clams as I go, and casting about for bluefish and rock.

My father could never sit still at the beach. He had to be in the water or foraging in the marshes. He fished, clammed, or crabbed and always came home with dinner, though not always the one he'd planned. My mother and mother-in-law were different. They went to the beach to do some serious beach-sitting, to watch pods of dolphins swim and occasionally perform just offshore, to count the brown pelican armadas, to comment on what people were wearing, and to read the juicy beach books they had been saving for months. And of course to have wine and cheese on the beach at five after everyone else had gone in for dinner. We all have our patterns and traditions at the beach.

Just seeing so many people laughing, sitting, and strolling makes me realize that there is something special about these eroding edges of our continent. Each one feels eternal, and their timelessness encourages me to come back and stay for a while, and I do, as often as I can. I like being on the beach first thing in the morning and last thing at night. One never tires of watching the sun, or the moon, rise out of the sea or melt back into it—the first rays in the morning and the green spot that follows the sun's setting at night. I take it all in, the sand, water, and people, the clouds and the birds, which are always there to heckle me. I like exploring on these sandy beaches, the silica necklace that borders America.

But our beaches face challenges. Those associated with sea level rise are described in the chapter on islands, trash and pollution in the chapter on oceans. In this chapter we'll examine the impact of oil spills that continuously threaten our coasts.

Santa Barbara's Buried Past — Kathy and I visited Santa Barbara, California in 1976, and after checking into our room went for a walk on the beach. The sunshine was brilliant and much warmer than it is on the East Coast during the fall of the year. After our long, cross-country flight, we just wanted to take our shoes off and walk along the sand to relax and rejuvenate. The beaches were beautiful. But where were all the people, all those who had moved west to enjoy the California sun? Partway up the empty beach Kathy stopped and bent over. She had stepped on something black. We both had stepped on something black. Our feet had sticky black blobs on the soles. This beach was different from the clean sand we were used to on the East Coast. The sand contained blobs of crude oil.

This was new to us. We tried to wipe off the oil, but it wasn't easy. We kept walking, trying to ignore the hidden oil and enjoy the vacation. It was as hard to get the oil out of our minds as it was to get it off our feet. When we got back to our room, we noticed we were leaving a trail of black spots on the sidewalk. It took quite a while to get the oil off our skin, not something you'd want to do every day. It certainly discour-

Santa Barbara Channel Blowout

Oil has been produced in the Santa Barbara area since the late 1800s. Initially most oil derricks were onshore, but the oil- and gas-rich anticlinal reservoir trended offshore, so drilling followed. The world's first offshore oil drilling was done from a pier extending out over the ocean in 1896. Then drilling was done from manmade islands built in shallow water close to shore. Legislative actions delayed actual oil platform construction and drilling until the mid-1960s, as the federal and state governments fought for ownership of submerged lands. Congress passed the Submerged Lands Act in 1953, but it was contested. In 1965 the Supreme Court finally settled the competing claims on the submerged lands outside a three-mile limit, giving them to the federal government. The states own the rights to oil and gas within three miles of shore.

Multiple platforms were deployed offshore over the next few years. Then a major blow-out occurred on January 28, 1969, on Union Oil's Platform A, which was drilling in 188 feet of water to a depth of 3,479 feet. The rig was six miles from shore. Oil, gas, and water rushed up the largely uncased hole and blew out at a pressure of 1,000 pounds per square inch, coating everybody and everything and sending a greasy geyser into the air.

Union Oil tried to seal the casing at the sea floor to stop the flow, but the well only had 238 feet of casing. When they closed the top of the well-hole, oil and gas blew out of the sides below the casing. The pressurized oil escaped into the surrounding soft sedimentary rocks and worked its way to the surface at numerous locations. Thick bubbling oil slicks quickly began to grow and spread from at least five separate leaks up to eight hundred feet away from the drilling platform. It took weeks to stop them all.

This spill, the largest ever up to that time, had a significant impact on marine life in the Santa Barbara Channel. Thousands of sea birds died, as well as dolphins, elephant seals, and sea lions. Public outrage resulted in several pieces of environmental legislation. Although the leasing of new tracts was curtailed, development of already leased lands continued. Union Oil's Platform A continues to operate today.

aged us from taking more walks on the beach, which was great to look at but not much else. No wonder it wasn't crowded. I had thought the lack of people was due to the famously cold water of the Pacific, not to globules of oil.

Is this what you have to put up with when developing oil deposits—inevitable spills and damage to wildlife as well as to beaches? As it turns out, California has extensive offshore and onshore oil reservoirs, natural seeps, and a long history of drilling and production. The largest oil spill in history (up until that time) had occurred close by in the Santa Barbara Channel in 1969, where five million gallons of oil spilled into the Pacific over a ten-day period. It had been a major news event, but I had not heard much about the clean-up. That had only been seven years earlier. Now I was standing on the beaches of Santa Barbara, and crude oil was present in the sand and on the soles of my feet. I was not sure if this crude oil was left over from that major spill or came from natural seeps. It could have been either. Either way, it was clear to me that a lot of oil could have a major impact on the value and usefulness of our beaches. I suppose people in this area and maybe along the Gulf Coast are used to this sort of thing.

Our walk on that oil-laden beach made me realize how difficult it is to protect all of our natural resources while trying to meet the energy demands of a growing population. It came back to mind when I was contracted by the U.S. Minerals Management Service in 1981 to calculate reserves of offshore oil and gas on our Pacific, Atlantic, and Gulf shores. That fascinating project gave me firsthand access to the geophysical logs from many of the wells that had been drilled on our continental margins, and hundreds of miles of seismic survey data from these offshore provinces. My job was to calculate U.S. offshore petroleum reserves by analyzing the data and mapping out the location and size of potential oil and gas reservoirs buried deep below the sea floor.

California offshore reservoirs have had a long history of development. The oil industry has learned the hard way that the offshore environment is a challenging place in which to operate. The data revealed that it is also a resource-rich area. The Santa Barbara spill slowed down leasing but didn't stop exploration and development work.

The data also revealed that there was a great deal of potential beneath the waters of the Gulf Coast, some in shallow areas and some in deep, high-pressure formations in much deeper water. I wondered at that time if we would ever develop the technology to safely extract the deep, higher-risk deposits of the Gulf. Now, thirty years later, we are attempting to tap those very reservoirs. The 2010 British Petroleum (BP) oil spill revealed some of the dangers of such drilling. We always seem to push the limits of our capabilities. I wonder what lessons we've learned from that unfortunate and deadly disaster.

What surprised me most in 1981 was the potential for offshore oil development along the East Coast. Much less data had been collected in the Atlantic and only a few wells had been drilled, but the wells did reveal thick accumulations of sediments here similar to those of the Gulf Coast. Thus far there has been no commercial development in U.S. waters, but production of oil and gas is ongoing from wells off Nova Scotia and Cuba. The question of further exploration along the Atlantic Coast comes up regularly, but for now this potential resource has been taken off the table, largely out of fear that spills will damage commercial fisheries and contaminate East Coast beaches. Following our experience in other areas, I certainly understand why. I suspect, though, that within my lifetime we will see this resource developed as well.

As successful as the oil industry has been in exploring, producing, and delivering billions of barrels of oil to all corners of this country and the world, whenever they have a big accident it can be a real disaster on many fronts. In 1989, twenty years after the big Santa Barbara spill, the

Exxon Valdez hit a reef in Alaska and spilled millions of gallons of crude oil from Prudhoe Bay into the pristine waters of glacier-rimmed Prince William Sound. Estimates vary, but between 11 and 25 million gallons of crude were released. Due to challenging weather conditions and difficulty in conducting timely response efforts, the oil spread across 1,300 miles of shoreline and killed large numbers of birds, mammals, and fish. This spill impacted wildlife for years and is still not completely cleaned up, even with the help of natural microbial degradation of the oil. This spill eclipsed the damage inflicted on Santa Barbara and was the largest offshore spill in U.S. history—up until that time.

Twenty-one years later, in 2010, an explosion on the Deepwater Horizon offshore drilling platform killed eleven crew members. A sea-floor oil gusher flowed unabated for *three months* spreading *210 million gallons* of crude oil into the Gulf of Mexico. As a result, BP has paid $42 billion in order to clean up some of the oil and repair the damage to the local economy. The oil released from the Macondo well threatened up to 1,074 miles of coastline. Fortunately, favorable weather conditions and a major cleanup effort prevented the impact from becoming as devastating as it might otherwise have been. Nonetheless, three years after the spill it is estimated that a third of the oil remains in the environment and continues to affect the health of a wide range of species. It is expected to be felt for a generation or more.

The Deepwater Horizon incident is now the largest offshore spill in U.S. history. Spills seem to be getting larger, paralleling the growing magnitude of our drilling technology needed to harvest oil from deep, high pressure reservoirs. A Department of the Interior/Coast Guard joint investigation found that BP, Transocean, and Halliburton violated a number of federal offshore safety regulations. Their report can be read at http://www.bsee.gov/uploadedFiles. The cause appears to be defective cement work by Halliburton, but there is plenty of blame to go around. This disaster will have a long-term impact on the environment and the economy. It will also increase our wariness regarding offshore drilling.

Imagine living along a coastline where you can't walk on the beach because oil buried in the sand will stain your feet. Imagine a ban on seafood consumption in an area dependent on seafood. Imagine the loss of all the businesses that rely on the ocean, the beaches, and towns along the coast. All of that has occurred on the West and Gulf coasts. The National Oceanic and Atmospheric Administration (NOAA) closed most of the Gulf to fishing during the three-month, uncontrolled blowout. Many businesses which relied on clean Gulf waters did not know when they could return. Now, three years later, some Gulf-wide fisheries have rebounded, but in many areas oil is still present in the marshes, and the reefs remain damaged. Oyster, shrimp, and crab catches are still off in Louisiana, even though BP has been doing a lot to reduce the long-term effects. That seems to be how we deal with man-made disasters—we spend money to clean up the mess and appease the anger, and we take some steps to heal the wounds to our natural resources and to the economy. But we rarely spend enough to fix all of the damage to the natural world, to our essential green infrastructure (reefs, beaches, wetlands). That deficit is often left for future generations to repay.

Imagine the disappointment and anger of the fishermen, local businesses, and families who live and work in the Gulf. If you have been raised dredging for oysters and have invested all of your savings into the equipment to do so, how do you meet your financial obligations when you can no longer go out and earn a living? Your losses ripple down to almost everyone in your community. Gulf Coast residents have been going through a tough couple of years of dribble-down economic woes. I wonder what it would have cost to have taken the steps to prevent this disaster?

What Can We Do? — The first thing we can do is to get informed about the risks of offshore exploration. There are a range of views on the future of our crude oil resources. The American Petroleum Institute is one of the best funded professional organizations in the country. It represents the major oil companies. A great deal of information about the industry can be found on their website. To foster objectivity and gain credibility, much of their work is jointly funded and performed by non-industry partners, including state and federal governments, non-government organizations (NGOs), and academics. Their studies are intended to address the concerns that arise from new exploration and production technologies and discoveries.

The Department of Energy (DOE) and its Energy Information Administration (EIA) are non-industry sources for information as well. Their job is to assess the risks, track progress, and project our energy needs and sources in the future. In addition to those sources of information there are a number of large NGO watchdogs that routinely investigate the oil industry including the Union of Concerned Scientists (UCS), the Natural Resource Defense Council (NRDC), and the Environmental Defense Fund (EDF). I have summarized below some of the steps that we could take as a nation to reduce the risks of future oil spills.

Professionalism, training, and oversight – We all value our beaches, our seafood, our wildlife, and our health. At the same time we are used to, or some would say addicted to, low-cost oil. We probably won't wean ourselves off oil in the near future, but there are things we can do to try to lower the risks associated with oil production in high-risk areas.

We must constantly push for higher professional standards for petroleum production and transport. It is a huge industry and normally it performs well. But as more people are involved in the complex work of exploration, production, and transportation, the likelihood of operator error increases. In order to operate in adverse settings and harness bigger, deeper, and higher pressure reservoirs, the industry needs a very high level of training and supervision. To ensure that there is adequate training and supervision requires a high level of oversight and monitoring. Based on past performance, this has to be done on both the private and public levels; based on the reports from past disasters, it has not been the case.

Reduce demand – Is it possible to reduce demand for petroleum? Could we at least slacken demand enough to reduce the need to drill in the highest risk areas? The answer is—yes. We have moved off petroleum for some of our energy needs such as the generation of electricity, and we could use less for transportation. Gasoline usage has already been dropping for the past five years, and that trend will probably continue as vehicles become ever more efficient. Americans are also driving less. We could, therefore, reduce our dependency on oil even more if we chose to. At the same time, hydraulic fracking in oil fields in Texas and North Dakota is resulting in greater yields. In the big picture, though, the easy oil has been produced—future oil production will require more technologies and will come from higher-risk reservoirs. So this might be a good time to move away from petroleum wherever possible.

Limit exploration – The government has the authority to limit exploration in some areas. Should it be stopped in the very high risk areas along our coasts? Should the deep water and deep reservoir areas of the Gulf be placed off-limits until the technology and the oversight is improved? Or is our dependence on oil so great that we need to develop it all.

It will be hard to limit exploration in the Gulf since petroleum is so much of the fabric of the local economy. The East Coast offers more of a choice. Efforts to open up offshore drilling of the Atlantic Continental Shelf will continue. States have the right to lease areas within three miles from shore. The federal government can sell leases up to 200 miles off shore. But do we want to drill on the East Coast? Are we prepared for the risks and the impacts? Do we have to exploit these potential reserves, or do we have less risky energy alternatives (see Chapter 13)?

Improve operations and response – Shipping disasters can happen almost anywhere because we ship oil into most ports of the U.S. Since the *Valdez* oil spill, most ships are now built with a double hull that should reduce the amount of fuel released in the event of an accident. As a back-up it is critical that local clean-up teams are well trained, well staffed, and well positioned. Let's hope they are never needed for a spill as large as the *Valdez* or Deepwater Horizon, but if they are needed, we want them to mobilize rapidly and to know what they are doing. That turned out to be a real problem in Alaska. The clean-up plans were inadequate, and the response, which was complicated by weather, was abysmal and too slow. Who were the individuals, the corporations, the communities, and the governments responsible for having crews ready to deploy when that spill occurred? All of these jobs are important and all of us have a role in making sure that our society is up to the task of producing and delivering fuel safely.

Financial risk – The good news is that no one wants to be the next BP. That was a financial and public relations nightmare, and they lost a great deal of business in the U.S. People did not like what BP did in the Gulf and responded at the pump and in the market. Their stock lost market value, and BP has shrunk from being #2 to #4 in the list of big oil companies. They still have a great deal of litigation to resolve. What would the cost to BP have been to prevent that disaster? I trust significant lessons were learned and are being applied industry-wide. I also hope that the agencies inspecting these industries are adequately funded and up to the task of monitoring new technologies as they come on line.

We must find a balance when managing our resources. If less-polluting energy options are available, there is less reason to risk damaging valuable resources. Where we don't have other options, we must see to it that our exploration, operating, and monitoring procedures are up to the task of damage-free development. That may not be possible, so it comes down to risk management and risk versus reward. Is one major spill every twenty years acceptable? It may be, but each generation will have to decide. Our beaches, our coastal businesses, and our fishing stocks are of great value, and we all have to do what we can to protect them.

CHAPTER 5

Islands

Tell me, what is it you plan to do with your one wild and precious life?
— Mary Oliver

Hurricane Donna, 1960 — Dad finished his work by mid-afternoon so we could take off early on our first family camping trip. A sense of adventure had been building all week—we were going camping on an island! Dad and Mom had picked an island because she wanted to swim, and he wanted to fish. They both loved the outdoors and wanted us to get a real sense of the sea. The day we left was sunny and warm. Dad decided to drive around the northern end of the Chesapeake Bay to avoid the normal Friday afternoon traffic on the two-lane Bay Bridge. We drove north to Elkton and then headed south toward Fenwick Island, passing the Susquehanna, Elk, and Sassafras rivers and the Intracoastal Waterway. As we pulled into the campground among the dunes we could smell the sea, hear the surf, and see for miles. The ocean was alive with whitecaps.

I look back on this trip wondering now whether my parents had even checked the weather report before setting out. Or was weather reporting so primitive back then that there was no warning of impending storms? Perhaps, since Dad was a farmer, he may not have believed in weather reports. In any case, he and Mom packed our robin's egg blue, '57 Chevy sedan with two kids and a borrowed tent and headed east toward the Atlantic. They planned to camp out in the elements, on a barrier island, one hundred feet from the ocean to give us a taste of the sea. Unbeknownst to any of us, our family was heading right into the eye of a storm.

The winds had picked up by the time we made it to the beach. Mom selected a site right behind the dunes to be out of the wind but still close to the water. We had the place to ourselves; Mom and Dad wondered why no one else was there. My sister Marsha and I set up the green canvas, four-person tent borrowed from our cousins. We spread out our borrowed sleeping bags and blew up air mattresses. Dad and Marsha got a fire started for dinner. The three of us then went to take a dip in the ocean while Mom prepared dinner. The waves were large and crashed menacingly onto shore. When we came back to the campsite, roughed up and coated with salt, we noticed that Mom looked worried. She said the campground manager had been around and spoken of a storm.

As evening progressed, the wind picked up and rain began to fall. Still wide awake with excitement and a growing concern about the weather, we moved into the tent and played cards by flashlight. Slowly we fell asleep with the sound of rain on the tent roof and little puffs of moisture floating down on us from the wet canvas ceiling. During the night the wind turned into a gale, and sheets of rain slashed the tent. Our shelter was not a twenty-first century waterproof *ripstop* nylon tent with a rain fly. It was made of canvas that absorbed the water and the flaps barely covered the screened windows even when tightly tied. All night long, Dad and I kept getting up to re-tie the canvas windows and re-stake the guy-wires to secure the tent as best we could.

We dug a trench around the tent in a failed attempt to keep water from flowing beneath the canvas floor. I kept dreaming I was floating out to sea and woke up several times with my air mattress floating on six inches of water *inside* the tent. The winds were so strong and gusty that they kept pulling the tent stakes out of the loose, wet sand. Dad apparently didn't sleep at all that night, doing his best to keep us safe if not dry. By morning when we woke up, the storm had passed, the tent was completely down on top of us, and everything in it was soaked. We spent an hour squeezing water out of our clothes and bedding and picking up our belongings strewn about the campsite.

Then it was time to explore the damage to the island. The storm had removed a great deal of sand from the beach, and the surf had breached the dunes at several places. There was still a high water table in the campground area and several large puddles with water up to our knees. Mom and Dad packed up all of our very wet belongings and went off to find a Laundromat where we spent several hours attempting to get things dry. At Mom's urging, Dad decided to go find a campground for the night that was farther inland and protected from the sea. We discovered Milburn Landing campground on the Pocomoke River (a state park) and set up our tent to dry under the tall loblolly pines. Here on the mainland, miles from the sea, and surrounded by trees, we felt safe from the elements and slowly recovered from a sleepless night and the storm.

It was, to say the least, quite an introduction to camping. We later learned that the eye of Hurricane Donna had passed by just off shore during the night. It was one of the ten most damaging storms of the twentieth century, costing over $28 billion. Fortunately, we lost only a night's sleep and dozens of quarters in the drying machine. My mother, who had camped a lot as a girl, rallied the troops and turned this trip into a great memory. Weathering a hurricane on an island turned out to be the beginning and not the end of our family camping adventures. I do recall more discussion about weather reports on later trips, but they never stopped us from going.

Threats to Islands — Islands are magical places to many of us. Our culture is full of references to fictional islands such as Bali Ha'i, Treasure Island, and Atlantis and real places like Bora-Bora, Santorini, Fiji, and Hawaii. Maybe they intrigue us because islands lie out there in precarious settings on the edges of our normal existence. They often create a sense of romance, solitude, and removal from the hubbub of everyday life. Maybe they just feel like an escape into another world. Whatever the cause of the attraction, I am glad that they exist and are accessible for all of us to enjoy.

Today islands around the world face three major threats. Most worrisome is the rising sea level and the increasing potential for damage from large storms. The second challenge is managing the amount and location of residential and commercial development that should be allowed on islands. Third is the need for islands to meet the increasing industrial infrastructure requirements of our country.

Challenge #1: Rising Sea Levels – The Gulf Coast and East Coast islands south of New England consist of sand, silt, and clay and lie at great risk of being washed away by sea level rise, storm surges, and erosion from rains and waves. I can attest to the power of the seas that night in 1960 when Hurricane Donna ripped through the barrier island on which we were camping. A larger surge easily could have taken out the dunes that protected us during that storm. It is highly likely that some, if not many, of these East and Gulf Coast sandy islands are at risk of disappearing.

Islands off the coast of New England and on the West Coast are mainly solid rock outcrops with a much longer natural life expectancy. However, all islands and the homes and piers on them are under threat of being badly battered from storms as the climate warms and sea levels rise.

Conservative projections of further sea level rise this century range from two to six feet. To put this into perspective, let's look at the Chesapeake Bay, where waters have already risen about a foot. As a result of only one foot of sea level rise, more than five hundred islands have sunk beneath the waves (Cronin, The Disappearing Islands of the Chesapeake). Their loose sand and clay substrate merely washes away in big storms. Many more islands, at least two of them (Smith and Tangier) inhabited, are doomed to disappear sometime this century. There is sadness and anger among the island watermen that their way of life is fast disappearing and that the waters they depend upon will one day rise up and engulf them. Few of them believe that the rest of us will do anything about global warming soon enough to save their homes.

We do go to great lengths to save some islands. In fact, we spend a lot of money each year saving our beach resorts, many of which are built on precarious, sand-rich, barrier islands. The barrier islands along the Atlantic Coast from Florida to New York are normally highly mobile, migrating toward the land or the sea depending on changes in sea level.

Smith and Tangier — The Vanishing Islands

Somewhere out there near the midpoint of the Chesapeake Bay lie two islands, one in Maryland and one in Virginia. About a hundred families living in these marshes still feed themselves and earn their living solely off the wildlife, the commons of the Chesapeake. They catch crabs, dredge for oysters, and fish for catfish, rockfish, and drum. They shoot geese and ducks. After four hundred years and twelve generations protecting their island culture, their days of living on these islands are numbered. Food is still there to harvest, but with rising sea levels and storm surges it won't take much to wash the watermen and their islands away. The islands cannot be saved without great cost and, with few inhabitants and even fewer visitors, there is little economic reason to save them.

I have walked around Smith Island. Old houses line a short street to nowhere, and even older homes with weathered soft-shell crab shacks stand by the water. A lone restaurant is open for business, managed by a woman who tells you what she's got today. Patrons still speak a Cornish dialect reflecting their English roots. I spent a night in a house available for rent and watched boats pass on the bay. They didn't stop. The next morning I got up, ate, and explored the wetlands until my "water taxi" took me back to the mainland.

As the kids grow up they go to the mainland for school and then for jobs. A few return to carry on the family traditions, but the end is in sight. The land is eroding because that is what islands do, they erode back into the sea. Since colonial days, Smith Island has already lost some 3,000 acres to the waters that incessantly pound its shores. Rising sea levels will only accelerate that process and then one day a great storm surge will take away their homes for good.

The state of Maryland recently floated a proposal to buy out the remaining residents. Nobody much liked the idea, but it might be the only solution left for the watermen and their families.

Since the seas have been rising over the last century, barrier islands would naturally migrate inland, pushed by the waves. However, having built so many hotels, houses, and boardwalks on some of them, we're now attempting to lock these migratory islands into place so as not to lose our extensive investments.

Keeping beaches and islands in one permanent location is accomplished by spending money each year on beach nourishment. Large pumps hydraulically dredge up offshore sand deposits and dump the sand onshore, rebuilding our beaches and dunes right where they were last summer. Of course this disrupts the offshore and onshore ecosystems and is very expensive, but it allows people to enjoy the shore in the way to which they have become accustomed. Yet this strategy is doomed to backfire as the climate warms and sea levels rise. The more we build on exposed beaches, the greater the calamity that will befall those unfortunates who happen to be there when the big one hits. The earth is a restless beast; barrier islands on the Atlantic and Gulf coasts will move again.

To see what would have happened if we did not rebuild barrier island beaches, all you have to do is to go to the south end of the boardwalk in Ocean City, Maryland, and look across the inlet to Assateague Island. The Assateague beach was just an extension of the beach at Ocean City until the 1933 Chesapeake-Potomac hurricane broke through and broke the barrier island into two separate islands. Assateague Island is thirty-seven miles long and is preserved as a national park and a wildlife refuge. No effort is spent to keep this island in one place; it is free to migrate naturally with the constantly changing level of the sea. As a result, it has migrated hundreds of feet landward over the past eighty years, as expected. It is a dramatic illustration of the different game plans pursued by man and nature.

Challenge #2: Island Development – Complicating the future of islands is the human desire to build on them. As our population grows, more and more people want to visit or build second homes on what in reality is a limited number of islands. That poses several serious problems. First of all, homes and businesses have already been built in areas that are at high risk and prone to flooding. Who (if anyone) should be insuring them? Many private insurance companies are smart enough to have pulled out of these areas of unacceptable business risk, and yet we, via the federal government, continue to pour money into the endless cycle of rebuilding homes in coastal areas. The federal program is deeply in the red after hurricanes Katrina and Sandy.

On hearing that the same home has been rebuilt multiple times by federally insured funds, one begins to question the wisdom of the system. In economic terms there is no justification for such subsidies. When you realize that large population centers like Miami or the Norfolk/Virginia Beach area might well be wiped out sometime this century, you start to wonder about the size of the reconstruction bill. In 2012, Sandy, a Category II hurricane at landfall, did a lot of damage to the islands and mainland of New York and New Jersey, at a cost of over $60 billion. There were 365,000 homes damaged or destroyed in New Jersey alone, and that was the impact of only a fourteen-foot storm surge. Katrina was a Category III hurricane at landfall, had a twenty-foot storm surge, and caused $100 billion in damage. Think what the cost of the next big one will be. If it is anything like Katrina, it might be too much to fix. After all, New Orleans, "The Big Easy," will never be the same—we will never rebuild it all—and we shouldn't. Many of its neighborhoods are unsafe because they lie in flood-prone areas that we cannot protect.

So the first thing we have to do is get a handle on where people can build on islands that does not put them at great risk and cost all of us a lot of money. The next step is to decide what levels of support services are required on an island to keep it, its residents, and its fragile ecosystem safe. Those islands that are heavily populated or close to shore may have all the conveniences of home. More remote islands don't necessarily have the modern conveniences to which we are accustomed, e.g., fresh water, electricity, and waste disposal services. That may be fine with the inhabitants. They may be used to scarce potable water, erratic electricity, and primitive waste disposal. Let me share an example of what it took to keep one rustic island viable.

The Isle of Shoals — My most intimate experience with islands comes from years spent on Star Island, part of the Isles of Shoals off of Portsmouth, New Hampshire. I first went to Star Island in the 1980s, though both my parents had spent time there in the 1930s. When Kathy and I began taking our kids *out there* for summer vacations, my folks came to visit and said that nothing had changed since their last trip, fifty years earlier. The weather-beaten cottages and grand old wooden hotel still needed painting, seagulls still owned the eastern promontory, and the views were still fantastic. That is the beauty of islands to many of us—leaving the fast pace of civilization back on the mainland. You come to the islands to slow down and to replenish your spirit. It is all about the rocks, the sea, and the camaraderie. The insert tries to capture a day on the Isle of Shoals.

One could say from a distance that not much has changed on Star Island, but behind the scenes things are constantly changing in order to maintain it for the enjoyment of an increasing number of visitors. The challenge of life on an island is that you have to learn how to live in balance with nature and the limited resources *ten miles out* from the mainland (McGill and McGill, 1989). On our island, fresh water was limited so we learned to use it sparingly. We did not have enough fresh water to waste it flushing toilets. For that we used our most abundant resource, sea water. Initially we had such a small volume of sewage that we piped it out into the strong currents that washed by the island, where it was quickly diluted.

Then, in the 1990s, a regulatory agency cited the island for dumping waste into the ocean. We were told we had to install an expensive and elaborate modern sewage treatment system before the island could open for the season. This created a great deal of concern, since most of us were used to living on the island in a very simple fashion, but in time we realized that the upgrade was important. The oceans are threatened with waste from a growing worldwide population, and we had to do our part. We had in fact been looking for a while to find a treatment system that worked with our saltwater-based plumbing. We found one. Star Island now has an expensive and effective water treatment facility that is constantly monitored to ensure its effluent meets federal discharge standards.

A Day on the Isle of Shoals

The foghorn drags me from a deep sleep. Seagulls cheer on the lobsterman as he harvests his daily crop. The fog condenses and drips from the screen in my window. And the wakeup chorus rouses me out of bed. What will this day bring? I have no idea, but I am up early, not about to miss out on a thing. I came to relax and be by the sea, but I will leave exhausted, having filled my cup with long active days and fond memories of life on this rocky isle.

Days are full of exploring the shores and sitting on the long, wooden front porch. Just like the one Hawthorne, Whittier, and Lowell strolled upon. I sit for hours, a book in my lap, gazing across the harbor to other islands. Sailboats, tides, children, and conversations come and go, but the islands seldom change. I take long walks in sunshine cooled by ocean breezes.

Late at night I glance down at the pier. The lone light reveals the effects of a full moon draining the water out to sea. At the end of the porch, the White Island Light circles and keeps me awake for just a few more minutes, helping me get my fill of the sea that will have to last throughout the coming year.

What is it about islands, the wind, the waves, the call of the gulls? They offer us a constant array of life that stimulates all our senses, so that we collapse at night and sleep soundly until the next day slowly cracks open.

Electricity is also a challenge. Where do you plug in? With no public utility to supply us, the island management had to run noisy and smelly diesel generators all summer. One year there was a spill while pumping the diesel fuel from a ship to the island's storage tanks. It was not extensive, but it *was* a clear warning to be more careful; larger spills could damage fragile local ecosystems. As a result of this concern and the air pollution caused by the generators, we are in the process of weaning the island from diesel. The community has tested wind turbines, since the wind is pretty constant and strong on an island ten miles from shore. The negatives were cost, potential damage from storms, damage to nesting and migratory birds, and the sound generated by the models we tested.

We have also taken a good look at solar photo-voltaic panels for generating electricity. Initially we thought solar would be too expensive. It is costly to install and there is only a need for electricity for a few months out of the year. As it turns out, though, shipping diesel to the island is so expensive that solar collectors are in fact cheaper than diesel. But then someone asked: "What about seagulls? Might they damage or coat the panels with seagull pucky?" Evidently they are not a problem; we have had an array of solar collectors on one building for fifteen years, and they have held up well in spite of the sea gulls. After much research, the current plan is to pursue solar energy.

Fresh water is hard to come by on many islands. Four hundred years ago the early settlers on Star Island carved cisterns out of the granite to capture rain to supply themselves, their livestock, and their crops with fresh water. Today, islanders collect rainwater from the roofs of buildings into large wooden cisterns. This works well except that seagulls also spend time on the roof ridgelines. The water is chlorinated and islanders use it for showers but not for drinking. During summers when we don't get much rain, we end up rationing showers and have to rely on more frequent dips in the brisk, sixty-degree ocean. These inconveniences are part of the rustic experience that we like to put up with—just part of life on a windswept isle.

For years, fresh drinking water arrived by boat but now an on-island reverse osmosis system desalinates seawater. So to maintain our *rustic* escape from the hectic lifestyles on the mainland, we've turned to modern technology, at great expense, in order to leave a smaller footprint and be in balance with nature on this remote island. For now we have met the challenges, but sooner or later new ones are likely to confront us.

How you manage an island all comes down to what you want it to be. Islands clearly have different values for different people. For me, the appeal of the Isle of Shoals is as a very rustic retreat. It may have more monetary value to someone who wants to build a fancy resort on it, or its location may be of value for industrial purposes. Some lie on the edges of continents and could serve as bridges from the ocean to the land and accommodate large-scale infrastructure. Islands therefore often become battlegrounds between preservationists and those developers. The big question is, who gets to decide?

Challenge #3: Infrastructure – The Isle of Shoals is one of those islands at great commercial risk. In 1974, island and mainland residents were faced with an issue critical to the future of the whole region. It was the height of the oil crisis and the country needed more oil and more jobs. Aristotle Onassis's Olympic Refineries wanted to deliver both by building an oil refinery on shore and fueling it with an underwater pipeline from the Isle of Shoals. He proposed to buy one of the islands as a deep water port for supertankers. The plans called for employing many local people and withdrawing the necessary fresh water from Lake Winnipesaukee to meet the needs of the plant. As one of the wealthiest men on the planet, he had the money to make it all happen. The firm optioned 1,000 acres of land on shore and set about convincing the affected communities of the economic benefits of the refinery.

Some saw new jobs, income, and the infusion of capital into the local economy, others their worst nightmare: oil spills, smokestacks, and supertankers damaging the coastline, the tourist economy, and the fishing industry. A wide range of residents from across the seacoast came together in opposition, forming a group called "Save Our Shores." A fight began, led by local people who had a different vision than Onassis for the future of this pristine coastline and the historic offshore islands.

The battle lasted six months. At stake was who had the legal jurisdiction to decide the future of the coast. Was it just an issue of buying the land? Did local citizens have any say in their future or was there a "greater good" here? Could the project go forward over the objection of the local towns because there was regional economic value in building the refinery? Which way would the townspeople vote? There was a recession going on and people needed work.

The local mainland town of Rye, voted overwhelmingly against the refinery, but it was not clear that their vote counted for anything. There were significant benefits for the state of New Hampshire and all of New England. Fortunately, the next day the legislature reaffirmed that towns do have "home-rule rights" in deciding on large projects such as the oil refinery. The company pursued other towns but did not prevail anywhere in this environmentally sensitive time and in this part of the country. After all, we, as a nation, had just awakened to the horrors of what we were doing to our environment all across the country. We had little faith in a large corporation's promise to protect our natural surroundings. We wanted to protect local businesses that depended on the health of the environment for their existence (fishing and tourism).

It was a victory for the local people who fought this battle, and the area has remained a beautiful, fiscally sound, and rustic getaway for all to enjoy. It shows what grassroots activism can do. The education and retreat center on the Isle of Shoals has continued to blossom, and Cornell University has built a world-class marine laboratory there as well. History, nature, and community continue to be celebrated on these shores every day of the summer. Nature reigns in the winter.

In many other cases, commercial interests have trumped local ones. Large interstate commerce projects usually win out over local objections, because often, people do not have "standing." But in this case against Onassis, the local preservationists and fishermen made the effort to involve a lot of people early on and got the political will behind them to save their coast. Key to their success was the ability to organize and mobilize their neighbors.

What Can We Do? — The biggest challenge (Challenge #1) facing islands is how to deal with the impacts of global warming, e.g., sea level rise and the increasing severity of storms. Islands will suffer significant damage unless we take individual and collective action to reduce climate change. Prevention is far cheaper than adaptation, and you cannot easily engineer around a problem of this magnitude. Saving islands and lives means acting now to slow population growth, reduce energy usage, and reduce our dependence on fossil fuels. What would a two-to-six-foot rise in sea level a storm surge twenty or thirty feet high do to your favorite places along the coast? I hope that your fear or your anger engages you to start taking action at home and at work to keep our country moving forward on this major issue.

Managing island development – Why do we just go along reactively rebuilding storm-devastated communities on islands at such great cost? We must be more careful in where we allow people to build homes and businesses. It is safer and cheaper to act now than suffer ever higher losses in terms of life and property in the future. On the local level we need to ensure that we have better planning that limits building in high-risk areas such as flood plains. This is a topic that merits your concern and your involvement on the local level.

Apparently, we are making progress on the national level with regard to the appropriate development of our islands. Congress is finally attempting to phase out the federally subsidized flood insurance program over the next few years, but there is a lot of push-back, from people with homes in dangerous areas so we must keep the pressure on our elected officials. We should not rebuild these homes multiple times; helping people once is enough. The Federal Emergency Management Agency (FEMA) is also wisely updating their Flood Insurance Rate Maps to reflect the fact that we are seeing bigger storms (thousand year floods) more frequently. This is a start, an area where fiscal conservatives, realists, and environmentalists can agree.

Island infrastructure – There is a real concern that large infrastructure projects will take over parts of many islands. With more of our population wanting to live or vacation on islands, more infrastructure may be needed. Yes, we should work to slow down population growth, but that may be difficult to accomplish. We should start now to ensure current residents have a say in these projects.

In recent years there has been a movement, usually on the township level, to pass laws giving people a say when a large project threatens to damage a local natural resource (see Barry Yeoman, "Rebel Towns").

Over and over again throughout the country conflicts arise when plans are proposed for coal, oil, and natural gas export and import terminals, big box retail stores, extracting groundwater, and fracking wells. To counter these threats, dozens of jurisdictions have passed ordinances that spell out the "rights of nature" and the "rights of local communities." These may not all hold up if contested on the state or national levels, but it is a start at realizing that our special places have more value than just their commercial potential. The great outdoors offers recreation, scenery, and health in addition to the economic value of the fishing and tourism industries. If nothing else, engaging people to begin monitoring and taking care of their local communities and resources is part of responsible self-government. That is especially important for island communities.

Islands are fragile and lie at the crossroads of nature and civilization. They may well prove to be the bellwether that informs us that our growth is out of control, that we need to rethink what it means to live and prosper on our planetary home. They are important places to protect.

CHAPTER 6

Forests

I went to the woods because I wished to live deliberately, to front
only the essential facts of life, and see if I could not learn what it had to teach,
and not, when I came to die, discover that I had not lived.
— Henry David Thoreau

A Walk in the Woods, 2013 — While walking through the woods one morning, my attention was snared by the antics of a red-bellied woodpecker. I had barely registered its routine tapping, but something else drew my eyes skyward, some sort of anxious scurrying. It was more than just a woodpecker at work. I stopped. About ten feet to my left was a dead tree snag. A woodpecker was indeed working a series of apple-sized holes about twenty feet above the ground. But he was jumping around, much more animated than he would be when looking for insects and seeds.

I then saw a furry commotion as he chased a small gray creature out of one hole and pounced on it. The creature broke loose, leaped off the tree in desperation, and fell in my direction. It spread out its limbs, stretching its skin, and fluttered like a kite down to the level of my head, and held fast to the bark of the tall tulip popular next to me. It was clearly a flying squirrel, the first one I had ever seen in flight. We both froze, startled to be in one another's presence. He was big-eyed and barely six inches from nose to the base of his tail. The tail was another four inches long and very flat as it pressed against the coarse rivulets of gray bark. We watched each other for several moments. He was catching his breath and adjusting to the daylight. I just stood there totally engaged in the moment.

Another flurry on the tree snag above me drew my attention back to the woodpecker as he rousted a second flying squirrel from its winter's nest. This one quickly found a second hole to dive into and disappeared, safe from his tormentor for the moment. Looking back at the first squirrel I noticed the extra skin on the back of the arms, not nearly as obvious now as when it was fully extended during flight. When he jumped, he had stretched out into a five-by-six-inch wavering sail. Walking around the tree, I continued to watch the tiny squirrel as it remained motionless. He must have thought he was camouflaged and hidden from me. In fact, he would have been easy to miss if I had not known he was there. His fur had colors and patterns very similar to the striped tree bark. Without the commotion, I would have walked right by this small gray bump on the large gray poplar.

Then in a flash the tiny squirrel took off, straight up the tree to a point maybe thirty feet higher. I backed up to get a better view and almost instantly he jumped again, steering deftly around branches and descending towards me once more. This time he landed near the base of a white oak after a good forty-foot flight. Up the oak he scrambled to a perch thirty feet higher and shortly thereafter took off on a fifty-foot, kamikaze-style flight through the crowded understory that ended when he disappeared into a large, multi-trunked, black oak. Standing there with my jaw gaping, I realized how lucky I was that the woodpecker had gotten my attention. What a gift!

Over the next week, I shared this story. Most people I spoke to had never seen a flying squirrel and were surprised that they live in our area, where there is so much development and so few trees. We rarely spot them because they are nocturnal and we are not. We don't think about or interact much with what happens at night in our forests. Owls, muskrats, raccoons, opossum, skunk, and coyotes are also quite common around here, and yet we rarely encounter them. We share the planet with strangers.

Our lack of knowledge about the life right outside our doors is also due in part to the fact that many of us don't get out in the woods much and don't really "see" things when we do. As Emerson said, "we only see what we expect to see." I realize that seeing flying squirrels is rare and a treat, but the experience only strengthened my resolve to see more of what's going on in the woods. Now that I know flying squirrels live here, I'll walk with heightened awareness, and hope to hear and see them again.

I have also encountered friends who don't appreciate flying squirrels. Two of my neighbors regard them as pests. A family of these little creatures had moved into the attic of their last house and awakened them every night. They were expensive to get rid of because they kept coming back. So my neighbors were not at all happy to learn that the little furry guys were in the neighborhood and were ready to call up our community association to cut down the dead trees to discourage the squirrels. I pointed out that we needed the trees, even the dead ones, because if we cut them down, it would be more likely the squirrels would move into their attic again. This gave them food for thought. There should be room on this planet for people of all persuasions—and for flying squirrels as well.

Discussions like this one make me think about the variety of perspectives about forests that I've encountered over the years. I often take people on hikes to get out and explore some of the natural wonders right in our own backyards. Most love to go, but I do hear some say they would never go into the woods. When asked why, they say they are afraid of snakes, bugs, and rabid raccoons. Others are concerned about getting dirty. Some feel they have evolved beyond the woods to a more sophisticated life and have no interest or time to go outside. They may like looking at nature but don't venture into it.

Because of these fears and ideas, there seems to be an increasing number of parents who won't let their kids wander in the woods. A teacher friend of mine said that she took her first-graders outside on a nice sunny day, and when she asked them to join her in sitting down in a circle on the grass, several refused. Their parents had never allowed them to do that. These children had already lost their innate playfulness, and fascination with nature had given way to fears and distrust.

Our society is made up of a wide range of people with an array of views. That is a good thing, but I'm really concerned that our focus on technology, consumption, and safety is producing a generation of people who are unfamiliar with nature, and, in some cases, afraid to go outside. At times it appears that we focus so much on the digital universe that we have abandoned the natural one. Richard Louv proposes ways to deal with this concern in his latest book, *The Nature Principle: Human Restoration and the End of Nature-Deficit Disorder.*

If we are unfamiliar with or afraid to venture into the woods, we are less likely to visit forests, appreciate their importance (e.g., rejuvenating our brains), or take action to preserve them. Our species has evolved over a period of two hundred thousand years, learning to live in balance with the rest of the natural world. Now, in just one generation, many of us have separated ourselves from nature. How can we learn to live centered and constructive lives without engaging with the breadth and depth of the natural world? If we and our children don't bond with nature, or at least with some special place in nature, who will grow up to care for future forests and their inhabitants?

Ralph Waldo Emerson, the country's foremost philosopher, led the charge 150 years ago that freed us from our societal shackles. He encouraged us to learn from nature, to observe how it is constantly changing. The Transcendental Movement he inspired convinced a whole generation that humans, as part of an ever-changing natural world, have the ability to change their circumstances. We are not stuck; we have the ability to pursue our passions, work our way out of the class in which we were born, and improve our lives. His disciples, Muir and Thoreau among them, carried the banner of learning from nature and opened our eyes to the valuable role nature can play in our individual and national psyches. I hope we have not lost what made America great in the past as we enter this new digital era.

My encounter with the flying squirrels certainly inspired me. They are wonderful examples of leaping into the unknown, navigating perils as they arise and bravely outmaneuvering obstacles as they soar. Emerson would have loved watching their acrobatics (perhaps he did) and would have considered using them as metaphors for human potential. Encounters within forests can teach us a great deal about ourselves.

Forests of the Past — Trees have been critical to our success as a nation. They were of such importance to the early settlers of North America that entire forests were cut down. They were simply a free resource waiting to be exploited. The same is true for most of the earth's forests. Fifty percent of the planet's land mass was once covered with forests. Today less than 9 percent of the land is covered with trees. Deforestation happened quickly here. Unlike in Europe, commercial exploitation of the forest and mineral wealth in the U.S. was largely unmanaged until about 1900. That was possible because our ancestors thought of our forests as an unlimited supply of lumber that "needed" no regulation. Early colonists were unaware and uninterested in the important role trees play in the health of our planet.

The timber industry started in the Maine woods (Boone, 2011), then swept through the upper Midwest, through the Southeast, and into the Pacific Northwest. Rutkow, in his excellent book *The American Canopy* (2012), reports that our ancestors first took down all the old growth white pine in New England because it was good for almost everything necessary to build and sail ships, construct and heat homes, and fuel the growth of our fledgling colonies. Next the lumber interests targeted the poplar, the best trees for creating wood pulp for making paper. Once those were all taken out, they went back to take out almost everything else in the northern woods as demand for wood and paper continued to grow.

After clear-cutting the northern forests, the timber interests jumped to the long-leafed pines of the Gulf Coastal Plains. Throughout the South, local politicians sold off the timber lands to generate jobs during Reconstruction. The jobs lasted only as long as the timber. During the First World War, the focus shifted to optimizing the removal of Sitka pine from the northwest. This was a light wood in great demand by our burgeoning air force. Just think about it—wooden planes.

The waves of unrestricted lumbering devastated a lot of woodland and wildlife, displaced families, and generated a wealth of anger. Although the timber industry (e.g., Weyerhaeuser Co.) employed a great many lumbermen, provided valuable resources to the nation, and opened up great swaths of land for farming, it was extremely disruptive. Lumbering played havoc with our woods, our rivers, small-scale farming, and hunting, which was, after all, the prevailing way of life. The huge timber interests chopped down large parts of the country with little care for the aftermath, which continued to be a problem for years. When they cut down trees they trimmed them and left a tinder keg of small dead branches behind. Nineteenth-century railroad locomotives spewed sparks and hot cinders from their stacks and became notorious for igniting fires. Fire swept through the areas where nothing but dried kindling was left (Tim Egan, *The Big Burn*). Once the brush was burned, the rich topsoil washed away, silting in and shutting down our ports. Towns went from boom to bust as the lumbering parties moved west. The lack of management and regulation of this short-sighted industry severely damaged many of our natural resources (water, soils, forests, and game) for decades to come.

When we finally realized late in the nineteenth century that uncontrolled lumbering was wiping out many of our most valuable resources, an increasing number of people turned their anger into lobbying for better forest management. Of course, then as now, there was no agreement on whether and how this should be done. For example, New York City businesses wanted the Adirondacks saved from any lumbering at all to maintain the quality of the water supply for the city. Some commercial interests wanted to harvest all the timber right away, and others wanted the forests managed so there would be plenty of trees left to cut in the future.

The Conservation Movement became one of the more effective voices in this debate. It focused on the need to manage our key natural resources, including trees, rivers, soils, fish, and wildlife, so they could be used today and also conserved for future use. The Preservation Movement grew up at about this same time, intent upon preserving places of natural beauty and wilderness as they were, without any commercial use.

Movements Across America

The Outdoor Movement was inspired by Rev. William Murray, who published a widely read book called *Adventures in the Wilderness: or Camp-Life in the Adirondacks* in 1869. This book, his public speaking, and his extensive writing, made Murray the "Father of the Outdoor Movement." His book mobilized the public and generated the political will to establish the Adirondack State Park.

The Conservation Movement sought better management of our forests, water, soils, and wildlife. Its first leaders saw themselves as champions of democracy, protecting the nation's natural resources from short-sighted exploitation by rapacious corporations. Farmers, fishermen, and hunters led the charge, which eventually resulted in national policies committed to the scientific management of resources by the National Forestry Service, the Bureau of Land Management, the Soil Conservation Service, and the National Fish and Wildlife Service. Much of our national land and many forests are managed today in a sustainable fashion that allows some hunting, fishing, pasturing, and mining.

The Preservation Movement wanted places of natural beauty to be left pristine for recreational or spiritual rejuvenation. The movement began in the mid-nineteenth century, when a group of artists and writers began to celebrate the undeveloped countryside as a romantic escape from civilization and a source of national pride. In the early twentieth century, a reaction to the growth of automobile tourism extended preservationist thinking to wilderness areas, where cars and all commercial activities were kept to a minimum. The National Park Service was created in 1916 to manage those lands.

The Environmental Movement. From 1865 to 1915, activists focused on the environmental ills of cities, and city officials responded by building sewer systems, taking responsibility for collecting garbage and cleaning streets, protecting sources of drinking water, establishing parks, and regulating "the smoke nuisance." The movement was re-energized and broadened in the 1960s with the nationwide environmental awakening and now serves as an umbrella term that covers a wide range of issues.

The Sustainability Movement began in the late twentieth century and has now permeated most of our culture. It is based on the concept that all decisions must balance economic, social, and environmental issues. Some businesses call this the *triple bottom line*. The goal is to ensure we use our resources without harming the future. Presidents Bush and Obama issued executive orders to require all federal departments to have sustainability plans. Most Fortune 500 firms have sustainability plans, goals, and directors. These efforts have lowered costs, waste, and the use of energy and other natural resources.

Passions flared on all sides. Regulations to restrict logging and hunting also made life difficult for many immigrants, Native Americans, itinerant laborers, and backwoods farmers. And that battle continues today in many areas such as in Alaska (see Chapter 11).

As the years passed, public sentiment slowly turned in favor of conservation of resources on some lands and outright preservation on others. Lobbying efforts finally convinced the federal government and state governments across the country to take action. Windows of political opportunity briefly opened, allowing our governments to save some of the forests and wilderness areas. But those windows did not remain open for long, and the struggle to better manage our resources rages today.

The first federal act of preservation occurred in 1864 when President Abraham Lincoln ceded the federally owned Yosemite Valley and the Mariposa Big Tree Grove to the state of California as the nation's first state park. Then Ulysses S. Grant created Yellowstone National Park in 1872, thanks in large part to the geologic reports of Ferdinand Hayden, who mapped these unique territories for the U.S. Geological Survey. Yellowstone became one of the first federally protected parks in the world.

These first steps were important, but it would be decades before additional legislation resulted in widespread forest protection.

People like John Muir, a self-taught naturalist and ardent preservationist, fell in love with the old growth trees of California and wanted much more of the Sierras preserved than just Yosemite Valley. Muir was an immigrant from Scotland who came to California via the Midwest. The beauty of the tall sequoia trees and majestic landscapes of the Sierras mesmerized him. He kept writing about the grandeur of these places and took many influential people (Ralph Waldo Emerson, Robert Underwood Johnson, Gifford Pinchot, and President Theodore Roosevelt) out to see the wilderness wonders of California. His focus was to preserve as much of the region as possible from sheep grazing and lumbering, both of which ran unchecked in the West during his lifetime.

In 1890, in great part due to Muir's writings and the lobbying efforts of his cohort, Robert Underwood Johnson, editor of the *Century Magazine*, Congress passed the National Parks Bill, which helped preserve a much larger area of the Sierras. Muir helped to found the Sierra Club in 1892, which became one of the largest grassroots preservation groups in the country. To this day its mission is still *to explore, enjoy, and protect the wild places of the earth*. Muir served as its president for twenty years and continued his efforts to preserve as many of "God's Temples" as possible. He is often referred to as "The Father of the National Parks."

In 1895, the Adirondacks in New York became the first state park created specifically to preserve a huge swath of forested land. It took a quarter- century battle and a state constitutional convention to not only set aside the land but to assure that it would never be timbered. It is the largest protected tract in America that "shall be forever kept as wild forest land." This success started out largely as a one-man effort. Verplanck Colvin not only surveyed the area he thought should be preserved but advocated for years that it be saved as a park.

Modern Forestry — The trend to preserve special areas and to conserve our natural resources peaked during the first years of the twentieth century. Theodore Roosevelt and his confidant and fellow outdoorsman,

Gifford Pinchot, were the right people at the right time who in a six-year window increased the amount of protected land in America from 40 million to 200 million acres. Pinchot, as the director of the Bureau of National Forests within the Department of Agriculture, created the modern-day concept of conservation. *"It is the government's role to protect and manage our natural resources in a sustainable manner for the benefit of current and future generations."* His view on responsible forestry was that it included land management, the prevention of forest fires, and treating timber supplies as a renewable resource, lumbering and replanting as necessary.

Because of their differing philosophies, conservationist Pinchot and preservationist Muir were sometimes allies and sometimes at odds. Muir wanted no lumbering on any of the land, whereas Pinchot was able to preserve our national forests only because he agreed to allow managed lumbering. Following Muir's lead, preservationists kept pushing for lands that would not be timbered, and in 1916 their efforts led to the creation of the National Park System (NPS) within the Department of the Interior to manage park lands. The NPS now manages 401 sites (including 59 parks) and 84 million acres. It is interesting to note that these two important land management agencies (NPS and the Bureau of National Forests) are in different departments of the federal government, Interior and Agriculture respectively, which reflects their different goals.

Pinchot's contributions did not end with his work with Teddy Roosevelt. He later advised Franklin D. Roosevelt (FDR) who became a leading convert to modern forestry management at his Hyde Park estate in New York, as governor of New York State, and as U.S. president. During the Great Depression, millions of acres of land had been abandoned across the country. One of the goals of the Civilian Conservation Corps (CCC), an agency of Roosevelt's New Deal, was to plant trees on this land. In a ten-year period, Roosevelt employed 2.5 million men, who planted over 3 billion trees and installed 100,000 miles of trails. This was part of his attempt to rehabilitate hundreds of millions of acres of state and federal park lands. Roosevelt's "Tree Army," managed by

General Douglas MacArthur, was not only a boon for morale and the economy at the time, but was a major investment in the future health and wealth of America.

Private logging firms demonstrated very little long-term interest in the land once they had stripped the timber so long as there was so much virgin timber to exploit. Few logging firms considered going to the time and expense of replanting forests. Not until many decades later, when most of the unprotected virgin lands had been stripped, did lumber companies themselves begin to think in terms of sustainable or renewable resources. In the 1940s they began treating trees as crops, planting and managing their land as tree farms.

Meanwhile, it was left up to the government to think about the long-term economic and strategic military implications of a healthy lumber supply. Lumber has always been an essential resource of a growing nation. It was clearly in the national interest to manage the woods in a way that would reduce forest fires and replenish them in a sustainable manner forever. Over the past century, governmental regulations and agencies have been critical to ensuring that our water, farmland, and forests are managed so that current and future generations have access to these critical resources. *The wealth of our nation today is due in part to the sustainable management of our resources* (Figure 5).

Accomplishing the incredible conservation effort that took place between the Civil War and the start of World War II required a major cultural change in the country that came about with the conversion of anger to passion and then to political will. People angered at the loss of their forests combined with the passion of outspoken leaders rallied enough political support to change our national priorities. The battles were long and hard, but they slowly changed the way Americans view our natural resources. We were beginning to realize that forests have lasting, intrinsic value in addition to their immediate value in cash. We now know they also provide us with clean water, clean air, a more diverse and healthy environment, and a place to retreat. Protecting our forests will probably be a never-ending battle. Each new generation will have to learn for itself the full value of our forests.

The Movements Evolve – In the last fifty years, forestry management has evolved even further. President Nixon signed the Endangered Species Act in 1973 to identify endangered plants and animals and protect them from hunters and development. We soon came to realize that you cannot save an endangered species without preserving its natural habitat. Our country led the shift from assessing the health of a forest by the number of board-feet it can generate to assessing its health based on its biodiversity. This has had a large impact on forestry management both in this country and in temperate and tropical areas around the globe. For example, we now recognize that we should preserve the ancient rainforests of the world because of their diverse array of species and habitats and their invaluable storehouse of genetic material. We have moved from commodity-based forestry to ecology-based forestry.

In many ways the forest conservation and land preservation movements of the nineteenth and early twentieth centuries expanded and morphed into the late twentieth-century Environmental Movement (though even today some conservationists do not think of themselves as environmentalists). When Senator Gaylord Nelson called for the first environmental teach-in (Earth Day) in 1970, a tremendous wave of support poured out onto the streets of America and carried a whole host of issues forward under the broader title of the *environment*. Over twenty million Americans participated in the initial event, the largest demonstration of any kind in American history. Worldwide, over two hundred million people participate in this annual event today. Earth Day ended up usurping Arbor Day, and forestry issues were combined with a host of related issues, helping to make the 1970s the *environmental decade*. The movement added ecological considerations to the debates that heretofore had been restricted to protection of the water supply, lumbering, and recreation.

The Outdoor Movement has also expanded dramatically, from primitive camps in the 1800s to automobile camping in the early 1900s, to a wide range of recreational sports today. John Muir and William Murray went by train, horseback, and on foot to explore the wilderness in the late 1800s. My grandfather, inspired by the annual automobile trips of

Ford, Edison, Firestone, and Burroughs, drove his family to state and national parks in a Ford Model T pulling a camping trailer in the 1920s and 1930s. In the 1960s, my childhood family camped at many of the national parks throughout the West traveling on interstate highways in a Greenbriar Sportsvan inspired by the "See the USA in your Chevrolet" ad campaign. Today my adult children camp and hike in the great outdoors but also bring their mountain bikes, rafts, and kayaks. As access has gotten easier, more and more people have visited our national lands and an increasing number of international guests come as well. In recent years, annual attendance has exceeded 170 million visitors to our national forests and 280 million visitors to our national parks.

As a result of this expanding number of visitors and their range of interests, forest rangers now oversee and regulate a variety of outdoor recreational activities in addition to the more traditional range, timber, wildlife, and fish management. The problem today is that *too many* people are visiting some of the national lands. Their presence damages the habitat of many of the species we are trying to preserve. We need more protected land.

To combat the advance of auto-tourism and the many roads that were constructed to open up access to people, Bob Marshall and Aldo Leopold began the Wilderness Society in 1935. Their goal was to keep some parts of our national forests free from new road construction and the onslaught of people—to keep it forever wild. As with most legislation, it took decades for the public to understand the importance of our wilderness areas. The Wilderness Act, drafted and promoted by Howard Zahniser, received strong support from President Kennedy, and was eventually passed and signed by President Johnson in 1965. Initially it identified nine million acres for wilderness designation, but with time the area protected by the Wilderness Act has grown to 110 million acres at 757 sites.

The effort continues. In 2009 President Obama signed the Omnibus Public Lands Management Act, which designated more than 2 million additional acres as wilderness, created thousands of miles of recreational and historic trails, and protected more than 1,000 miles of rivers. We should keep our eyes open for more opportunities. The goal should be to maintain a balance between preservation, conservation, and development. There are other efforts to preserve land in the Congress right now such as a bill to preserve the red rocks area of Utah (http://www.suwa. org/issues/arrwa/cosponsors-of-americas-red-rock-wilderness-act-in-the-113th-congress). I am sure they would love your support.

Forest Resources Today — Trees and forests do remain important to our society. And yet, even today with all of the efforts of the last century, woods are cut down all too often for housing developments, ball fields, and new highways, with little appreciation for their value outside of the value of the land on which they grow. More progressive jurisdictions require the replanting of saplings when trees are cut down for development, but replacing mature oaks with tiny saplings, although a step in the right direction, is poor compensation for the loss of the myriad ecological services provided by the large oak. Eventually, some of the saplings may make it to full size, but we live at a deficit while the new forest grows.

Of all the environmental challenges we face today, the one I hear about most is when a majestic tree or local woods are taken down "for progress." It happens all the time and is perhaps the most obvious detrimental impact from development. Recently, our local blogosphere lit up in anger when several acres of trees were cut down in order to build a nature center.

Communities often identify with their natural landmarks. The loss of an iconic tree or a patch of woods has emotional as well as real tangible impacts. The look and the feel of a town is changed, a reference point and the place of countless memories has vanished. There is the loss of habitat and the wildlife that depended on it. Property values often decline. People of all political persuasions feel the loss, become angry, and in most cases feel helpless to do anything about it. Sometimes their anger turns to violence, but normally it can be channeled into positive action. Even though it may be too late to save a particular tree, this sense of loss, this anger, can morph into a movement to save other special parts of the community. Strong community involvement in the planning process can preserve trees and forests that are important to you and your community.

Rebuilding Our Forests — The efforts to rebuild our forests have been going on for well over a century. Here in Maryland, the concept of creating forested parks was clearly incorporated into the 1904 Olmsted Plan for rebuilding the city of Baltimore after the great Baltimore fire. The Baltimore plan recommended a continuous integrated green belt around the city as well as along the rivers through the city for the citizens to retreat to as needed. The Olmsteds knew that forests and park lands should be close to the people, and easily accessible.

Once it had been built, the people of Baltimore flocked to Patapsco Park for picnics and camping, and some even stayed the whole summer. (Anyone who has endured a Baltimore summer will understand why.) Of course, then as now there were competing interests, and many aspects of the Olmsted plans were not fully implemented. But thank goodness for our ancestors who thought ahead, and for the ongoing efforts to restore and preserve what is left of these beautiful wooded valleys. The preservation and restoration of parks and forests, near and within cities, is an ongoing effort that will always be worth supporting.

Maryland hired Fred Besley in 1906 to be its first state forester. Besley was a protégé of Pinchot and a graduate of the Yale Forestry School (which had been created by an endowment from the Pinchot family). He developed the Patapsco Forest Reserve starting with 2,000 acres along a river where much of the valley had been denuded of trees. This Forest Reserve has grown to be the 14,000-acre Patapsco State Park that runs for miles along the now heavily wooded valley carved out by the Patapsco River. By the 1930s the state had accumulated 55,000 acres of land across the state and under the Civilian Conservation Corps program qualified for ten work camps of 200 men each to plant trees and build trails.

Today Maryland, a small state, has over 145,000 acres of state forests that are well loved and used today by equestrians, mountain bikers, hunters, birders, fishermen, campers, kayakers, hikers, and joggers. Patapsco Park offers a great escape from urban and suburban living and is heavily utilized, so heavily in fact that it often has to turn people away on weekends. Here as in many parts of the country, more land and forests are needed to meet the needs of our growing population.

Like the Patapsco State Park, the most continuous stretches of woodlands outside the large national forests tend to be along stream valleys and on mountain ridges. These are places that are hard to develop or are areas where we as a society have discouraged development. In modern-day America, we decide where nature will be allowed to exist. Unfortunately these bits of forest are often fragmented, and resemble oases in a desert of development.

Across the country we have not saved enough contiguous land for all of our native species to thrive. Where are the elk in all the towns called Elkridge, Elkton, or Elk River? Where are the bison, quail, and meadowlarks? The loss of each species creates a domino effect, a trophic cascade, on a whole host of other species. We must find ways to do more. We have to follow Pinchot's example and find ways to balance the competing needs of commerce, nature, and people. We have to find much larger areas to preserve and to rewild, to let Mother Nature take her course (see George Monbiot, *Feral*).

To start we have to work with what we have preserved thus far and expand from there. Counties and states all across the country are trying to figure out new ways to do just that. Our county (Howard County, Maryland), like a few others, has created what in modern parlance is called a *Green Infrastructure Plan*. This is a systematic attempt to identify the most ecologically important areas on lands both private and public. The goal is to try to connect them into a hub and corridor complex. The hubs are the larger, more biologically diverse wooded areas and the corridors normally lie along streams that connect the hubs. This design concept should encourage the health of a wide range of species, especially ones that need to migrate or travel, by providing corridors for them to follow. It turns out I live adjacent to a hub—no wonder I have so much wildlife around me.

We will use our *Green Infrastructure Plan* to target and acquire miss-

Violence Comes to Vail

The process of finding the right balance between commerce and preservation has not always been one of debate, negotiation, and peaceful outcomes. In some cases the disagreements between developers and local residents have resulted in violence.

One such episode occurred in Colorado in 1998. Several people identifying themselves as members of the Earth Liberation Front (ELF) did not think that the Vail ski resort should expand into the last good lynx habitat in Colorado. In a last ditch attempt to stop development, someone chose to burn down the resort's restaurant shortly after it was built.

Similar vigilante actions have occurred on other development sites when it was perceived that due process, lobbying, and negotiation failed to resolve an issue. It is a choice people make when they get frustrated or angry, when they feel disfranchised. Anger is understandable when our environment is being consumed or damaged; when some groups benefit while others suffer the consequences; when *the commons* (the air, water, and forest resources owned by us all) are exploited for the benefit of some and the detriment of others. This "violence as a last resort" tactic may have been inspired by the 1975 Edward Abbey novel *The Monkey Wrench Gang*.

The Vail saboteurs did not think they were the bad guys. They targeted specific development interests, and they did not injure people or animals—in contrast to the developers, who were destroying part of our national treasure (national forests) and the lynx habitat. The federal government did not see it that way and pursued and prosecuted the perpetrators. In March 2001, ELF was classified as the top "domestic terror" threat in the United States by the Bush Administration. This was six months before the 9/11 terrorist attacks on the New York Trade Center and the Pentagon, where we learned who the real terrorists were.

ing links of ecologically important tracts and to encourage better management practices on tracts that are privately held. Some landowners object to having their private land classified as part of an ecologically important region. They are concerned that it would restrict what they wanted to do with it. In general, though, these programs don't force compliance. They provide information, management options, and in some cases offer incentives to manage the land in an ecologically healthier manner for the benefit of the landowner and the community. Check with your local or state planning office to see if they have a Greenprint or Green Infrastructure map for your area. Your community may be able to increase natural areas, wildlife, *and property values* by understanding how best to manage lands to have the greatest ecological value.

Other Challenges to Our Forests — Preserving large tracts of land is critical for the long-term health of our woods, wildlife, and humankind, but it is only a first step. There are a host of other threats to our woodlands. Forests may have healthy individual trees but are not sustainable because runaway deer populations have removed the understory—the trees of the future. This is a common problem in many suburban settings. In many areas we have to reduce the deer population so that the thousands of other plants, mammals, fish, and birds that depend on a healthy understory can flourish. That may mean harvesting (shooting) deer to keep their numbers at a healthy level. Some will object to this practice; there are always competing interests and perspectives. However, the bottom line is that we do need to proactively manage our forests and their biological ecosystems, especially if our population continues to grow. That is, after all, what the top predator's job is, to keep things in a healthy balance. This will result in smaller but healthier deer herds as well as a healthier ecosystem for all species, including humans. If man was not here, wolves, bears, and mountain lions would return and keep the deer population in check, and restore the necessary ecological balance. Unfortunately, in their absence, it is incumbent on us to do so, unpleasant as the thought may be. In addition to deer, beaver have returned to many parts of the U.S. They are certainly making their presence felt around the lake where I live. Once, they were widespread and attracted the first Europeans, who developed a valuable trade in their pelts. Even today there is a market for beaver skins ($37 per pelt in 2014). But they were not common in this area when I was growing up—their numbers had been kept low by widespread farming and trapping. I had a friend in high school who earned enough money for a new trombone, and later a car, by trapping muskrat, beaver, and mink. He would check his traps each day before school.

As the suburbs expanded, trapping became less common, and these once scarce mammals have repopulated local lakes and streams. This past fall and through the winter, beaver have been cutting down dozens of trees, stripping the bark, and dragging branches into the lake near their dens. I have counted at least six of them at one time on the thirty-seven-acre lake near my home. They have damaged a *lot* of trees. The local home owner association puts up wire mesh around any tree that has been attacked to discourage further damage. That keeps them from felling the tree, but some trees do not make it after the initial damage. It is a difficult problem for the community. Most people like having the beaver around but are disappointed when the trees are damaged. As with deer, we have to learn how to manage their population as well.

In addition to deer and beaver, disease can wreak havoc on our trees. The American chestnut was once a dominant shade tree, lumber source, and food supply throughout the Eastern Woodlands. It is estimated that they made up 25 percent of the forest and that the canopy of a mature chestnut was large enough to shade an acre of ground. Thus the line by Henry Wadsworth Longfellow, "Under the spreading chestnut tree the village smithy stands," must have had a more impressive meaning to folks when it was first penned in 1840. I have read early accounts of the American chestnut and the forests that existed when Captain John Smith first sailed up the Chesapeake Bay. It's been said that in those days a squirrel could start off in Georgia and make it all the way to Maine without ever coming to the ground. I like picturing how those cathedral-like forests must have looked, and how it must have felt to walk beneath those majestic old chestnuts.

Unfortunately, a fungus was accidently introduced in 1904 (a result of unregulated international commerce) that wiped out literally all of the chestnuts (4 billion trees). The devastation peaked in the 1930s. If trees successfully resisted the fungus, their lumber was quickly salvaged by men who feared losing the value of those trees as well. Chestnuts were so important that a lot of effort was devoted to trying to save them, but in the end, our forests today are generally devoid of American chestnuts. Sprouts still grow from the old, dead tree stumps, but generally the fungus kills them with time. This was a great economic and emotional loss to many people who had relied on the wood and nuts for income, the trees for shade, and who loved the trees for their beauty. The fungus is believed to have arrived in America along with imported Japanese chestnut trees. The U.S. has tightened up on its import and quarantine programs as a result of this devastating fungus, but the border is still quite porous. Everyone should know the story of this widespread devastation to appreciate why we must be vigilant on what we import.

Shortly thereafter the Dutch elm disease wreaked havoc across Europe. The U.S. spent a great deal of time trying to prevent the same outcome here. Like Europe, we had gone through several generations of lining the streets of our great cities with stately elms. We planted some 25 million elms nationwide; some cities planted over 600,000 trees (Minneapolis). But the disease crossed the Atlantic in 1928 and has been spreading across the U.S. ever since. We have lost about 75 percent of our elms in this country, about 77 million trees. Many of our cities have lost their soaring green arches.

It turns out that the beetles carrying the fungus were unknowingly imported by furniture dealers across the country when they imported logs and burls from infected trees in Europe. The U.S. tried a range of solutions to reduce the impact. In one of our failed attempts to save the elms, we almost wiped out all of our raptors at the same time. We sprayed high concentrations of DDT (a biocide lauded by some at the time as the "insect bomb") to kill the Dutch elm disease beetle, but ended up nearly wiping out falcons, eagles, hawks, and other wildlife.

Rachel Carson was largely responsible for raising the nation's knowl-

Bringing Back the American Chestnut

Wanting to be part of the revival of the American chestnut, our local land trust, the Howard County Conservancy, partnered with a group trying to find a strain of resistant chestnut. At least two groups in the U.S. are trying to cultivate chestnuts. The American Chestnut Foundation (TACF) crossed the American chestnut with the Chinese chestnut, which is resistant to the fungus. They are rebreeding these trees with other American chestnuts to work back to a close genetic and hopefully resistant kin to the original. Another group, the American Chestnut Cooperators' Foundation is trying to produce a resistant strain by inoculating original American chestnuts and planting them in groves around the country waiting to see how many of them will thrive.

The Howard County Conservancy planted original American chestnuts in one of their fields at the Mount Pleasant Farm in Woodstock, Maryland. Several of them are now up to six inches in diameter and twenty feet tall, mature enough to cross-pollinate and bear fruit. One tree bears several scars on its trunk but continues to grow. Another reveals no evidence of damage. These trees cross-pollinated this past year, and the conservancy is planning to plant their offspring with the hope that in time they will have fully resistant stock. Someday our descendants might see American chestnuts towering above our forests once again.

edge about the harm of excessive use of chemical pesticides, such as DDT, to bird populations. She was a marine biologist in the U.S. Fish and Wildlife Service (FWS) and an award-winning nature writer. Certain politicians and the chemical industry aggressively attacked her and her work, but the work was validated by others. Her writings proved decisive in the battle against unregulated and overuse of these toxic chemicals and eventually stopped the widespread indiscriminate use of synthetic pesticides. Her 1962 book *Silent Spring* informed an unprecedented number of Americans of the problems inherent in the misuse of man-made chemicals, and sparked the modern environmental movement. As a direct result of her efforts, the U.S. created the Environmental Protection Agency (EPA) in 1970 to better regulate the appropriate use of man-made chemicals and banned DDT in 1972. Carson died of cancer in 1964. She posthumously received the Presidential Medal of Freedom, and since the ban on DDT, raptors have returned to our skies.

Today we are facing an arboreal threat similar to the one we faced a century ago. The emerald ash borer is endangering all species of North American ash. This insect was probably introduced into Michigan from the Far East about a decade ago and has already killed millions of trees. In Maryland, as in many places of the country, we are cutting down all the ash trees for miles around any infected tree in an attempt to stop the advance of the beetle. This may be a good line of defense initially, but at some point we have to leave as many ash trees as possible hoping some will have a natural genetic resistance to the beetle. There are *billions* of ash trees in the country, and just the cost of taking them down, dead or alive, will be enormous.

The mammalian and bacterial attacks on trees are not their only dangers. In the last ten years we have also had severe wind damage to trees and forests. In 2012 the Baltimore-Washington corridor was hit by a "derecho," a widespread, long-lived, straight-line wind storm. Strong winds took down branches and some of the tallest and oldest trees in our woods. If we are going into a period of more damaging storms brought on by climate change, we might lose even more of the tall trees. So in addition to managing beaver and deer in this area, we have to take climate change seriously, too. It is amazing how much effort it takes to maintain a balance in nature, but we'll have to continue it, if we want our forest remnants to flourish for future generations.

What Can We Do? — With all of these challenges to our forest, what can we do to help protect them? The National Forest Service website is a great resource for tracking the challenges to our forests. They recom-

Leading Conservation Non-profit Organizations

The Audubon Society (1905) uses science, education, and grass-roots advocacy to advance its preservation mission, which is: *To conserve and restore natural ecosystems, focusing on birds, other wildlife, and their habitats for the benefit of humanity and the earth's biological diversity.* It has played a significant role in the preservation of the Alaskan Natural Wildlife Preserve and the Everglades. The society is named after famed ornithologist, John James Audubon, whose major work was a color-plate book entitled *The Birds of America* (1827–1839).

The Sierra Club (1892) initially focused on preserving the Sierras in California, then expanded to preservation activities across the country. Its mission: *To explore, enjoy, and protect the wild places of the earth; To practice and promote the responsible use of the earth's ecosystems and resources; To educate and enlist humanity to protect and restore the quality of the natural and human environment; and to use all lawful means to carry out these objectives.* They publish the *Sierra Magazine.*

The Izaak Walton League of America (1922) consists of fishermen and hunters who work to conserve wild open spaces. It is named for the author of *The Compleat Angler*, 1653, the first book promoting conservation, and is considered to be one of the founding organizations of the Conservation Movement. Its mission: *To conserve, restore, and promote the sustainable use and enjoyment of our natural resources.* Many members will say that they joined the League for sporting activities and stayed because of its involvement in conservation projects. It publishes *Outdoor America.*

The Nature Conservancy (1951) has preserved more than 119 million acres of land and thousands of miles of rivers worldwide. Their mission is: *To conserve the lands and waters on which all life depends.* Their success is the result of their search for pragmatic answers and their partnerships with communities, businesses, governments, multilateral institutions, and other non-profits. They publish the *Nature Conservancy Magazine*.

American Forests, 1990 – Their mission is: *To protect and restore forests, helping to preserve the health of our planet for the benefit of its inhabitants.* They have planted more than 40 million trees and work in all 50 states and in 30 other countries replanting forests destroyed by natural disasters and human activities. They have planted native trees in Michoacán, Mexico, to restore winter habitat for migrating Monarch butterflies.

mend actions and practices that local groups and individuals can take. Most states have their own forest services and many have on-line advice on tree and forest maintenance, native species, and where to find champion trees. Many counties and local jurisdictions have forestry boards that maintain arboretums, advise local planning and resource agencies, and often lead field trips and hold lectures. So there are plenty of resources to help you learn more about the area where you live. Here are a few ideas to help you get started.

Plant trees – Planting more trees in rural, suburban and urban areas is one of the most important things you can do. Trees provide valuable services that will benefit us and the natural world. Most communities today have opportunities for getting involved in planting trees and maintaining forests. Many land trusts throughout the country have tree planting projects and there are nonprofits like American Forests that work throughout the U.S. and in many countries abroad. All of these groups rely on financial and volunteer support to achieve their missions, so they need your help. But be careful what you plant. As individuals we can help prevent the next arboreal tragedy by following import laws and only buying and planting native trees, shrubs, and wood. This will reduce the likelihood of the introduction of new diseases into the country and reduce deforestation of third world countries.

Public involvement – We can encourage better management of forests and wildlife, from the federal government all the way down to the local land owners. We can certainly encourage local governments to create Green Infrastructure Plans to save and restore critical areas. But it will take a lot more. We will all have to manage our own woods in as sustainable a way as possible. We must develop a culture that appreciates, plants, and maintains trees. Therefore, one of the biggest needs is to get more people, businesses, and community organizations involved in preserving forests.

A recent survey of leading conservation organizations revealed what they see as the biggest obstacles impeding a strong conservation ethic in America today. The first is the lack of public knowledge on the importance of this topic. Second is the difficulty in getting public engagement in caring for the land. The third is that the biggest gap in interest is with young adults, eighteen-to-thirty-year-olds! Fewer of them have been brought up experiencing nature because they are so immersed in the digital universe.

The passion for nature starts when we are very young and are trying to absorb and understand our environment. If we are inside all the time, indoors becomes the only environment we know. On the other hand, if we spend time outside, we will become inspired by the world around us. This early passion is enhanced by the activities we engage in throughout our lives. I know that a balance of indoor and outside activities was certainly important to me as a child and remains so today. Busy as they are, I try to encourage my family and friends to spend at least thirty minutes outside every day.

Create outdoor opportunities – Expanding outdoor recreational opportunities is probably the best means we have to engage people with nature. Once engaged they will most likely understand the need for effective conservation. Historically, outdoor recreation meant hiking, hunting, and fishing. Today this has expanded to include a whole array of options including mountain biking, running, horseback riding, photography, geocaching, birding, orienteering, and other activities. The more *often that people get out into the woods, the more likely it is that* they will become good stewards.

Coalitions – To protect our remaining forests we will have to work with all the various groups who enjoy the outdoors. Our efforts should include the more traditional outdoor organizations like the Sierra Club (hikers), the Audubon Society (birders), and the Izaak Walton League of America (fishermen and hunters). But we also have to enlist the newer groups such as the bikers and joggers who are out using the trails.

A more recent organization, the International Mountain Bike Association (IMBA), formed in 1998, has been attempting to bring out the best in mountain biking by encouraging low-impact riding, volunteer trail work, cooperation among different trail user groups, grassroots advocacy, and innovative trail management. They currently have hundreds of chapters throughout the U.S. and overseas. As their membership grows, let's hope they learn how they can become stewards of the woods as well as users of the paths.

Today, we are all needed to speak out and be the voice of the forests, for ours and future generations.

CHAPTER 7

Rivers

Do unto those downstream as you would have those upstream do unto you.
—Wendell Berry

The Role of Rivers — There is something timeless about sitting on the banks of a major river like the Mississippi and watching huge barges and boats glide by. Such rivers seem to flow out of the past and into the future. Their banks are a good place to sit and contemplate the flow of one's life. In awe I watch the river's relentless flow, its power, and feel its transformative ability to inspire us. Like gazing up at the heavens at night, rivers help me put my life into perspective.

Rivers have been heavily utilized and exploited during the development of this nation. Rivers were the avenues of discovery for early explorers. They were the sixteenth- and seventeenth-century pathways of trade for French trappers and Native Americans. Later they served as highways for Lewis and Clark's Corps of Discovery (1803–1806), John Wesley Powell's Colorado River Expeditions (1869–1872), and others during the period of westward expansion. During the nineteenth century, billions of trees were transported downstream to saw mills by floating them on the swollen, early spring flows. Even today, the country's major rivers are significant transportation routes. Sixty percent of U.S. farm exports—largely corn and soybeans—move along the Mississippi, as do many coal, oil, fertilizer, and salt products needed by American cities and farms. Boat and barge traffic along these rivers remains one of the cheapest forms of transport in our country.

Above all, rivers are nature's way to move water off the land and carry it to the sea. Major rivers like the Mississippi, Susquehanna, Colorado, Columbia, and Sacramento are not single water bodies but a vast dendritic network of arteries that stretch across their watersheds right up to your back door. Yes, all of us live in a watershed. Where does the rain that falls on your roof, driveway, and yard flow when it runs off your backyard? What is your watershed address?

Three and a half million miles of rivers tie us all together (Figure 6). The mightiest, the 2,530-mile-long Mississippi system, has a watershed that drains the rain from thirty-one states. Large rivers like the Missouri, Ohio, Arkansas, Illinois, and Tennessee all feed into the Mississippi, bringing debris from the Rockies, the Great Plains, and the Appalachians and delivering it all to the bird's foot delta at its mouth. Note that the size of the rivers in Figure 6 reflects the volume of the water flow at any given point. It is easy to see from the map that the Mississippi carries more water than any other river in the U.S. It is a vast network of natural and man-made pathways that has served us well— except when it doesn't.

The Great Mississippi Flood of 1927 in the lower Mississippi Valley was one of the worst natural disasters in the country's history (see, John Barry, *Rising Tide*), destroying many of the towns and much of the farmland along the lower reaches of the river. In 1982, I flew over the mid-continent and saw the Mississippi and her major tributaries in full flood stage. The waters filled floodplains sometimes ten times wider than the normal width of the rivers. Flood waters were covering towns and washing away topsoil and crops. As the sun set, the brightly reflecting waters etched a permanent and powerful image in my mind, as if the whole country was underwater and washing away.

The Mississippi is called the "Big Muddy" for the amount of silt and clay it carries to the Gulf of Mexico. Rivers are the arteries that drive the hydrologic and geologic cycles of our planet and have been doing so for billions of years. Rivers wear down the mountains and feed the debris onto the plate tectonic conveyor belts under our oceans. One day, this same continental debris (the sand, silt, and clay) will be recycled into the mountains of the future.

Many of us grew up on a river and others have stories of their adventures on rivers. They have become one of our favorite places and we enjoy them for a whole host of reasons. They provide us with a real connection with nature, a place we go to see wildlife, to relax, and to challenge ourselves. That is why rafting, canoeing, and kayaking are so popular. As a seasoned river guide my daughter Anna likes the challenge of mastering a river. She likes training her passengers to paddle as a team, and guiding them through Class III and IV rapids. She also enjoys retelling the local yarns, trying to keep everyone guessing at what they might encounter on a trip down the river and through the wild woods. She introduces them to the beauty of our world.

I may not have floated down the Mississippi like Huck and Jim in Mark Twain's *Adventures of Huckleberry Finn,* or the Colorado like John Wesley Powell (Worster, 2002), but I sure feel a sense of freedom every time I paddle down a river. In fact, a number of my favorite adventures have been on rivers such as the Potomac in Maryland; Shenandoah in Virginia; Verde in Arizona; Yellowstone in Wyoming; Madison in Montana; and the Susitna in Alaska. On some of those trips, I found myself alone on quiet water, fly rod in hand. On others, I was running rapids with a raft full of family and friends. Both could be considered spiritual moments (see Norman MacLean's *A River Runs Through It*). These are man-sized rivers; rivers for canoeing, swimming, or fishing; rivers for exploring; rivers that took me out into the wild, tossed me around a bit, and taught me something about life and living it well. I will do what I can during my lifetime to preserve these experiences for generations to come. I will do what I can to restore the rivers that have been degraded by man.

Down the Patapsco, 2010 — Six of us launched four kayaks and a canoe into the Patapsco River near Avalon, heading downstream toward the Chesapeake Bay. It would be a five-hour paddle to the take-out point near Baltimore. Our goal was to cross the fall line, floating from the whitewater of the Piedmont into the calmer, tidal waters of the Atlantic Coastal Plain. Normally we prefer the rapidly flowing waters of the Piedmont, where the river does much of the work and where there is more challenge in navigating rapids. However, on this trip we wanted to retrace the 1608 path of Captain John Smith from what is now Elkridge down into Baltimore Harbor. We would have to paddle hard to get there by dark.

We were a motley but experienced crew off on another adventure (we've been doing this for three decades), yet my colleagues and I were a little rusty carrying our blue, yellow, and red watercraft down to the river and launching them. Tom, in no-tread boat shoes, slipped on the muddy bank and fell in, making for a wet start. The boats were dusty and full of cobwebs but stayed afloat. This group is lucky to get out once or twice a year and our joints needed to warm up and adjust as we took our first few strokes and used long latent muscles. Max, Jim, Peter, and Tom tried surfing a ripple and keeping their kayaks going in a straight line. I like sitting up high in a canoe, the better to see rocks ahead and watch fish dart by as we float downstream. My paddling partner, Doug, was along for the ride, taking it all in, and regaling me with stories of past trips.

As we paddled downstream, an ominous sound bubbled up from the river valley we were entering. The valley narrowed, the current picked up speed, the sound grew louder, and I looked off the bow of the Old Town canoe to see what lay ahead. As usual, I felt myself come alive as we paddled into the unknown.

"Rapids ahead, keep left!" someone shouted as we spread out and pulled into eddies to watch how each of us would navigate the current, various fallen trees, and rocks of all sizes. Like NASCAR spectators, we were watching others and waiting for a crash! In more than twenty-five years of river kayaking we have not lost anyone yet, though we often get wet. Once we left an aluminum canoe behind, crumpled flat and wrapped around a large rock sitting smack in the middle of the Potomac.

"Go left, go left!" I shouted at Doug as we headed straight for a large, mostly submerged boulder. We barely slid by. Max's kayak got hung up on a sand bar dead ahead of us. We clumsily attempted a ninety-degree turn to avoid him. As usual there was a lot of shouting, flailing, and

What Happened to Elk Ridge Landing?

In 1608, Captain John Smith and his crew sailed a 30-foot shallop up the Patapsco River. Later during the 17th and 18th centuries seafaring vessels came to the well-established port of Elk Ridge Landing (now Elkridge, Maryland) to transport tobacco and iron back to England. Records suggest the river was hundreds of feet wide and 14 feet deep at this old port. Today, it is 50 feet wide and generally 1 to 2 feet deep.

There is not much left to the old town, and the silted-in river certainly cannot accommodate anything bigger than a canoe. One can only wonder, "Where did it all go?" The river and what used to be the port city of Elk Ridge Landing have changed dramatically since colonial times (Sharp, 2001). I try to picture what life must have been like in those early days of settlement. All I can imagine is the challenge of frontier life and the squalor of living conditions faced by the common man, perhaps best expressed by John Barth in *The Sot-Weed Factor* (1960).

Scanning the stream valley we can see evidence of the decline and fall of the old port. Here, the bottom of the river and its banks are all silt, sand, and mud, burying the old international port. By cutting all the trees and planting a monoculture of tobacco, our ancestors destroyed the topsoil, then storms washed the topsoil into this stream valley and harbor creating a malarial swamp and putting an end to this former port town.

The ports at Elk Ridge Landing and Joppa Towne farther east, became un-navigable due to siltation and ceased their existence as port cities. Development throughout the watershed and a series of dams have further affected water flow in the river. It is worth the trip to see how this stretch of the river has been reclaimed by nature over the past 200 years. Our ancestors conquered the wilderness along this valley through very hard work, and then due to poor stewardship of the land, the port silted in and died.

strong pulls with the paddles—our manly show of strength and agility. We'd be feeling those muscles over the next several days.

We left the rush of the Piedmont behind, crossed the illusive fall line, and entered the calm of the Atlantic Coastal Plain. Schools of yellow perch darted out of our way. We passed the old Elk Ridge Tavern (circa 1744) which is now a restaurant of some repute, but we didn't stop because we still had a long way to go. There were no other buildings of that era. We wondered what happened to the port at Elk Ridge Landing as we silently floated past the site where it used to be.

Once beyond Elkridge, the river was all smooth paddling except for the occasional water hazard such as a "sweeper" or "strainer." These natural traps occur in areas with undercut ledges regularly drop trees across the river, impeding our passage. We did our best to avoid these potentially dangerous traps that let water flow through but could easily flip or trap a canoe in their branches. They are no fun to get tangled in.

Where the water was low we got out and dragged our boats. Kingfishers and great blue herons flew by and we paddled around a few families of mallards. The riverine passageway was a multi-hued, green tunnel, with a tree canopy overhead and vines hanging down the banks. It was a good day to be on the water.

We were enjoying the day until the river widened out to several hundred feet from bank to bank. We were in the tidewater stretch and the tide was coming in. No more being carried along easily with the current. We began paddling in earnest to make it before dark to where our cars were stationed. We had a ways to go.

We left our pristine wooded valley and approached civilization, marked by a complex, crisscrossing pattern of concrete and steel bridges. Passing beneath the bridges we noticed the first pieces of trash floating on the water. As we paddled, the amount of trash increased dramatically. Most of it by far was composed of plastic bottles. Then bottles were all around us, a raft stretching from shore to shore and as far as we could see in front and behind us, tens of thousands of plastic bottles floating on the river, quite a change from the bucolic paddling of the morning.

Why Plastic Bottles?

As I paddled through the wasteland of bottles at the mouth of the Patapsco, I thought about how much plastic we dump into our rivers and oceans and what it must do to sea-life (see Chapter 12). Thinking how we routinely trash our rivers still angers me today, and anger has pushed me to make a pact with myself to use *reusable containers* whenever possible and never buy plastic bottles.

This pledge is difficult to keep because, today, plastic bottles are ubiquitous. About 100 billion beverage bottles were thrown away last year. They ended up in our rivers or in our landfills. The abuse of this material is enormous— just think how often you see plastic bottles on the ground. Then picture all those bottles flowing down your favorite stream and winding up in a lake or ocean. Why do we need so many plastic bottles anyway? They epitomize the worst of our throwaway culture. What an awful concept—designing anything that would be intended from the start to be trashed within minutes of purchase. Drinking sugar-sweetened beverages is bad enough—they are the single largest source of sugar in our diets—but buying water in plastic bottles seems even crazier. Jenkins (2011) reports that a host of chemicals have been found in bottled water that are not found in tap water. When I first heard that I was skeptical. It was hard to believe that we had all been "taken" by the marketing campaigns of water bottling companies, who repeatedly claim how pure their product is, "as pure as mountain spring water." I had to find out for myself.

I ran tests on six popular brands of bottled water bought off the shelf at a local grocery store. I also ran samples of office water collected directly from the tap and samples from faucets at the homes of my friends. Those samples came from our city water supply and from private wells. I found that the bottled water from the store was no better than tap water and in several cases contained a wider range of chemicals.

So why do we pay for bottled water? I have to conclude that many people don't know that the U.S. spends a lot of money to ensure our water supply is safe to drink, right from the tap. Extensive marketing campaigns have convinced many Americans to pay a lot of money for something they can get for free. We pay more per gallon for water in a bottle than for gasoline at the pump. Then we throw the bottle away. This makes no sense.

We were shaken. Our first reaction was anger at the people who lived near here who must be the source of all this trash. "Don't they care?" Then someone pointed out that many of these bottles probably came from the same place we just did, moving right down the river along with the water, the sediment, and us. Over a hundred thousand people live in the thirty-five-mile Patapsco's watershed. If one bottle fell off the porch or out of the recycle bin from each of those homes then, yes, this is what you'd get. Leaving one piece of trash behind may seem negligible, but not when there are so many of us. We are all responsible for the trash, the debris, the chemicals, and the sediment that ends up in our waterways. It is sobering to realize that we are the culprits behind many of today's environmental problems.

The River that Caught Fire, 1969 — Of course it is not just plastics that have damaged our rivers. One of the most famous American rivers, from an environmental perspective, is the Cuyahoga, which flows through Akron and Cleveland, Ohio, and empties into Lake Erie. At least thirteen fires were reported on the Cuyahoga in the industrial age, the first documented event occurring in 1868. The largest river fire, in 1952, caused over $1 million in damage to boats and a riverfront office building. These were not small events, but neither did they receive much national attention. There was a time in our past when negative aspects of industrialization were not talked about. They were considered one of the costs of progress, just something we all had to "put up with."

Then, on June 22, 1969, a fire started on the Cuyahoga and burned for two hours. It was picked up by national media, and it *did* capture the attention of the nation. The timing was right. The entire country started asking the obvious question, "How can a river catch on fire? "

This outrage came right at the time when America *was* starting to pay attention. A time when our national consciousness was being raised on a whole host of dangerous corporate practices, not the least of which was dumping toxic chemicals directly into rivers. It was as though we were just waiting for a poster child, and there it was. The Cuyahoga stepped up to help usher in the environmental era. The incident spurred an avalanche of water pollution regulations—the Clean Water Act (CWA), the Great Lakes Water Quality Agreement, and the creation of the federal Environmental Protection Agency (EPA). Every movement needs a spark, and this one ignited Americans to change.

The Cuyahoga caught fire because flammable petroleum products were being directly and indirectly dumped into it. The CWA ended much of the direct dumping of pollutants into our streams and rivers, but it did not happen overnight. It took a great deal of enforcement, lawsuits and changes in industrial operations (best practice guidelines). It also required the introduction of processes and technologies to capture, manage, and safely discharge contaminants. All of that happened through a combination of behavioral and technical changes driven by regulations and regulators, and implemented by staff who had been inspired by professional societies and consultants. *This is how we create change in America.* The process is complex, but in the long run it is effective at changing our cultural and professional values and behaviors. *Organic waste discharges into the nation's waterways declined by 98 percent as a result of these actions.*

Spilling volatile petroleum and other chemicals into the river was clearly a big part of the problem with the Cuyahoga, but as it turned out, surface dumping is not the whole issue with our rivers. Some contamination comes along with groundwater that seeps out from riverbanks. Tens of thousands of new, man-made chemicals were created during the twentieth century, and some of them were found in natural seeps from our vast supply of underground fresh water! Yes, by the 1960s, we had been so negligent in the handling of a wide array of chemicals that we had contaminated our precious groundwater, our essential drinking water supply buried in aquifers all across the country! That was an even bigger problem, and at first we were not prepared to deal with it.

Testing the Groundwater, 1986 — Not until the late 1980s did we get serious about dealing with contaminated groundwater supplies. I remember being called in by the Maryland Department of Health to help solve a problem for a local landowner. The water from his well smelled bad. He was a farmer and was at wit's end about what to do about it.

"How long has this been a problem?" I asked.

"My wife says it's been bad for a while. I know it's getting worse. It used to be good water. We stopped drinking it last year and now buy all our drinking water. It's not cheap you know. Seems like a damn shame to have so much water and not be able to drink it. It just tastes bad. I can smell it throughout the house."

They were clearly more than a little angry. They had spent their lives on this land and now the water had gone bad. They were also frustrated. After multiple calls to their elected officials and to the local government agencies, they realized that no one had direct responsibility to deal with contaminated well water. In the early days of environmental cleanups, there was no clear path for getting help. Initially, health departments got involved. With time, public works or environmental departments picked up the cases of water-well complaints. It turned out that there were a lot of contaminated wells all across the country and people were angry. Our abuse of the land was coming back to haunt us.

I took samples of water from the farmer's faucet and from a seep on their farm that emptied directly into the adjacent creek. I could smell the contamination in the samples as I collected them in small glass vials. Back at my lab, we ran them on a gas chromatograph. Sure enough, they were contaminated with fairly high levels of petroleum hydrocarbons. I also found significant concentrations of cleaning solvents. I scheduled a follow-up meeting back at the farm.

"Here are the results. Note the water clearly is contaminated. Have you ever dumped any extra fuel, pesticides, or cleaning liquids into the ground?"

"No, we wouldn't do that," the farmer's wife said. "We burn everything out back in the trash heap."

"Do you have any underground storage tanks?" I asked.

The farmer said, "We have a heating oil tank on the back porch and a gasoline tank buried out by the barn, but we stopped using that years ago."

"Can you show me where they are?"

"Sure, let me get my boots on." Which he did, and then we walked around his house and barn. As we walked I sketched a map in my notebook showing the buildings and the slope of the land.

"I see some staining in the soils beneath your oil tank. Did that ever leak?"

"No, that stain came when the oil company over-filled the tank once. He got busy talking and stopped paying attention to what he was doing."

I drew the location of the tanks and the location of the well on my map.

"Why did you stop using the underground gasoline storage tank?"

"About ten years ago it failed - would not hold gasoline. I was pouring good money after bad, so I abandoned it," he said.

His wife said, "We lost some of our elm trees down the lane at about that same time. But we did not have the water problem back then. We have it now. It's been a long time since the tank failed."

I said, "I think it would be a good idea to do a soil vapor survey across your property to see if there's a connection between these sources and your well. When liquids soak into the ground, they often migrate down to the groundwater table and follow it as it flows downhill to a stream. The compounds we found in the water sample are all volatile, and they give off gases that will rise to the surface. By taking vapor samples at shallow depths, we can usually trace contamination along its migration pathway back to its source."

The lab analysis had cost $200. This next phase was going to cost $4,000. The farmer said he did not have that kind of money and would just continue buying water. He was ticked, felt trapped, and was starting to give up. I went to the state and said that this could be a larger problem and asked how they were going to find the source of the contamination. They were concerned about how widespread this water problem could be and who else might be affected. They agreed to pay for the survey.

My team came in and poked holes the size of your forefinger four feet into the ground and drew out small volumes of soil vapor. We analyzed the samples and found the same compounds in some of the samples but not in all of them. The relative concentrations varied across the farm. We plotted the results on the map I had made of the farm buildings and the potential sources. I drew "contour" lines connecting areas of equal concentration. This process is like solving a mystery. First collect data, then analyze it, and finally interpret it. Sometimes our interpretations need further testing, and other times it's pretty clear to everyone.

At our next meeting we showed the results.

"Take a look at these sampling points that have the most circles around them. That's where the highest concentrations of the contaminants are in the subsurface. There is no evidence of a significant spill around the heating oil tank. There is evidence that the gasoline that leaked out of your underground gasoline tank did migrate down to the water table and then flowed 200 feet downhill. It probably killed those elms, but it did not go in the direction of your well and did not reach the stream. Notice we also found a spot by the woods where there is a small occurrence of contaminants. It looks like an old dump site."

"Yeah, we often throw things away back there, we burn most of it and then we bury the rest. We drain our sprayers there, too," the farmer said. His wife looked at him, wondering if he had said too much.

"Well you see what happens. That area has been contaminated, so I wouldn't do that anymore. It's illegal to do that today. But what the data are also telling us is that there's a large, contaminated plume of groundwater coming downhill from offsite, moving directly toward your well and continuing on to the stream. It looks like it's coming from the strip mall on the highway uphill from your place, probably from the gas station and the dry cleaning store."

The farmer exploded. "Those bastards, they poisoned my well! What am I supposed to do about it?"

The data were very convincing, so the state opened cases on both of these sources of contamination. The owners of both sites were required to stop contaminating the soil and water and to clean up the groundwater. That's not easy to do, and it will take many years to clean up the contaminated area. In the meantime, the owners of these "sources" were required to pay for fresh drinking water for the farmer and his livestock. They chose to put in a new well away from any of the contamination—not the perfect solution but the best compromise for all involved. The state has been keeping track of the cleanup efforts for the past two decades. Cleanups are neither cheap nor quick.

This is a typical example of problems that were occurring all across the country in those days. Many of us contaminated the soil and groundwater with our "normal practices" of dumping excess fertilizer and pesticides, used oils, antifreeze, and other waste liquids right into the ground. That was just what you did with your waste chemicals up to the last quarter of the twentieth century. What else were you supposed to do with it? There were no recycling centers. We had not yet learned that we were fouling our nests. But there was plenty of land, and we thought these small amounts of leftover chemicals would degrade away over time. Many of them do degrade, but it often takes a long time. We didn't know the impact of what we were doing.

Some of our past practices were worse than others, but we had to stop all of those activities contaminating our groundwater. They all add up. In addition to surface disposal of pollutants that got into our streams, there were over two million underground gasoline storage tanks in the country, many of which were leaking. My company alone handled over 3,000 projects trying to find sources of contamination from a wide range of surface and subsurface discharges. Much of this work was triggered by bad-tasting well water, the discovery of contamination (e.g., iridescent slicks) during excavation projects, contamination found in streams, and accidental spill releases. Much of it was coming from gas stations, dry cleaners, and manufacturing and commercial sites. Much of it came from our homes. We are all to blame.

I recently taught a course on sustainability to Russian businessmen. They told me they have so much land that they just dump all of their wastes on it. They haven't reached the critical point where population density would force them to follow less polluting practices. Land is cheap and abundant in Siberia. This philosophy has caused a great deal of environmental damage across Russia and the former Soviet Union. Vast areas are highly contaminated, but according to these businessmen, that is a low priority. They are just trying to make money and feed their people. This sounds all too familiar to the pushback we heard fifty years ago in this country. Today, I think most Americans are glad we took the steps we did to improve the health of our people and our country. The social, environmental and economic benefits outweighed the costs.

Cuyahoga River Follow-up, 2013 — The Cuyahoga River became the poster child for a time when we did not focus on disposal practices, the health of our rivers, or even the health of our communities. Our culture has changed now to one where we do care about these things. The Cuyahoga has been cleaned up dramatically as a result of the enforcement of regulations born from its misery. Stretches of the river once devoid of fish now support up to forty-four different species. Today we can hold it up as a poster child not of carelessness but for a new period of awareness, a major success story of the last fifty years.

Americans and our institutions have done an incredibly good job cleaning up our waterways. We have passed laws. We have stopped dumping the most toxic chemicals. People who did not follow the laws have gone to jail. Corporations have been fined, and most have changed their ways. It has taken a long time and quite a bit of effort, and it did *not* result in the economic catastrophe that many predicted when we required a change to our most egregious corporate practices. Workplaces are *healthier* today, the environment is *healthier*, and business bottom lines are *healthier* as a result. Our GDP continued to rise. It is a success story we should all be proud of, one that we can learn from, and one we can replicate.

Aside from these successes, more clearly needs to be done. The challenge we face today in America is not the dumping of toxic materials by large manufacturing plants and refineries. Much of that is under control. The problem today is the residue generated by everyday living: the exhaust from our cars; the fertilizer we put on our lawns and farmlands; our widespread use of highly polluting fossil fuels; and the polluted rain water and sediment running off our backyards. All of this, yes, *all* of it gets transported downstream by our marvelous network of streams and rivers. On its way it damages not only communities and the base of our food chain but also many of the places we hold dear. Our streams, lakes, bays, beaches, and oceans are being damaged. According to the EPA, 55 percent of all rivers in the U.S. are still under duress. Over 30 percent of all rivers have high nitrogen and phosphorus concentrations.

The health of the Cuyahoga, although better than it was in the 1960s, is not perfect today. The challenge it faces today is no longer that it will catch fire. Elevated awareness has clearly changed our culture. But the Cuyahoga River now faces the same problem that so many other rivers across the country do, the runoff of stormwater pollution from farms and yards.

In much of the nation, fertilizer from agricultural operations makes up the largest part of the pollution. We have developed a series of best management practices for farms which, where they are used, do help. But the use of best management standards can be tricky. Farm conditions and practices vary. The Natural Resources Conservation Service is one of the best places to find more information on this topic (www.nrcs.usda.gov). No-till farming is a best practice that has reduced runoff of fertilizers and silt, but it requires the substantial use of pesticides. Furthermore, in farm fields where tile drains have been installed, the waters that flow out of these drains may have to be treated. Unfortunately, the latest U.S. Geological Survey (USGS) data for the Mississippi River basin shows the nutrient levels are still rising. They are also rising in most urban and suburban areas of the country. Those nutrients are coming from homeowner use of fertilizer and the nitrates that fall on our land from fossil fuel power plants. We are now dealing with the widespread challenges of managing the residue of everyday life in an overcrowded twenty-first century.

Trying to get a handle on pollution in rivers is exacerbated where the rivers are used for a variety of purposes. The Klamath River that flows from Oregon to California is under duress because it attempts to accommodate so many competing interests. In that watershed, multi-party agreements, facilitated by the EPA, are being used in an attempt to keep the needs of nature, agriculture, and watershed residents in balance. It is an ongoing example of the challenges of managing rivers.

What Can We Do? — In 1968, President Johnson signed into law the Wild and Scenic River Act, which has helped guide us in preserving and restoring the nation's rivers. To learn more about how our federal government is trying to preserve our rivers, explore the National Wild and Scenic River System website (www.rivers.gov).

Behavior change – Improving the health of our society will require us all to recognize our role in polluting our rivers. Some of our habits will have to change. That may sound hard, but it is the easiest, cheapest, and quickest way to solve this and many of our other environmental problems. When you think about it, a relentless marketing campaign persuaded us to drink bottled water in a country where the tap water is so good. If our drinking habits can be changed by advertising, why can't we change our behavior with an information campaign that helps us learn the truth about how we are damaging our rivers.

Recycling – Let's start with the easy one: polluting streams with plastic bottles. Recycling has caught on in many areas and we must take steps to increase what can be recycled. Unfortunately, even today, the rate of recycling plastic bottles is only about 20 percent. Most of us still throw away bottles and many other things that can be recycled. Rates are higher where single-stream recycling takes a wide assortment of materials. Keep asking what can be recycled in your area—it changes all the time.

The Future of the Klamath River

Last summer I revisited and explored the Klamath River, a 255-mile-long, federally protected "Wild and Scenic River," that flows from Oregon through northern California to the Pacific Coast. It is beautiful, in places cutting through both semi-arid and forested habitats. The upper regions of the Klamath are known as the "Everglades of the West" and serve as a wonderful refuge for migratory birds. The lower parts have supported the third-largest salmon run on the West Coast, following closely behind the Sacramento and Columbia rivers. It is an amazing resource that runs through park, agricultural, and tribal lands.

While traveling along the river on this latest trip, I was disheartened to see so much algae in the river, so I inquired about it. The Klamath has had contentious resource issues for years, including water allocation, water quality, and threatened and endangered species. In 2002, a massive die-off of over 33,000 adult salmon on the Klamath brought renewed attention to the area. The die-off had a major impact on the Yurok Tribe, which has fishing rights to the lower 43 miles of the river.

The river is degraded by widespread blue-green algae blooms. The blooms resulted from high nutrient loads from agriculture, water impoundment (and warming) behind four dams, and diversion of water for irrigation. All of this takes place way upstream from the tribal lands. A series of lawsuits have been aimed at removal of the dams and for restrictions on the use of water for agriculture. The EPA has been brokering discussions and implementing consent decrees to force all parties to work together to balance competing needs for this wonderful resource.

Now, after a long and contentious battle, all parties are trying to implement a recently reached agreement that involves balancing upstream uses of the resource with nature's ability to maintain a healthy ecosystem downstream that can support the wildlife and the people who live along the river. This is a landmark case and well worth following. It will be interesting to see how effectively the different interests work together over the next several years as they implement the process (http://www..epa.gov/region9/water/watershed/klamath.html).

Bottle bills – Since recycling is not capturing all the discarded bottles, many states have passed bottle bills (CA, MI, NY, VT, OR, ME, MA, IA, CT, and HI). These require stores to pay people for returning plastic and glass bottles and aluminum cans so that more of them are recycled or reused. I remember how widespread and successful this approach was back in the 1950s. I earned spare change by collecting bottles and taking them to our corner store. It gave us all the chance to make a little money while cleaning up our neighborhood.

Re-useable containers – Get healthy. Drink tap water. The push to use fewer throwaway containers is helped today by our country's emerging efforts to reduce childhood obesity. An increasing number of health organizations, realizing that obesity leads to a large number of preventable diseases (high blood pressure, diabetes, heart disease) and deaths, are doing their best to inform parents about the addictive problems created by offering sugar-sweetened beverages to kids at home and at school. Kids who grow up with regular access to sweet drinks have much higher rates of obesity-related illnesses when they grow up. Water right out of the tap is a great alternative and better for us and the environment. We all could be carrying reusable containers of tap water with us wherever we go. Reducing our use of plastic bottles (and all other wastes) is a big step toward restoring our rivers.

Stormwater runoff – Like the Klamath and Cuyahoga, the future health of rivers will depend on all of us learning to manage the water that falls on our property in a more responsible way. To meet these goals, small landowners can start collecting water in barrels, rain gardens, or infiltration trenches and let it seep gradually back into the soil. In our community we have begun to install rain gardens as the best backyard

Community Organizing

Community organizing will be necessary to achieve many of our river restoration and stormwater management goals. An example of this is the work being done by PATH (People Acting Together in Howard), a consortium of local, faith-based organizations in Howard County, Maryland. PATH is an affiliate of the nationwide Industrial Areas Foundation. In our county, the congregations within PATH have advocated for and implemented several important initiatives, including a grassroots stormwater management effort.

A faith-based coalition may seem like an unusual advocate for stormwater abatement, but it came right out of their desire to help their member congregations. They asked them to hold one-on-one meetings among their parishioners in order to find out what issues were most important to them, i.e., "What keeps you up at night?"

Two of the most common answers across the county were 1) finding meaningful jobs for their teenaged and young adult children and 2) preventing further environmental degradation of our planet. In discussions across faiths (Christian, Muslim, Jewish, Unitarian), they decided they could do both by forming a youth conservation corps to build rain gardens.. A local non-profit, Alliance for the Bay, set up a program called READY (Restoring the Environment and Developing Youth) to run the program.

During the first summer (2012), 31 students were trained in the mechanics of rain garden installation, landscaping, and teamwork, and they built dozens of rain gardens. Forty-five students were trained for work during the summer of 2013, and they built even more. Equally important to this outcome is that 18 congregations learned about and mobilized on the issue of stormwater management. More than four hundred people came out to public meetings to show their support for cleaning up our rivers. Over 4,000 members from these congregations are now aware of the stormwater challenge, and many are installing rain gardens in their own backyards, at the offices where they work, and at their places of worship. You might want to consider starting a group like PATH in your community. http://www.industrialareasfoundation.org/).

solution for individual residences. They are man-made depressions in yards, located and designed to collect rain water from impervious surfaces (roofs, driveways, etc.). The gardens are planted with specific water-absorbing plants, and lined with a substrate that allows water to filter slowly into the ground. Rain gardens allow our natural groundwater tables to be recharged. A higher groundwater table will then feed water into our streams continuously throughout the year. That helps prevent flash flooding and the scouring of our stream banks when it rains. The gardens, which mimic the natural hydrologic system, also help us keep fertilizer on our property and prevent trash and chemicals from washing into our streams, lakes, and oceans.

Collective action – It will take community commitment throughout the watershed to save our rivers. The good news is that the process for fixing stormwater runoff has already begun. It started with the Clean Water Act of 1972. Over the years the regulations have been refined and strengthened (2006) to meet the needs in areas where continued population growth has increased the stress on natural systems. The EPA is helping by requiring water quality improvement plans for most water bodies. This will take different approaches in the various hydrologic regimes around the country. It will be interesting to watch how communities take responsibility for and figure out how best to handle their stormwater runoff. Individuals and communities don't have to do it all themselves. A range of organizations are focused on these issues. Some have raised funds for a local youth conservation corps to build rain gardens. Others work to get policies changed. One local group (PATH) has been very effective at organizing the faith community to pursue both.

In addition to what you can do in your own backyard and in your

The Waterkeeper Alliance

One national group that pursues an advocacy model for restoring rivers is the Waterkeeper Alliance. Their grass roots affiliates around the country often seek to obtain legal standing in order to assert enforcement actions. Bobby Kennedy is the chairman of this umbrella organization for over 200 individual Waterkeepers, Baykeepers, and Riverkeepers around the world. The organization grew out of the efforts of the Hudson River Fisherman's Association in the 1960s. In their fight against Consolidated Edison's proposed hydropower facility at Storm King Mountain, New York, they won the right for citizens to have standing in protecting environmental lands based on recreational and scenic issues without having to show tangible economic harm, "the Storm King Doctrine."

By reasserting *public ownership of common resources*, Waterkeepers protect communities, the environment, and the democratic rights of citizens. They have established that any harm incurred by the "commons" (see Glossary) is an act of thievery against every community member. This idea is a big step forward for protecting our rights to clean air and water.

The Waterkeeper Alliance is made up of people and organizations who pursue a range of activities for protecting a specific river. These actions take the form of investigations; environmental review of development projects; regulatory review and comment; litigation; and local, state, and federal policy issue advocacy. These river advocates are always on the lookout, checking on new sources of runoff and contamination and opportunities for improving their river. Their job is to find out what is damaging the river and to work with all interested parties to improve things. Their work led to the genesis of the citizen lawsuit provision of the Clean Water Act, which they have utilized to achieve their goals.

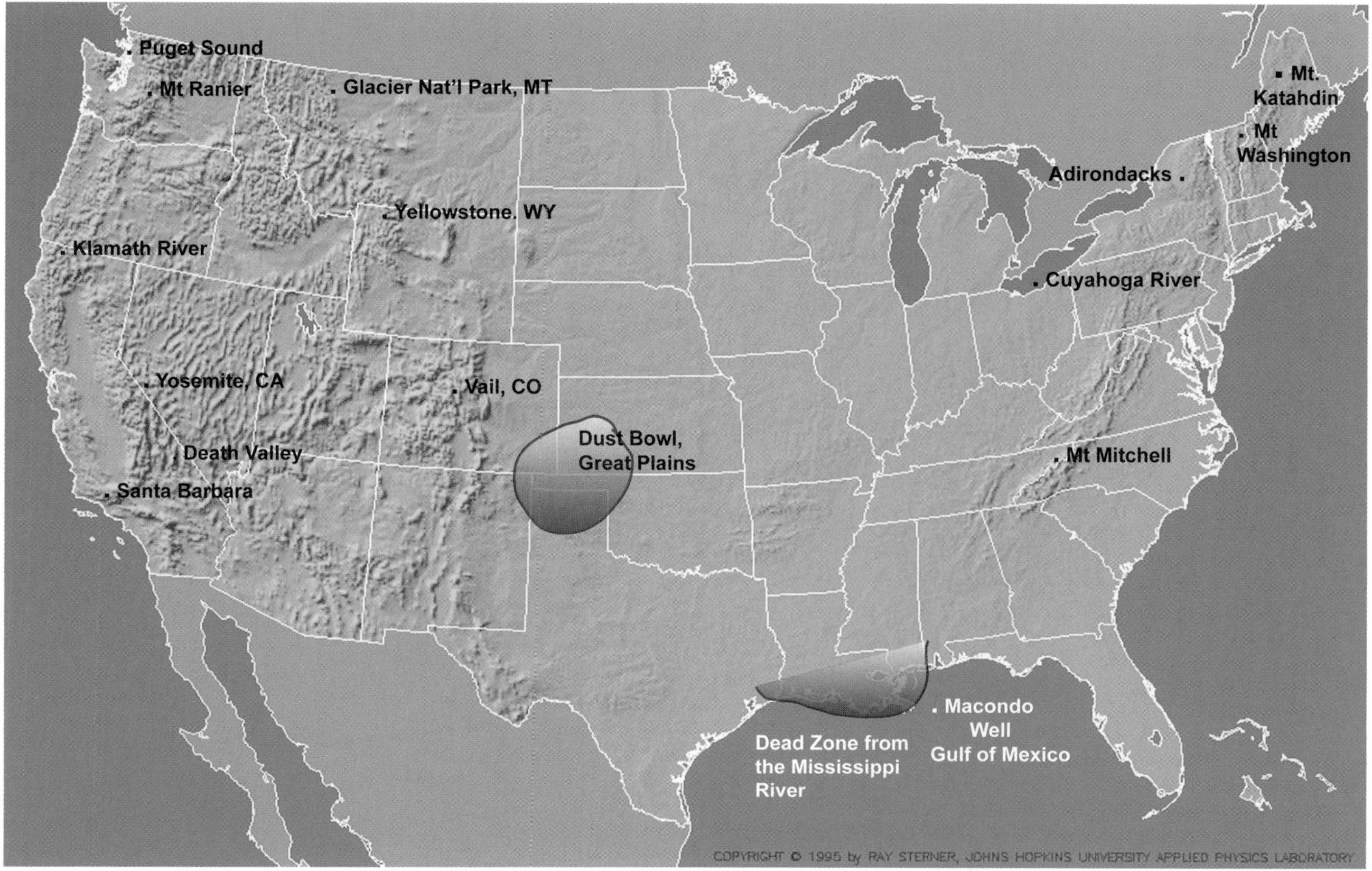
Puget Sound
Mt Ranier
Glacier Nat'l Park, MT
Mt. Katahdin
Mt Washington
Adirondacks
Yellowstone. WY
Klamath River
Cuyahoga River
Yosemite, CA
Vail, CO
Dust Bowl, Great Plains
Death Valley
Mt Mitchell
Santa Barbara
Macondo Well Gulf of Mexico
Dead Zone from the Mississippi River
COPYRIGHT © 1995 by RAY STERNER, JOHNS HOPKINS UNIVERSITY APPLIED PHYSICS LABORATORY

Figure 1: Places discussed in *Saving the Places We Love.*

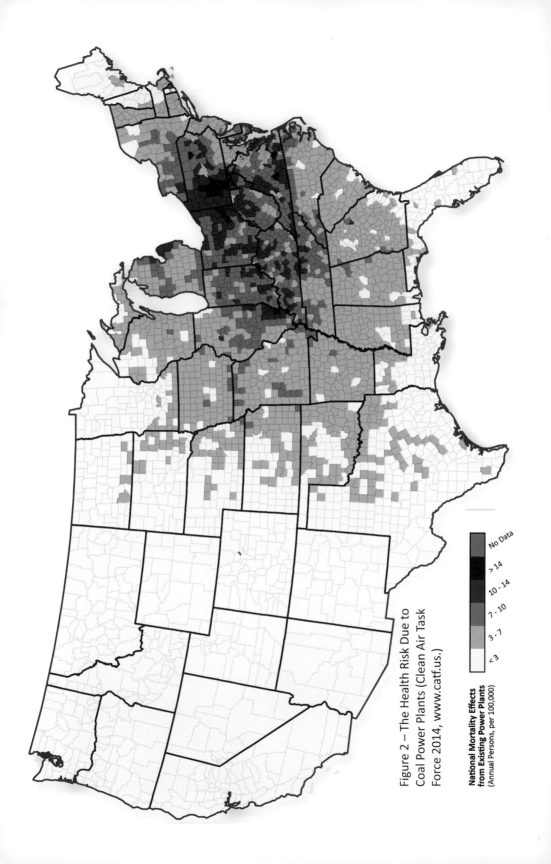

Figure 2 – The Health Risk Due to Coal Power Plants (Clean Air Task Force 2014, www.catf.us.)

National Mortality Effects from Existing Power Plants
(Annual Persons, per 100,000)

No Data
> 14
10 - 14
7 - 10
3 - 7
< 3

Rain garden installed by PATH at the Franciscan Friary in Ellicott City, Maryland, 2013. (Photo by Don Tsusaki.)

Figure 3: Residential Rain Garden Design (http://vienna-wv.com/portal/2013/07/18/what-is-a-a-raingarden/).

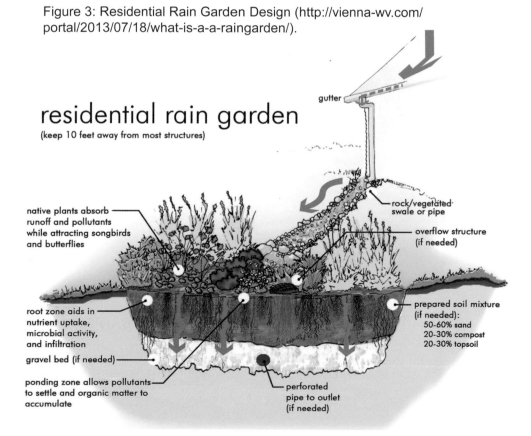

residential rain garden
(keep 10 feet away from most structures)

gutter

native plants absorb runoff and pollutants while attracting songbirds and butterflies

rock/vegetated swale or pipe

overflow structure (if needed)

root zone aids in nutrient uptake, microbial activity, and infiltration

prepared soil mixture (if needed):
50-60% sand
20-30% compost
20-30% topsoil

gravel bed (if needed)

ponding zone allows pollutants to settle and organic matter to accumulate

perforated pipe to outlet (if needed)

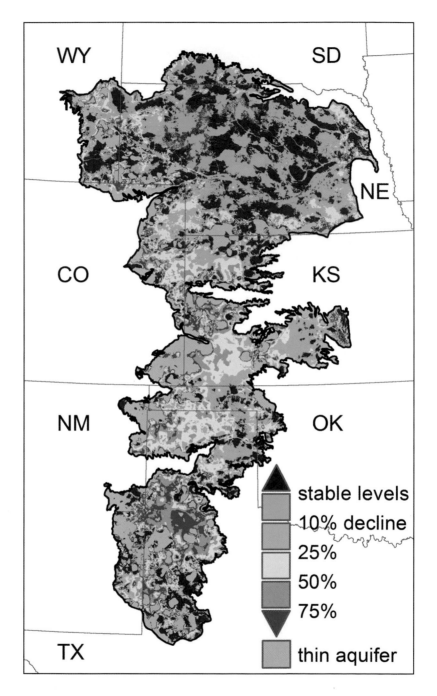

Figure 4 – Ogallala Aquifer Depletion Risk. (From Basso, et al., "The Future of Agriculture Over the Ogallala Aquifer: Solutions to Grow Crops More Efficiently with Limited Water," 2013.)

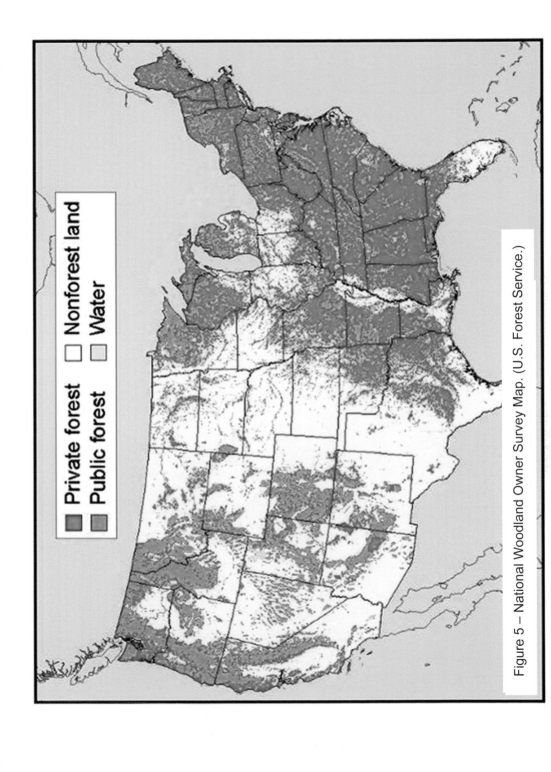

Figure 5 – National Woodland Owner Survey Map. (U.S. Forest Service.)

Legend:
- Private forest
- Public forest
- Nonforest land
- Water

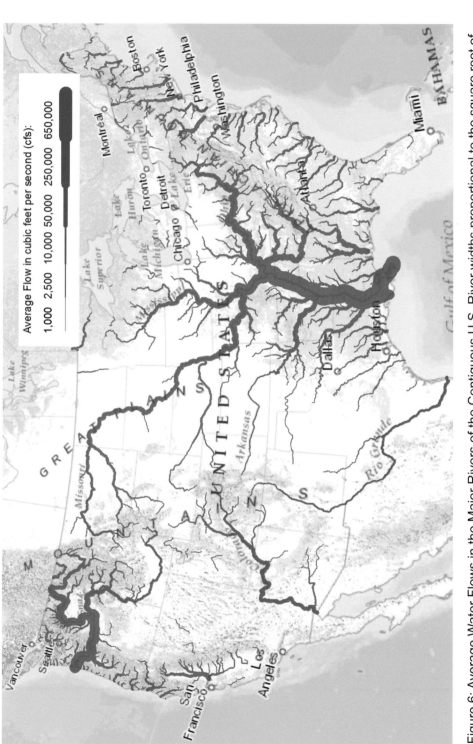

Figure 6: Average Water Flows in the Major Rivers of the Contiguous U.S. River widths proportional to the square root of the rivers' estimated average annual discharge. Data from NHDPlus v2. (Prepared by Matthew Heberger, 2013.)

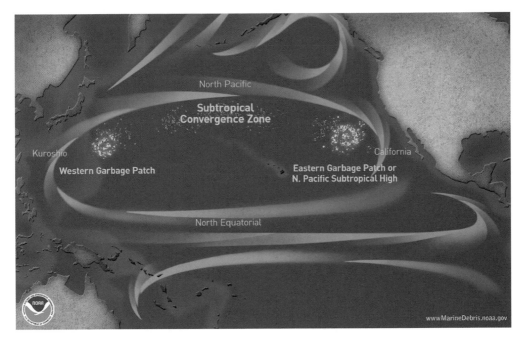

Figure 7: Map of Pacific Ocean gyres showing where trash accumulates. (National Oceanic and Atmospheric Administration.)

Plastic bottles collecting at the mouth of the Patapsco River. (Photo by Stephen Brown-Pearn.)

Pipeline Incidents Since 1986

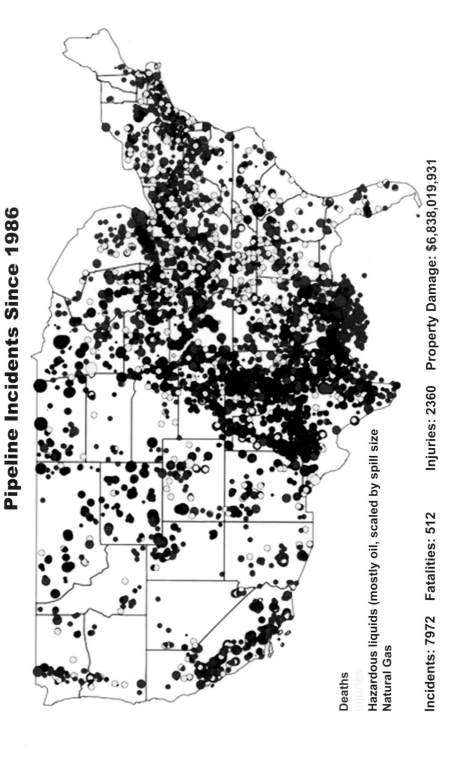

Deaths
Injuries
Hazardous liquids (mostly oil, scaled by spill size
Natural Gas

Incidents: 7972   Fatalities: 512   Injuries: 2360   Property Damage: $6,838,019,931

Figure 8: Toxic Liquid Spills from Pipelines. (Department of Transportation, Pipeline and Hazardous Materials Safety Administration.)

Figure 9: Gas Production from Conventional Fields. (U.S. Energy Information Administration, based on data from HDPI, Indiana Geological Survey, USGS. Updated April 8, 2009.)

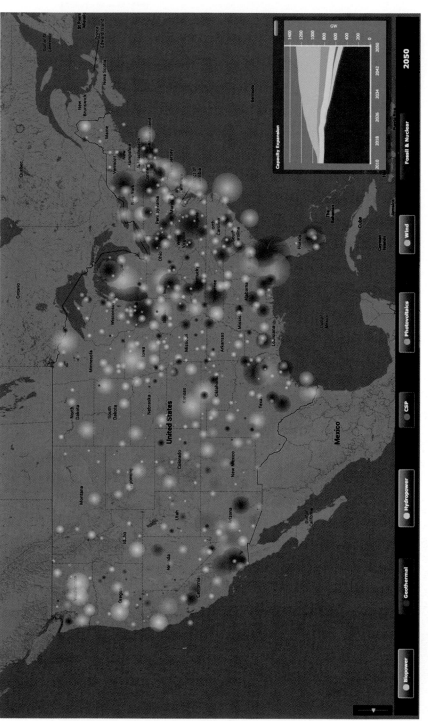

Figure 10: Projection of Power Sources in the Year 2050. (National Renewable Energy Laboratory.) Dark Blue=Fossil and Nuclear, Pink=Wind, Yellow=Photovoltaics, Orange=Concentrated Solar Photovoltaics, Gray=Hydropower, Purple=Geothermal, and light green=Biopower.

Mt. Katahdin, Maine, showing the infamous Knife Edge Trail. (Imagery ©2014 Google; Map data©2014 Google.)

Algal blooms in Lake Erie (Photo by NASA Earth Observatory). Note the recent algal blooms at bottom center.

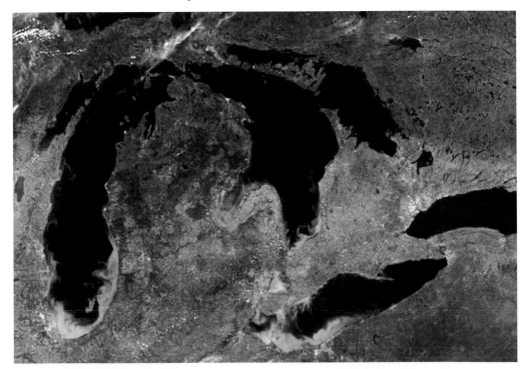

Dust storm engulfing homes in 1935. (Kansas Historical Society.)

A more recent storm threatening homes in 2011. (Viewer-submitted photo from KCBD-TV Lubbock website.)

Crop circles in the Great Plains. (Water Encylopedia – Ogallala aquifer.)

Aerial view of the Prairie Pothole Region of the northern Great Plains, near Wing, North Dakota. (Photo: Jim Ringelman, Ducks Unlimited.)

Barrier islands. Assateague Island (top) has migrated westward, while Ocean City, Md., has not. (Jane Thomas, ian.umces.edu/imagelibrary.)

BP's Deepwater Horizon offshore drilling platform blowout and fire in 2010. (Photo: U.S. Coast Guard.)

Mount McKinley and Denali National Park, Alaska. (NPS Photo / Jacob W. Frank.)

How the West once looked. Buffalo grazing on the National Bison Range in western Montana. (US Fish and Wildlife Service.)

Rocky shoreline of the Pacific Coast near Half Moon Bay, California.
(Author's photo.)

Federally preserved northern Cascade mountains in Washington State.
(Author's photo.)

community, you might also want to consider what you can do in a larger river or watershed group. Many rivers have teams of volunteers (e.g., Tributary Teams) that do their best to monitor, clean up, and become stewards of the river near where they live. Your local environmental, public works, or planning department could steer you to these groups. Some families, businesses, or church groups adopt sections of rivers to keep clean. Other groups pursue more of an advocacy model. One national group, the Waterkeeper Alliance, seeks to obtain legal standing in order to assert enforcement actions.

There are many organizations and campaigns that could use your support. American Rivers is a national nonprofit formed in 1973, which works to protect wild rivers and restore those that have suffered damage. They have protected or restored 150,000 miles of rivers through their efforts. They conduct an annual America's Most Endangered Rivers® campaign (www.americanrivers.org).

Ask around to find an organization that has achieved the goals that are important to you. I support some groups financially and others with my volunteer time. I find it helpful to work with both local and national groups to gain perspective of what is important and effective. I connect people and groups who are pursuing similar goals. It is important to collaborate with as many people and groups as possible to build the broadest coalition to save your favorite river.

It is also important to get people outside, to encourage them to literally go out and walk or canoe a river so they have a chance to fall in love with the outdoors. We also want them to see the trash and the algae blooms. We all need to experience the earth's beauty, and to see the impacts of our mistakes. We need families, schools, clubs, companies, and churches to get involved. We need more people to take their fear and their anger and go speak at meetings, give testimony, and lobby so that we have adequate knowledge, laws, and regulations to ensure that future development is as sustainable as possible. We have a lot of work to do. *Rivers should be places that are safe, inviting to visit, and full of wildlife. They should be places where we go to get recharged and marvel at the beauty of the universe. They are a place where our restorative actions will touch the future.*

CHAPTER 8

Backyards

Your property is a wildlife preserve representing the last chance we have to sustain plants and animals that were once common throughout the U.S.
— Doug Tallamy

Manor Lane, Maryland, 1983 — One day I heard through the neighborhood grapevine that an overgrown cornfield down the street was going on the market. I was intrigued by the possibilities and immediately walked over to survey the site. Topographically, the field was a high point, so no one lived upstream. The wide-open view to the west would be great for watching sunsets. A ten-acre forest to the north was full of majestic, century-old, hundred-foot-tall trees. I already knew that the neighborhood was a great place to live. Right then and there, I decided to turn this field into my family homestead. I would clear part of it, build a house, and bring up my kids on this land.

Kathy and I made an offer and signed the deal within a month. Now the question came up about what to do first with a piece of "unimproved land." This field had been productive farmland for three hundred years, and like so many other fields during the twentieth century it would now metamorphose from once productive farmland into a house, a yard, and several small fields. Yes, there was a house to be designed and built. That would probably take up most of our efforts, attention, and money. But I was more interested in what we were going to do with the rest of the land. We decided this was a wonderful opportunity to put some thought into planning a backyard, and deliberately create a lifestyle for ourselves.

Over the next year I walked the land every week, wanting to get a sense of it, seeing where the sun shone and tracking the shadows of tall trees. I wanted to meet all the creatures with whom we'd be sharing the land. I began to develop a real sense of place with this little hill and could visualize the house, the barns, and the fields. I could almost see what the trees would look like in twenty years.

We opened the discussion to the family: what are the main elements we want in our backyard? Do we want it open to the woods, to our neighbor's backyards, to the street, or do we want it to be private? Do we want it all in grass to play on, or do we want as little grass to mow as possible? Should it be sunny and open for a garden, or do we want to plant trees for shade and to serve as a windbreak? There were many questions.

The kids wanted horses and a tree house. Kathy wanted chickens and gardens. I wanted to be as self-sufficient as possible, with a woodlot for fuel, sun to warm a passive solar home, a private well, a vegetable garden, and room to raise sheep. It was a real luxury just to be able to consider all these options for creating a life.

When we got down to actually taking some of these steps, it got even more complicated. We had to start asking ourselves about native versus non-native trees and shrubs, how would the water flow across the land, and what types of gardens to put in. It was quite a process, but one that would set the stage for our lives to come. It was fascinating, listening to everyone's dreams and trying to figure out how to make them come true.

American Backyards — To own a lush, green backyard is a luxury of our time and place compared to our ancestors and to the majority of people throughout the world today. Even in America, many city dwellers or apartment renters do not have their own backyards. For those who do, this land around our homes that we call "our yard" is where we spend much of our outdoor time and much of our money. We have picnics, host our guests, turn the kids loose, and even as adults, get outside for a breath of fresh air, an escape from everyday life and family chaos. We *retreat* to the backyard.

I can personally attest that it was essential for our family's mental health to have a place outside the house to go and relax. We often sent the kids out to play when the house was too small for the emotions running rampant in our growing family. We would shout "Go run around the house!" or "Go climb a tree!" and the kids would comply, happy to leave the turmoil as well. I admit that instead of doing inside house work or engaging in a discussion on interior decorating, I was often all too happy to go cut the grass or go out to chop wood. We kid about it now, but to this day we still claim that my domain was outside and Kathy's was inside.

The backyard of course was more than just an escape; it was also a place where we got to touch nature, watch the seasons change, and center ourselves in a place of beauty. It was also the first place our children learned really about the natural order of things, and the place we went to be awestruck by the complexity and power of the universe. It was where they first witnessed the death of a pet and assisted in the birth of a lamb. It was where we created memories of our family growing up.

Historically, backyards have served a wide variety of purposes. The most fun backyards I know are those owned by farmers, artists, gardeners, or folks with hobbies. No telling what you'll find around their houses. To gain a deeper appreciation of what is important to someone, I like to check out their backyard. You can learn a lot about a person's interests and values by just suggesting "Why don't you show me around your place."

When my father bought his farm in the 1950s, he had no time to mow a lawn, so once a week he would let the sheep out to do it for him. Mom didn't like that idea much since sheep left a mess wherever they went and ate her flowers, so she lobbied for a well-defined and protected lawn. A tug-of-war between farm and yard ensued that was settled when my parents put up an electric fence fifty feet from the house. That kept the mowing to a minimum, helped feed the sheep, and provided an area for my sister and me to play. We learned very quickly not to run into the fence, though I think I was the slower to learn. It was never completely clear to me whether the fence was there to keep the sheep out or to keep me in.

Madison Avenue marketers, Levittown type developers, and Hollywood directors have done us a great disservice by promoting the stereotype of a house surrounded by nothing more than a lawn of manicured grass, sometimes with a white picket fence. At some point this vision of lawns got out of hand, and now many houses are set in the middle of 1/4-acre, 3-acre, and even 10-acre tracts of carefully mowed, fertilized, raked, but otherwise ignored grass. The lawns are rarely used. And, yes, I was caught up in this too. I have enjoyed the solitude and sense of accomplishment when mowing my lawn, making my homestead look well-manicured.

But, I'm having second thoughts about lawns. In the Chesapeake Bay watershed, turf is the number one *crop* (see Schuler, *The Clipping Point*). More land is dedicated to growing grass on lawns (close to 4 million acres in this single watershed), than any individual agricultural crop—corn, soybeans, wheat, and other row crops. There are 6.8 million lawns that drain into the Chesapeake Bay, and their owners spend $4 billion a year—mainly on fertilizer, gasoline, pesticides, and lawnmowers—to maintain them. Lawns in the watershed receive about 19 million pounds of pesticides per year and 215 million pounds of nitrogen, much of which ends up in our streams that carry it to the bay. In addition, lawn and garden equipment (e.g., lawn mowers and tractors), which generally have poor pollution controls, are the second leading emitters of smog-causing pollutants in this area during the summer, just a bit behind cars and trucks.

This monoculture has very little value. Lawns are largely ecological deserts, providing little support, food, or shelter for other living things. Give me a garden, a meadow, or a forest anytime. Maybe it is time to start thinking about our backyards in a new way, one that changes them from ecological deserts into life-affirming landscapes with flora and fauna.

The Challenge of Lawns — Why have I included backyards as a chapter in a book about saving your favorite places? There is no threat to your

The History of Backyards

Colonial yards often consisted of stockaded vegetable gardens around primitive log cabins. Fences kept vermin out and protected the food that kept settlers alive. The American backyard of the nineteenth century was usually a farmyard with chickens and pigs running loose, and rusting, farming equipment scattered about. Farmyards were well used for raising animals and staging farming activities to support the household.

When did these interesting yards morph into manicured greens? Lawns, it turns out, are a fairly recent development. Fencing an area for grass may have developed from the idea of *the commons* in small towns, or from outdoor places of worship at convents. In England, areas left for intensive grazing by sheep, horses, or rabbits were referred to as lawns. European aristocrats created vast, landscaped lawns around their estates to demonstrate their power and wealth.

In the U.S., lawns became popular in the second half of the nineteenth century and throughout the twentieth, as setback rules moved houses back from their customary location close to a road or street. Next came the development of specialized grass seeds, sprinklers, and lawn mowers. With the advent of the forty-hour week in 1938, people had more time for outdoor activities and maintaining a lawn. Games such as badminton, horseshoes, croquet, and lawn bowling became popular as did taking meals outdoors. The stage was set for the postwar population boom and appearance of the suburb.

The use of lawns has fallen off as air-conditioning has become widespread. We used to go outside on summer evenings to cool off; now we go inside. As our focus has evolved from radio to television, and now to the internet, we are moving indoors, abandoning our relationship with nature. Most Americans today reside in the indoor, digital universe.

backyard, but just the opposite: how we manage our backyards poses a threat to most of the other wonderful places in our lives. Our lawn mowers pollute the air; the fertilizer and pesticides we apply harm reservoirs for drinking water and food supplies downstream; the stormwater that runs off your roof, patio, driveway, and lawn harms downstream neighbors, creeks, lakes, bays, and the ocean. Without knowing it, *we and our everyday behavior have become a dominant environmental threat to our own health, our way of life, and many of the special places that we love.* Fortunately, fixing the backyard is not very hard and is something we can do all by ourselves. It can also prove to be fun and rewarding. Let's see what we can do.

Historically, in our original, finely tuned natural hydrologic system, rain fell to earth, filtered into the ground, and slowly recharged our subsurface groundwater tables. Those water tables then continuously recharged our streams with a year-round supply of fresh, clean water that supported a wide array of aquatic life. It was a good, sustainable system that served life on earth for billions of years.

Now that we have largely replaced forests and meadows with lawns and with impervious surfaces that prevent infiltration entirely, rushing stormwater carries the residue and waste from our roofs, driveways, patios, and yards downriver into lakes, bays, and the ocean. It contaminates the base of our food chain, the phytoplankton, which is concentrated along our coasts, right where the waste arrives. We have to stop human-enhanced runoff. We must find a way to capture the runoff in our front and backyards and allow it to filter into the ground, as nature intended.

You might say, "All I do is put fertilizer on my lawn. What's the harm in that?" The harm is that the next heavy rain carries about half of that fertilizer to streams and lakes and causes major algal blooms. Aside from being unsightly, algal blooms keep sunlight from plants and fish that need light to live. Moreover, when the algae die, bacteria use up the available oxygen during decomposition, which leads to massive, oxygen-depleted underwater *dead zones.* The dead zone in the Chesapeake Bay this year extended for more than a hundred miles and covered over half of the bay's main channel (see the Chesapeake Bay Foundation's

Love Canal

Backyards are not always benign. Contamination may be buried in yours or it may be flowing from a neighboring property (see Chapter 7). This is less likely to happen today, but not so long ago burying wastes was common.

You might recall the story of Love Canal in Niagara Falls, New York. In 1953, the school board, the town, and the developer wanted a particular piece of land so much that they overlooked a clause in the contract. Hooker Chemical clearly disclosed how they had gotten permission from the Niagara Power and Development Company in 1942 to dispose of drums of chemical waste in a buried canal built by William Love circa 1900 for shipping purposes. The city had disposed of waste in the canal as well.

The city took the deal because they got the land for a dollar. They also got 21,000 tons of toxic waste. Remember, this happened at a time when people dumped all sorts of chemicals into the ground assuming they would dissipate. The problem in Niagara was exacerbated during construction when heavy rains breached the canal and chemicals washed into adjacent soils. The chemicals were not cleaned up at that time. Much later, an investigation by the local newspaper (from 1976 to 1978) revealed a great many illnesses in the new neighborhood built around the canal. Subsurface investigations found that many backyards contained buried chemical waste. Two schools and 900 homes were affected. In the end, the chemicals in the canal were left in place but securely capped with clay and plastic. The canal area was fenced off from any further intrusion, and the surrounding area cleaned up. The site has been closely monitored for the past 35 years. It was a major urban planning scandal.

What is the lesson? It is important to check on the past use when buying a property. Find out if there have been underground storage tanks or areas where farmers once dumped their excess chemicals. If there is any suggestion of potential contamination, water and or soil samples should be collected and analyzed. If you have concerns, contact your county or state Department of the Environment and ask if they have any records on spills on or near your property. Local health officials may also have water quality data on nearby wells that can reveal the health of the aquifer.

annual report on the state of the bay). Some four hundred other large dead zones around the world have formed at the mouths of major rivers. They result from inappropriate and overuse of fertilizer upstream, largely from farms but increasingly from backyards. The dead zone in the Gulf of Mexico, spawned from runoff in the Mississippi River, is about the size of Massachusetts. Visit http://wwwgulfhypoxia.net to see the latest information collected by MacArthur Fellow Nancy Rabalais of the Louisiana Universities Marine Consortium.

But runoff is not just a problem at the mouths of rivers. Many of us live downstream from at least one neighbor's lawn. When your uphill neighbor sprays chemicals on his lawn and the next rain washes chemical residue onto yours, it might affect your pets, your plants, and your children. What do you do? Many people resort to fences, but fences can't hold back air or water. Sharing information on where the chemicals go and what their impact is downstream may help. Feel free to share information with them. You could also invite Master Gardeners or Master Naturalists in to speak to your community or neighborhood association. None of us wants unknown chemicals drifting or washing onto our land, into our windows, or into our seas. We all have to be more aware. Chemicals can also migrate onto your land via subsurface groundwater. Or there could be contamination in your backyard that you don't know about. Such was the case with New York's Love Canal.

Trees and Shrubs — Trees and shrubs can help restore the natural processes of rainfall capture and infiltration. They reduce the amount of chemical residues in our streams by absorbing and slowing runoff. Trees shade and cool our homes and yards during the summer, and, if they are deciduous, they let the sun warm our homes during the winter and reduce our energy bills and use of electricity year-round. (Less electricity used = less fossil fuels burned to generate that electricity = less air pollution falling on your backyard). Trees also clean the air of chemicals and process much of the carbon dioxide that we exhale. Coniferous trees and shrubs serve as windbreaks. They are great to have in winter, keeping our homes warmer, and keeping dust down when things are dry. Trees and shrubs retain far more water than short, grass-rich lawns. In fact, grass is often so compacted and cut so short that water runs right off and into streams in sheets, as if the lawn was pavement.

Native trees and plants are even better. They are great hosts of other native species such as butterflies and birds. They have evolved here and do well in this climate. Often, when non-natives are planted, they do not do as well in periods of drought and may not support other native species. For example, migratory birds plan on certain berries ripening and insects hatching at key intervals during their spring and fall migrations. If those key plants and insects have been crowded out by others with different timing, migration is affected. What we plant and how we maintain our gardens is important because it is so easy for non-native and invasive plants to take over. Doug Tallamy has written an excellent book titled *Bringing Nature Home* that provides what you need to know to get started on a native plant backyard. Another good source is *Tree Biology Notebook: An Introduction to the Science and Ecology of Trees*, by Richard Murray.

Natives are best because they have had a long time to adapt to the conditions found in your area. They can thrive with the normal pattern of rainfall, the extremes of local temperatures, and the variety of local diseases and pests. Ideally you would select shrubs and trees that blossom at different times—spring, summer, and fall. Their blossoms will support the native pollinators (e.g., the bumblebees) in your area. Our native bees tend to be generalists that will pollinate everything in your garden.

Importing exotic trees, plants, animals, and specialty wood is clearly part of our history and culture. We import trees and shrubs because we like how they look or their fruit and don't realize they can damage the delicate balance of local ecosystems. As discussed in Chapter 6 (Forests) this practice of importing trees resulted in the devastation of some iconic and valuable American trees—the chestnut, the elm, and now the ash. The problem with non-native trees, in addition to their potential for introducing damaging fungi and disease, is that some of them can become invasive. When introduced into an area where they have no natural competition or predation, they can replace other flora or whole ecosystems. They did not evolve in balance with the rest of the ecosystem and therefore do not play as much of a role in keeping everything in balance.

What Can We Do? — Lawns don't look so attractive to me anymore, in fact they look sterile. Maybe it's time we all stood back and redefined what is beautiful about a back yard, or a front yard, and what is just a boring expanse of turf grass, which is not a very interesting or useful plant.

Converting lawns – All it takes to start restoring nature in your front or backyard is to let Mother Nature do her thing, with a little bit of help from us. If you do nothing, your lawn will become a meadow, but it will take time for the native seed bank in the soil to outcompete the non-native grasses in your yard. Fortunately, there are a lot of creative things you can do. Sure, we can leave some areas of lawn if we choose, but the trick is to get off our mowers and our couches and into gardening or other backyard hobbies. Your backyard is a wide open palette. I have friends who have begun raising bees, chickens, hops, and award-winning flowers, all sorts of things, right in their backyards.

My father converted a large part of his backyard to growing grapes and apples. He, like Johnny "Appleseed" Chapman, had something in mind that was more than meets the eye. We did eat a lot of grapes and apples and even canned grape juice when we had more than we could drink, but the bulk of the grape crop was pressed, fermented, and turned

Non-natives and Invasives

Invasive plants are non-natives that have few competitors and therefore can dominate a habitat, eventually squeezing out native plants. A good example is crabgrass, which is probably a challenge to many people who like a perfect lawn. It is native to Europe and was introduced into the U.S. in 1849 as a potential forage crop. Today it is widespread and grows best when conventional cool-season lawn grasses are dormant in mid-summer. During the winter months it dies off and turns brown. Other invasive plants include bamboo, Russian olive, hyacinth, Japanese barberry, multi-flora rose, oriental bittersweet, Chinese wisteria, English ivy, Japanese knotweed, cheatgrass, Canada thistle, garlic mustard, Japanese honeysuckle, and kudzu.

Some were introduced by accident and traveled here in the ballast of ships, in packaging, and with other imported goods. Others were brought here intentionally for aesthetic or economic reasons. They are responsible for billions of dollars of crop and fire damage every year and crowd out important native species. I recall the Soil Conservation Service in the 1950s advising my father to strengthen his fences with multi-flora roses. They suggested these natural fence lines would be more effective, require less work, and provide habitat and food for birds. They were right about the habitat. Unfortunately birds spread the seeds across all our fields and meadows until multi-flora became the bane of our farm, showing up in the hay, tangled in wool, and a nightmare when we had to go into a mass of thorny rosebushes to repair a fence. When I bought my overgrown tract of land it was infested with multi-flora rosebushes, Canada thistle, and Russian olive. I've been fighting them ever since. It has been estimated that 50,000 non-native species (including livestock, crops, and pets) have been introduced into the United States. The costs associated with the damage they cause are estimated at $120 billion per year (Pimental, et al., 2005). To find out what you can do to fight invasives, visit the BLM Plant Conservation Alliance website: (http://www.blm.gov/wo/st/en/ prog/more/weeds/taking_action.html).

into wine. I can still hear corks popping prematurely from bottles in the basement and smell the aroma of fermenting wine wafting up through the old wooden floorboards. We had a feeling that something magical was happening in the basement. Indeed it was.

Permaculture – At my next home, I plan to start with a permaculture expert who could come in and create a design that connects the house to the natural setting. A gradual wilding, if you will. I'll have lots of native blueberries and blackberries, milkweed plants, butterfly bushes, and other shrubs to attract and support insects and birds. Rainwater will be collected from impervious surfaces and used to water the gardens. A kitchen herb garden will be just outside the back door, and there will be plenty of room for vegetables. We might even put in a high-hoop green-house to keep our table filled with fresh greens throughout the year. Pathways will allow us to enjoy the mix of trees and shrubs, and there won't be a blade of grass to mow. If any of us want to play on grass, there are always grassy public spots around town—and then there are all my neighbors, who may still be raising grass—no need for me to grow any grass on my land.

It's time each of us rethought our yards. It will require changing some of our habits, but let's take a few steps toward making our back-yards better for us and for other species. We can redesign them so they enhance, and not damage, our environment and all the lakes, rivers, beaches, and oceans downstream that we treasure so much. There is much we can do. We do not have to be perfect to make a difference but we do have to take action. Why not start in our own backyard?

Resources – Master Gardener and Master Naturalist groups can pro-vide you with the information you need to revitalize your backyards. These volunteer groups are usually sponsored by the state's land grant universities and have programs and plans that are customized for your area. They can recommend specific trees, shrubs, and flowers that will grow well in your area and support the local pollinators.

They also provide information on installing rain gardens to slow down runoff (Figure 3). Their gardens focus on native species that provide habitat for indigenous birds and butterflies and many of the species which have become endangered due to the loss of meadows, woods, and wetlands. Rain gardens can be beautiful additions to your yard. I love to walk through them and see all of the life they support.

There are a lot of source materials for rain gardens on-line. Start with the EPA site on best management practices using green infrastructure methods (http://water.epa.gov/infrastructure/gi_what.cfm). A good nonprofit on-line resource for selecting native plants is the Center for Plant Conservation (http://www.centerforplantconservation.org/). A good place to start to learn more about planting native shrubs is http://www.fws.gov/pollinators/polllinatorpages/yourhelp.html.

Neighborhood efforts – Once we have begun managing the water flow across our own backyards, it becomes clearer what should be done to manage storm waters throughout the neighborhood. By banning together with neighbors, one can install joint projects and plan out the most effective strategies for the whole micro-watershed. Thinking in terms of neighborhoods might also result in obtaining funds from local non-profits and local governments who may be very supportive of effective community programs. Jurisdictions at all levels are trying to improve their *green infrastructure* because it is the cheapest and best use of their limited funds for reducing stormwater runoff. Form coalitions whenever you can to help get the word out, and encourage people to install rain gardens and to become leaders in restoring their backyards and their communities.

CHAPTER 9

Farmlands

. . . the care of the earth is our most ancient and most worthy and, after all,
our most pleasing responsibility. To cherish what remains of it,
and to foster its renewal, is our only legitimate hope.
— Wendell Berry

Manor Lane in Winter, 2003 — Blackbirds blanketed the backyard. One moment all was calm, and the next moment, thousands swooped in to peck the ground while keeping up a constant chatter as only blackbirds do. I opened the door to be part of the excitement, and they all took off, first a small flurry off to one side of the yard and then the rest lifted up like a great wave rising, cresting, and preparing to crash. They circled, flew over the hedgerow, and cascaded down onto Clark's fallow field.

To better view this invading horde, I climbed a tulip poplar. Looking out over the fields I saw that these birds were part of a long serpentine trail of what looked like millions of black specks, some clusters on the ground, some in flight, that extended across neighboring fields as far as I could see. Where were they from, and where were they going? I wondered if they flock together for protection or to find food more efficiently. I could only guess. Watching their accordion-like theatrics, I pictured them extending across the entire country in one continuous, wavy line.

I kept my perch in the poplar until the visitors finished their inspection of Clark's field. They lifted once again with a loud whir of wings only to descend once more on my yard. I was now engulfed by their chatter as they alighted in the tree all around me, ignoring my presence, and apparently enjoying their camaraderie. They stripped the dogwoods

147

by the house of every red berry, and fifteen of them emptied the bird feeder while others tried to land on their backs to join in the feast.

The birds covered the garden, gleaning what seeds had been left behind after the harvest. They were welcome to all they could find. I was hoping they would eat all the weed seeds that would otherwise sprout in my gardens next spring. It was fun to see the blackbirds come through searching, pecking, and fertilizing my land. They scoured the pasture and scattered to the far reaches of the lawn, and then, at some hidden signal, they rose in unison and moved on to the next meal on their march across the countryside.

The yard grew eerily quiet. I sat there for a few more minutes, surveying our land from this bird's eye view. What a difference a few feet can make. We are such earthbound creatures. I felt like a foreigner spying on my everyday life, creating a list in my head of all the things that had to be done, now that it was the off-season. I saw the half-emptied woodpile and felt the urge to fill it up. I watched the sheep amble out of the barn to graze in the field. They were in need of shearing. I inspected the henhouse roof from the tree's vantage point and made a mental note of loose chicken wire and a sagging joist. Yes, there were things to do, plenty of chores calling me from my perch in the tree. Yet I lingered for a few more minutes, enjoying the view of my neighbors' farms, hundreds of acres that had produced crops consistently for hundreds of years. I treasured this bucolic setting. I was glad to be part of it but wondered how many of these farms would be here in ten years, in two years. There was a real threat to our neighborhood. Not just blackbirds were invading our countryside, people were streaming in, too.

Vanishing Farmlands — We live on a small piece of land right on the edge of suburbia. A town has sprung up over the past forty-five years in what used to be premier farmland for growing some of the best corn in the country. Over one hundred thousand people have moved into this new town. The county's population keeps growing as well with suburbs encroaching on this once rural farming community.

Our land is wedged between several larger agricultural operations that grow corn or soybeans year in and year out. Neighbors to the north have been farming for a very long time. Their family has owned the land since 1727. When I look to the southwest, though, the view is different, a ridgeline recently reshaped with houses. This had been a very productive field for centuries and then just two years ago the fields disappeared, the topsoil was removed, and the ground cut up and paved over, not to be farmed again. The ridgeline now serves as a constant reminder of the future and the challenges we face as a county.

But we are no different from many other parts of the country. The postwar population boom has resulted in widespread development. New houses, townhouse complexes, offices, and shopping centers are popping up all across America. We've seen an explosion of people out of our urban centers and the suburbanization of our countryside. Over the past few decades, 3,000 acres of productive farmland have been lost to development *each day*. The U.S. population has doubled during my lifetime. The population of the suburban county where I live has grown over ten-fold in that same short period. We've grown from 25,000 farmers in the 1950s to 280,000 suburbanites today. It seems like overnight, but the process has been anything but easy. We have struggled to preserve vestiges of our agricultural past and the ability to feed ourselves from local farms.

There is an even larger struggle going on across this country for the future of rural America. Can we afford to let rich farmland to be paved over? What is in the long-term interest of our citizens? We need farms, farmers, and the produce they raise for our security, but the population keeps growing, and we keep eating up our countryside. We are devouring the breadbasket that has built and fed the country for centuries.

Part of the problem is that many of us move to the country because we like the beauty, the slower pace of life, and less congestion, and some of us like working with our hands, with animals, and working outside. Many non-farmers like driving through farmland because they are mesmerized by the wide open spaces, a wheat field turning golden brown, a hayfield littered with bales, corn growing right before your eyes, and farmhouses. We relate to this history of cultivating the land,

and we rely on the sophisticated breadbasket that feeds the world. So, yes, the farmlands of America are one of those favorite places that we want to save for their pastoral beauty, our connection with the past, and most importantly for their ability to feed us all. However, it is hard for all parties when farming communities are invaded by suburbia.

On a Country Road — "Get off the road," the driver mumbled under his breath, but just then he saw his chance. The BMW flashed past the tractor and its driver, a bearded farmer in a sun-faded plaid shirt. The farmer continued on his way, pulling a load of hay from *his* fields to *his* barn. He had noticed the BMW behind him but had no options, no shoulder on which to pull off. It wasn't his fault that his neighbors had sold their land to be developed, but now he had to contend with new neighbors, lots of them, some of whom forget that he was here first. Farming had become harder now that he had to contend with commuters trying to get home for dinner.

"Damn farmers," the BMW owner complained to his wife when he got home. "I had to wait until Peters got his dairy herd across the road. Then I lost another five minutes because Jones was on his tractor going ten miles an hour on a curvy road. He is going to get himself killed. That's ten minutes wasted at the end of a sixty-minute commute!"

His wife said, "I had to put up with those awful smells all day long. Smith must have been spreading manure on his fields again. That shouldn't be allowed in this day and age."

"Well I heard he's selling out so that may not be a problem much longer."

She replied, "He can't do that, we moved here to be in the country! If they develop his farm we'll have even more traffic. All these people want is to sell their farms and get rich quick."

I hear similar stories all the time here in Howard County, Maryland. We are midway between Baltimore and Washington, and overnight we went from a rural to a bedroom community—people moving to the country to live but keeping their jobs in the cities. It's happening almost everywhere, the downside of cheap oil and a good interstate system.

People commute more, and they put up with the commute because they like living next to beautiful farmland. Unfortunately, some newcomers soon start complaining about the unintended consequences of their choices. Often they take it out on the farmers, wanting them to change how they do things to satisfy the newcomers. New residents sometimes dislike certain smells and activities in their new communities. Some object to the steps farmers are now taking to stay in business, such as agro-tourism or creating vineyards. It seems ironic, but we might have to pass a "right-to-farm" bill to stop these threats to farming.

Thirty years ago the farmers here, fearing that the whole county would become one large suburb, decided to be proactive about saving their highly productive farmland. That has not been easy to do. Farmers and planners have been trying for years to come up with the right mix of regulations and incentives to protect and support farming in the community.

Maryland passed legislation that resulted in lower property taxes for farm land. Federal tax breaks could be obtained if the landowner agreed to put an easement on his farm that would prohibit development. Land trusts were formed to hold the easements and to monitor the properties to make sure they were kept in agriculture. To encourage even more farmers to preserve their land, the county also initiated an easement purchase program and a transfer-of-development-rights option. Over a thousand farmers in the state saved their farms by placing an easement on their land. That lowered their costs and let them pass the land on to their children. Other states have developed similar programs. We've successfully preserved over a million acres of farmland nationwide in this manner. At the same time, counties and states without these easement options have lost a lot of farms to development.

Our county has designated areas where they support development and other areas where they support agriculture. In the area targeted for development, water and sewer services are provided. In the agricultural areas, the county has limited the amount of building that can occur. These steps have helped. Most of my neighbors have placed their farms in agricultural preservation programs, so the rural character of our neighborhood has been preserved. Tractors and other farm equipment are common and welcome on our lane.

Key to the preservation of farmland is the planning and zoning process. As issues arise, all parties get the chance to discuss the pros and cons of proposed changes within a public forum. These discussions can get quite heated and colorful. I recall meetings where one faction of farmers drove their $200,000 tractors right downtown to the hearings in an attempt to make a point. Most decisions, though, are not black and white, and farmers can end up on both sides. It is hard to craft a regulation that meets the needs of everyone.

Farm Heritage — If you go back far enough, many of us came from farming backgrounds. In 1800 about 90 percent of Americans lived on farms. Today less than 2 percent of us do. My grandfather grew up on a farm large enough to support a family of ten. My father's farm was downsized by Interstate I-95 from 110 to 70 acres, and he worked at the copper plant downtown in addition to working on the farm. Our place was smaller still, and my wife and I worked elsewhere, but our land kept us in fresh vegetables, fruit, eggs, and enough lamb for much of the year. We found that fresh food tasted a lot better than anything we could buy in a store and was more nutritious. Farming is in our blood and we know how hard it is to earn a living from it. Farming is dependent on the vagaries of the weather and changing climatic patterns. Farmers are at the mercy of insects that could be a boom or a bust depending whether they pollinated or consumed crops. We struggled with the need for and costs of chemical amendments to the soil, pesticides, and what to do with the wastes we generated. Our place was labor-intensive and required constant attention. It was also a very satisfying, family-focused way of life that we appreciated.

Farming has changed dramatically in the past fifty years, from the labor-intensive, family farm to a machine-centric, agribusiness heavily dependent on chemicals and devoted to monoculture. It is also much more productive. When farmers talk about "The Green Revolution" of the mid-twentieth century, they refer to the great increase in productivity brought about by the industrialization of farming and the widespread use of chemically derived fertilizers and pesticides. This dramatic revolution has resulted in the specialization of farming and the globalization of the food marketplace. Farmers have invested heavily in the equipment to grow large volumes of specialized crops, and the systems are in place for acquiring seed, pesticides, and for delivering crops to market. It's a finely tuned business and one that older farmers can pursue since it uses machines and is less dependent on manpower.

Before the Green Revolution, what you raised depended solely on the local market for your crops. Now it depends on the global demand for a product. It also relies on genetically modified seeds from Monsanto, etc., approvals from the U.S. Food and Drug Administration (FDA), incentives and insurance from the Farm Bill, and a series of state and federal conservation policies. Farmers now consider what subsidies and insurances are available and they watch the commodities market to manage the risks of planting a single crop. In the past decade, they've had to pay attention to non-food markets, specifically the energy market, with our nation's foray into using corn for ethanol production. That has shaken up the market price of corn and corn products throughout the U.S. and Mexico.

Food distribution has also changed dramatically over the past fifty years. We now buy produce from faraway places because it's more efficient and cheaper to do so. What was seasonally limited produce is now available throughout the year because it is flown in from areas with different climates (e.g., the southern hemisphere). Having strawberries in January in Minnesota or Maine would have been a marvel fifty years ago, but today you can have your favorite fresh fruit nearly any day of the year. In addition to the year-round availability of most foods, some would argue that food quality is better as well. Others argue that the taste and nutritional value have diminished because we are now growing varieties that ship and store well. There may be some truth to both claims.

The Locavore Movement — As efficient as the industrial agricultural system is, many Americans are turning back to local farms for some or all of their produce. There are over 7,000 farmers' markets in the U.S. selling locally grown food. That may sound like a lot, but the whole local food marketplace probably only represents about 1 percent of our total food distribution network. But it is growing rapidly all across the country. Why is this happening with all the success of the international food marketplace? Is it just creative marketing by local farmers, or is a real difference driving this increasing demand for locally grown food?

The trend toward buying local, seasonal food is referred to as the *locavore movement*. An increasing number of people and restaurants are buying from local farmers because they believe the food is fresher, tastier, and more nutritious. Some consumers also prefer buying food from a local farmer than from some unknown source thousands of miles away. Some buyers are concerned about food from overseas where environmental, human rights, and health standards may be lower or unknown. Many locavore consumers assert that the food is tastier, since the varieties chosen by the farmer can be selected for taste and not necessarily for hardiness in shipping or long shelf life. Of course when food is fresher, it is more nutritious because nutrition decreases with time. The local food movement is also often a community-building effort where people have come together to create a more locally based, self-reliant food economy.

Go to any farmers market and what do you see? Usually, lots of people are milling around, comparing prices, and chatting directly with the farmers and with each other. Going to a weekly farmers' market is much more of a community event than shopping in a big box store. Friendly farmers of all ages, often multiple generations, unload boxes from their trucks and spread ripe produce out on the tables in front of them. None of this food had to be preserved for long periods of time, no gassing, chilling, or repackaging. As you walk around, you see a range of locally sourced products from fruits, vegetables, and eggs to grass-fed meats, cheeses, and bakery products. You can ask the farmers about their farm, about any herbicides used, and when the produce was picked. In most cases it was picked that same morning and often by the person you are speaking with. That compares quite favorably with produce picked a week or more ago in a different country. Chicken eggs may have been laid fresh this morning in contrast to eggs from a store that typically are weeks or months old. You find this out by asking the people behind the table. Friendly conversations give you a sense of the farmer's integrity and the quality of the food you are buying.

Farmers engaged in this marketplace range from small operations, farming a few acres largely by hand, all the way up to more ambitious operations that work more land with more equipment and labor. When I was a kid, we used to buy many of these same products from farm stands and trucks parked along the highway; now these foods are marketed in a whole variety of ways. In addition to farmers' markets and produce stands, some farmers sell directly to restaurants or stores. In many cases the distribution system is less sophisticated than that used in large grocery or "big box" stores. Quite often delivery and sales are made by the same hands that sowed and picked the produce in the first place.

Some locavore farmers follow the community supported agriculture (CSA) model. CSAs usually have buyers sign up and pay to be members at the beginning of the season. Members then pick up their share of whatever the farmer has harvested on a weekly basis. CSA members are in fact sharing in the risk of farming and in the bounty of the harvest. The challenge for a CSA farmer is to have a sufficient variety of food for their customers each week so no one gets stuck with too much kale or too many zucchini. Some farmers become brokers for other farmers. As a result, CSA members might get a box of food each week with a wider variety of products than usual.

Many of us are willing to pay more for locally grown food. This is good because otherwise it is hard to make money in this complex, labor-intensive, hands-on business. If one took into account a farmer's costs for land, equipment, soil amendments (e.g., nutrients), labor, delivery, and marketing the cost would be high. Local farmers don't have the efficiencies of scale that large agri-businesses have, so the *buyer* has to be interested in better nutrition, taste, and knowing where the food is grown. To keep his prices low, the *farmer* has to somehow get his land for minimal cost and not count his labor into the equation in order to make money on his/her crops. Some farmers are predicting that as fuel prices rise, the cost of shipping food thousands of miles from farm to table will get more expensive, thus helping the local farmer compete.

The locavore movement appears to be working in smaller, interconnected communities with word-of-mouth advertising. I've seen great examples of this in Pennsylvania, Maine, Vermont, North Carolina, Kentucky, California, and Oregon, and it appears to be spreading across the country. It is strongest where a lot of young people are willing to put in the physical effort and form strong bonds that support one another's operations. The locavore trend harkens back to the small businesses of our past but could prove to be a model for the future. In our area the demand for locally grown food is greater than the supply, and we are looking at ways to increase both sides of this equation.

It will be interesting to see where the locavore movement goes from here. At present, demand seems to be steadily increasing. The respect for and the demand for locally grown food has been enhanced by the successful sales of several popular books: *The Omnivore's Dilemma* by Michael Pollan and *Vegetable, Mineral, Miracle* by Barbara Kingsolver. But it is very hard to earn a living so local producers depend on the support of the community. Farms of all sizes are important, and the more involvement we have buying our food from local farmers, the more we will want to support them, their farms, and the farming way of life. Go visit your local farmers' markets or local CSA to learn more and to enjoy the taste of locally grown food. Some say that if you go for the food you'll come back for the community.

What Can We Do? — Farms of all sizes are threatened by our growing population and the increasing demand for land (for building new homes, schools, highways and businesses). On top of that, farmers across the country face decreasing water supplies for irrigation, the contamination of our water bodies with too much silt and fertilizer from current farming practices, and agriculture's heavy dependence on fossil fuels. Several of these issues will be treated in other chapters. Here we will focus just on preserving farm land.

As discussed above, the U.S. has been working for decades to develop the right mix of tax incentives and zoning to help farmers keep their farms in agriculture. It has not been easy. Ann Jones, a land preservation consultant, suggests that right now there appear to be three major trends affecting farms and farming that are relevant to this discussion. They are: 1) The very encouraging trend of young people coming back to the land; 2) increasing environmental regulations that bring uncertainty to the aging farm population that currently owns the land, and; 3) land preservation programs that have been patterned largely on zoning that puts regulations down "in perpetuity." Strict zoning regulations make it harder for the farm community to be flexible in meeting the changing needs of the community and the marketplace.

The challenge to each of our communities therefore is to figure out how we can support young farmers, assist in the transfer of farmlands, and help all farmers deal with the environmental and zoning regulations that are necessary to correct the impact of our growing population. We will have to be flexible as we learn how to build the system that will work in the future.

It is not always easy to interest local farms in selling produce locally. First of all, most farmers are committed to agribusiness these days and are geared up to provide a single product to the agricultural industrial complex. They are no longer well equipped to grow fruit and vegetables. Furthermore, farmers who are retiring may be tempted to sell their land for development, especially if there is no young farmer coming along who can pay a comparable price. Let's take a look at what could be done to preserve farms and increase access to local produce in our communities.

Access to land – A major hurdle to the expansion of locally grown produce is getting land into the hands of farmers who want to grow and sell food to the community. Land near suburban settings is very expensive. One solution is to encourage current land owners to lease their land to younger farmers. Older farmers could also serve as mentors to

Portland, Maine, CSA

My daughter, Leigh, has the farming gene, enjoys physical exercise, and loves to provide good quality food to her friends and local community. These are all important ingredients for running a produce farming operation, which she has done for the past 5 years. It's not a bad life for someone who loves to be outside during the summer. Her produce is wonderful. She learned how to garden from one of the leaders in the organic grower movement, Eliot Coleman (*The New Organic Grower*), so she knows a bit about what she is doing.

Leigh doesn't own any land. She farms on a one-acre plot at a vineyard where she used to help tend the vines. She has developed a strong bond with the owners. The cost to buy (and maybe even to lease land) would be prohibitive to her scale of operation.

Each spring during the Maine mud season, Leigh starts her vegetable "sets" in a greenhouse she built herself. You can often find her in there while it's still snowing outside. Timing is important. She wants the sets ready to transplant right after the last frost. When the soil at the vineyard dries out and becomes tillable, a neighboring farmer graciously comes over and tills the garden. She is then all set to start the labor intensive process of prepping beds, adding soil amendments, planting, mulching, irrigating, weeding, harvesting, and selling her crops.

From June to October, as the food ripens, she is out picking early on Wednesday mornings. She then brings boxes of produce to the side porch of her home, where her customers stop by to chat and pick up their share on Wednesday afternoons. In some cases she has to explain what some of the vegetables are and the best ways to eat them. Leigh also sends musings by email each week ("The Kale Patch") that contain stories about the farming process and recipes keyed to the weekly harvest (for example: mashed roots with herbs). She is a great cook, so she's always experiment-

ing with how to prepare the week's vegetables. She has also sup-
plied greens to restaurants and grocery stores in the Portland area
(listed as "Leigh's Greens"). In the weekly "share," she sometimes
complements her vegetable produce with seaweed and sea salt that
she and her friends have harvested, and elderberry syrup she has
made. She sees her efforts as a way to eat well and build community all around the food she loves to grow.

younger apprentices. Another option would be for the community to
purchase the land and lease it to one or more farmers for growing local
produce. In a number of areas around the country, large farms have been
bought for development, but they leave the old farmstead intact along
with room for vegetable gardens so that locally grown produce and a
farming coop can be offered as an amenity to buyers.

Community ownership of close-in farms is similar to what is happening in cities where vacant lots or blocks are being taken over at
no cost to start neighborhood gardens. To train the farmers, numerous
training programs are popping up around the country, operating through
colleges or organizations such as Future Harvest (Chesapeake Alliance
for Sustainable Agriculture). This group is a network of farmers, agriculture professionals, landowners, and consumers that promotes profit-
able, environmentally sound, and socially acceptable food and farming
systems that sustain local communities. There are also new "land link"
programs around the country designed to link farmers looking for land
with farmers who have land to lease or buy. More information on these
options can probably be found from Master Gardener networks, land
grant colleges, agricultural departments in schools, or local planning
and zoning departments.

Food distribution – Efficient distribution systems are necessary in
order to reduce the costs of getting local food into consumer's hands.
Our county has decided to create a central distribution hub to get local
food to restaurants, hospitals, prisons, schools, and the general public.

The goal is to aggregate, distribute, and market local food products to local consumers. For this to work we will have to make sure that there is enough supply and demand to be self-sustaining and beneficial to all parties. This is not a new idea. Currently, the USDA recognizes 188 local food hubs around the country. So there is a lot of experience out there where you can learn how best to make a food hub work. In addition to five stationary farmers' markets, our county is also planning a mobile farmers' market that can go into neighborhoods where the residents may not have transportation to get to the stationary markets. This farmers' market on wheels will be equipped to take SNAP (formerly the Food Stamp Program) EBT cards as well. The goal is to get high-quality food to everyone in our community.

Food incubator – There is also a need for food-based, business incubators, where entrepreneurs can process fresh produce into more value-added products, such as converting fruit into jams, canning tomatoes, processing meats, etc. Food processing requires well-equipped and inspected facilities, a trained labor force, time and funds for research and development of new ideas and services, and marketing channels. Incubators can be supported with training and expertise from state agricultural extension services and community colleges. Once operating, they can be invaluable in helping start-ups deal with the high risks and costs of creating the infrastructure needed for processing. Incubators can be designed to help in the licensing, permitting, health and safety regulations, slaughtering, processing, preservation, storage, and distribution of the product.

The success of these programs will require training new farmers and educating consumers about the health, economic, and environmental benefits of eating locally grown food. We will have to be sure not to squeeze out family farms that often grow a combination of grains and local produce. In addition to supporting farms, we should also support growth in back yard gardens, front yard foodscapes, and community gardens. We must also be careful not to zone farming out of our lives with overly restrictive covenants. In some communities, covenants prevent raising chickens, honey bees, or other animals and crops. It will be a fine balance to meet the needs of all of our citizens.

With the increased interest in healthy eating, I think we will see a marked resurgence of the local food movement. Americans will create a brighter future and stronger communities by growing more of their food in their own backyards. This is not hard to do. In addition to baby boomers and millennials getting back into farming and gardening, whole families may end up turning off the digital universe for a few hours each week and going outside to tend their gardens. I bet we'll see more people cutting back on empty expanses of grass and having enough vegetables and fruit trees in their yards to supply some of their needs. They will probably take the excess bounty to the local farmers' market. Entire neighborhoods would go every Saturday morning to barter what they brought with them and to do a part of their shopping for the week. This is all consistent with a return to preparing our own food and meals from scratch. It will result in physically and mentally happier families and communities all tied in with each other and with their local farms simply because they have changed their relationship with the food they eat.

CHAPTER 10

Cities

People who spend as little as 30 minutes a day out in nature are happier,
healthier, more productive, and more creative than those who do not.
—Rachel and Stephen Kaplan

St. Bernard Parish, March, 2006 — Kathy and I visited New Orleans
seven months after Hurricane Katrina did its best to wash that city off
the map. We came to help, to learn, and to support the residents who
had lost their homes and their communities. We returned home thinking we had been to two different cities: the French Quarter still showing
the glitz of old New Orleans, and downriver parishes where the devastation was nearly total and left us with the feeling we'd been in a third
world country.

Yes, the French Quarter looked fine, as it had in the past, but it felt
deserted. Residents and tourists had not yet returned. What was not fine
were the miles and miles of destruction and desolation we passed on
our way through residential New Orleans, the Ninth Ward, and the strip
through St. Bernard Parish. We had rented a car and were on our way to
visit a non-profit, where our daughter had been helping for the past several months. Homes and neighborhoods of all economic levels were gutted. McDonalds, Wal-Mart stores, and strip mall after strip mall had been
damaged and abandoned. Temporary stop signs had popped up at the
intersections since none of the traffic lights were working—nothing was
working. No gas stations, laundromats, fast food, or ATM machines were
operable. Streets were empty. Seven months after Katrina, we saw few
signs of life, aid, restoration, or *hope* aside from hundreds of white FEMA
trailers and pockets of idealistic youths who had come to town to help.

Most disturbing to me were the X-codes painted on the abandoned buildings, a system devised by the National Urban Search and Rescue teams. Each quadrant of the large, painted "X" provided information about what was found when a rescue team searched the premises—the number of people living and dead, the extent of the damage, and other hazards they had encountered. The visual state of the homes was shocking enough, but then to see the number of people who had died in their homes during the hurricane was wrenching.

Driving was slow going. A lot of trash remained in the roads, along with the ever-present potholes. I stopped at every intersection to look both ways, though there was no traffic. Waterlogged furnishings were piled next to front and back doors and outside windows. Homeowners and volunteers had gutted hundreds of houses. Mildewed furniture, clothing, electronics, games, and dolls were scattered across the yards. A few people were trying to rebuild their lives, but the utilities were all out, so they were constrained to life in a self-contained, four-person, FEMA trailer. The future was unclear. Was it even worth trying to rebuild under these circumstances of total uncertainty? Even the U.S. Army Corps of Engineers, who promised that the levees would be rebuilt, admitted that the levees would still not be strong enough for a big storm. During our little snapshot of a visit, I kept thinking that New Orleans was trapped in a waiting game. Residents who had lived through Katrina realized that all they could do was bide their time until the next big storm came their way. Mother Nature has a way of reclaiming her land, and New Orleans is right on the precarious edge of land and sea.

Many had already made their decision and left. Of the 70,000 residents of St. Bernard Parish, only 10,000 remained. It felt deserted and yet safe to walk the streets. We found most people were resolved to the hardships and were very pleasant. However, there was anger at the lack of progress, at FEMA, at the wages being paid to contractors from other areas, and just not knowing what would happen to their homes, their neighborhoods, their parish, and their city.

These were the struggles of a city trying to breathe again after a so-

The Role of Disaster Volunteers

In our 2006 trip to New Orleans, we were fortunate to be hosted by one of the groups of young Americans that had been drawn, like white blood cells, to this festering wound in the underbelly of Louisiana. America becomes one community at times of hardship. The national body had been injured and people, corporations, money, and food all flocked to New Orleans in a mass mobilization to fix the problem. It is the "good Samaritan" phenomenon: when disaster strikes, the natural human instinct is to rally around the devastated communities and help them out. But I kept wondering if we could fix such a major catastrophe, or are we only offering hope?

Non-profit organizations created web presences and attracted volunteers from all over the country to come to New Orleans to help. Thousands came, spreading out around the city, creating community kitchens, clinics, and distribution centers—whatever was needed. Some places were more structured than others. Leigh, our daughter, started at Common Ground Relief and ended up at a Baptist Church with a dozen other twenty-somethings where they created Project H.O.P.E. (Helping Other People in Every Way). They restored the church and turned it into a food and supply distribution center and a host site for college kids who came to help for a week at a time. They fed and housed the students on cots in one big sanctuary, and trained and organized them into groups that went out into the community to gut houses and remove the mold growing on the walls.

Management at the center was horizontal. As challenges came up they were addressed. It worked. The college kids went home and spread the word. Some returned. Some sent supplies. They were enamored by the commitment, lifestyle, and hard creative work of the long-termers, and the chance to be part of the reconstruction of New Orleans. We all felt this deep desire to help the local people get through their nightmare. Most of the locals were touched by the efforts of the volunteers operating out of the Baptist church. As a thank you, one day a 70-pound bucket of crayfish "showed up" for a joint neighborhood/volunteer "Louisiana Boil." They were all in this effort of rebuilding together.

cial, economic, and environmental disaster. A city where 1,833 people died, 350,000 cars were destroyed, 160,000 homes were flooded, and nine million gallons of oil were spilled from two oil refineries in St. Bernard's Parish. That is a volume of oil similar to that spilled by the *Exxon Valdez* in Alaska. In addition 27 hazardous waste Superfund sites were flooded in the impacted areas, and 60 million cubic yards of debris still had to be moved.

During the disaster, over half of New Orleans' residents moved away. Eight years later the population is still only three-quarters of what it had been prior to the storm. The commercial core of the city has been rebuilt, night life for tourists has returned, but the communities are still reeling from the disaster. The people of New Orleans need the jobs generated by tourism, but they also need housing, social services, good education, and safe streets. It all must fit together in a fully functioning city. A lot more work needs to be done if the goal is to restore the life of this heavily damaged and very iconic American city.

How they and we as a nation deal with this catastrophe and this issue will speak volumes about our humanity, our rationality, and our society. I came away realizing that we all have a responsibility to do what we can to decrease the likelihood of this level of destruction from ever happening again.

What Next? — Does it make sense to save all of New Orleans? How much effort do we put into rebuilding a city that is at an increasing risk of destruction as the Gulf waters and the planet continue to warm? The climate models predict that bigger storms are coming unless we reduce our greenhouse gas emissions. So maybe that should be our first step, the place where we should be investing to prevent more Katrinas.

Unfortunately, much of the talk today is focused less on reducing emissions and more on "how can we make our cities more resilient?" The problem with fortifying city defenses is that you can never do enough to save every neighborhood in every threatened city, and hundreds of cities are at risk. This approach does not address the root of the problem. We have to do something to reduce global warming and the frequency of big storms. If we don't, many of us will become the collateral damage when the next one hits. We could be the St. Bernard Parish of some future storm.

New Orleans has its own significant challenges due to the rising sea levels and mega-storms accompanying global warming, but so do many other coastal cities. The World Bank has created a list of the ten cities on the planet at greatest risk from climate change. I was surprised to learn that five of them are in the U.S. Miami is at greatest risk, followed by New York, New Orleans, Tampa, and Boston. What's more, Norfolk, Newark, Los Angeles, Seattle, Jacksonville, and Charleston are at risk as well, and the list goes on.

Many people do not realize that not just our coastal cities are at risk. The global climate change models predict higher temperatures and drier conditions throughout much of the southern U.S. As water supplies dwindle and the land dries up and catches fire, many cities there will suffer a wide range of heat- and drought-related disasters and illnesses as well. Phoenix, Las Vegas, Tucson, Houston, Dallas, and San Antonio, would all be better off if we slowed or stopped the rate of global warming. Even in the northern tier of states, problems are expected. Lower rainfalls are predicted to result in the shrinkage of the Great Lakes, which will result in higher levels of pollution.

But how can cities focus on preventing future catastrophes when they are threatened every day with a host of other environmental, social, and economic problems? One of the biggest challenges they face is the flight of residents and businesses to the suburbs. That has resulted in a major loss of the tax base and a greater concentration of poverty than can be supported with the remaining funds. Detroit has had the most difficult time. "Motor City" lost its auto manufacturing base and the well-paying jobs that went along with it. It has dramatically shrunk in size and has declared bankruptcy. Other cities are also fighting job and population loss and the threat of bankruptcy. All of these issues are important, intertwined, and must be dealt with in conjunction with the threats from climate change. How can they deal with these competing needs? Successful cities have learned how to keep all these interests in balance. Cities fail when they do not consider the interconnectedness of their challenges.

Past Efforts at Saving Our Cities — As discussed in Chapter 6, the Environmental Health Movement actually began in cities in the latter decades of the nineteenth century, when cities were perceived to have become too congested and disease-ridden. In fact, conditions then were much worse than today. Rudimentary sanitation and poor air and water quality affected public health, and those with means spent summers in the country. Spurred by advances in the understanding of disease, reformers advocated for and eventually convinced politicians of the need for sewage systems, cleaner water supplies, and more public parks. These steps led to significant improvements in health and tremendous economic growth during the first half of the twentieth century.

As part of this community enhancement effort, city planners found that town squares or parks that draw people can have a major influence on the social and economic life of a city. Frederick Law Olmsted (1822–1903) became a key figure in the greening of cities. He cut his teeth creating Central Park in New York City, basically following the theories of Englishman Andrew Jackson Downing and by teaming with Downing's protégé, Calvert Vaux. These men were the fathers of landscape architecture in America. Olmsted went from his work on Central Park to work on city plans and park plans all across the country, and his work was carried on by his sons. Olmsted thought parks should be places where all classes of society could go for rejuvenation.

Olmsted and his sons' work turned the American metropolis green, which was one of the steps that led to the heyday of American cities. Millions of trees were planted during the late nineteenth century. Unfortunately, our cities lost some of that "greenness" over the years. Commercial interests won out over livability. Cities became unbalanced—too much commerce and too little space purely for enjoyment and camaraderie, requirements of a thriving community. Many cities became glass and concrete jungles that were deserted at night as employees fled to the suburbs. We are slowly reversing that trend, but we need city planners and developers who will follow reignite Olmsted's vision.

What Can We Do? — With the likelihood of more storms, droughts, fires and job and population losses, how our cities go about saving themselves? To address the impacts of global climate change and other major concerns, many cities have set up sustainability offices to examine how best to balance and integrate economic, social, and environmental issues. It is not easy but at least it is a way to keep all the issues on the table. When effort and money are spent to fix one problem, the impact on the other problems can be taken into consideration. Contact your local city planning (or environmental) office and ask them for a copy of their sustainability plan and their general plan. I hope you will find programs already underway to help rebuild your city. There are no quick fixes, but your city should have a process in place to create a healthy, sustainable, and livable city (http://www.icleiusa.ort/sustainability).

Creating a sense of place – One of the major drivers of success for many cities in recent decades is the revitalization of their natural setting. In a surprising number of cases that place has been a city's waterfront (http://www.epa.gov/dced/sg-coastal.html). Many cities grew up as river, lake, or ocean transportation hubs. It was the great value of their natural setting that made them successful in the first place. As options for transportation multiplied (rail, air, and trucking) many waterfronts fell into ruin from neglect and were often used for waste disposal. I recall visiting the docks to pick up fresh seafood with my dad in the 1950s and finding them to be fascinating but scary places. Old, collapsing wooden piers, wooden gangplanks leading to floating barges, smoke, grime, and water you would not want to venture too close to. Cities in those days were industrial centers, billowing smoke into the air and waste into the water. There were very few reasons to go to these dilapidated edges of society, where culverts dumped waste and residue. They did not feel safe. My wife was frightened the first time we visited the waterfront in my hometown of Baltimore. That was as recently as 1970.

A huge achievement of the past fifty years is that we have dramatically resurrected, often through the use of public-private partnerships, the allure of the waterfront. They have become *the places* to go for entertainment, for leisurely walks, to spend time on a Sunday afternoon, and yes, even to buy a condo so one can live close to the action. By restoring the natural amenities, they have attracted people back into their centers, resulting in urban revival. The integration of environmental, social, and economic interests has been the key to their turnarounds.

Baltimore's rebound was led by William Donald Schaeffer, who served as mayor from 1971 to 1987, and governor of Maryland from 1987 to 1995. A practical and demanding leader, he worked hard to create the rebirth of Baltimore's most valuable environmental asset, its waterfront. His efforts resulted in the building of the National Aquarium, the Maryland Science Center, and Jim Rouse's Harbor Place (a commercial shopping and entertainment center), key destinations that attract millions of visitors to the Inner Harbor in downtown Baltimore. This initial investment attracted money, jobs, restaurants, hotels, stadiums (for the Orioles and Ravens), and eventually marinas and condominiums right on the waterfront. Baltimore now has a five-mile waterfront trail that connects many of these features to one another and to the older neighborhoods that have gone through their own periods of restoration. The transformation has been marvelous. The best place I have found to watch all of these changes is from the top of Federal Hill Park, a 150-foot-high, green refuge overlooking the harbor and downtown. Here you can watch all sorts of vessels return at the end of the day as the sun sets and the lights come on across the city. The restoration has been so successful that we go to Baltimore's waterfront all the time to walk, picnic, visit museums, and dine. We've

The Value Nature in Cities

Professors Rachel and Stephen Kaplan of the University of Michigan have shown that people who spend as little as 30 minutes a day out in nature are happier, healthier, more productive, and more creative than those who do not. They found that people often resort to TV, sporting activities, music, and action movies to escape the discomforts of mental fatigue, but that although these activities may captivate the brain, they don't allow it to rest and recover. In contrast, a walk in the woods, a park, or along a waterfront allows the brain to soak up pleasing images and to wander, reflect, and recuperate. The Kaplans have shown that watching television is the fastest way to burnout; whereas, outdoor activities such as a walk in the woods or gardening, have profound, positive impacts on both mental and physical health.

Cities are struggling to provide their residents with the means to live healthy lives. Re-greening efforts are being made in many cities, in which thousands of trees are planted to create an urban canopy. Cities used to be greener but lost much of their canopy to Dutch Elm disease. Trees tend to cool neighborhoods and encourage people to go outside. More people outside translates into increased safety. The best cities today have wonderful parks and greenways that invite their residents to go outdoors.

The Trust for Public Land has ranked U.S. cities with the best park systems. The list includes: Minneapolis, New York, Boston, Sacramento, San Francisco, Washington, D.C., Portland (OR), Virginia Beach, San Diego, and Seattle. In addition to parks, Portland, OR, is one of the best biking cities in America, with 200 miles of dedicated bike trails. Cambridge, MA, is one of the best walking cities. Austin, TX has devoted a great deal of acreage to green spaces including 206 parks, 12 preserves, 26 greenbelts and more than 50 miles of trails. All of these forward-thinking places are widely viewed as lively, economically successful, people-oriented cities.

even thought of living there—a far cry from my wife's first impressions forty years ago.

A wide range of vested business, community, and government interests now see the value of keeping waterfronts viable. This extends even to the point of cleaning up the water. The private, public, and non-profit sectors are partnering to do just that. It is now in everyone's interest to create some version of the old "swimmable and fishable waters" vision of the 1972 Clean Water Act and to do it right downtown. In some cases it is being done with the use of green infrastructure for reducing the impact of storms and the resulting stormwater runoff from upstream communities. It is another way to get upstream suburbs to help in the restoration of our cities. More and more people are coming to recognize the benefits of integrating social, environmental, and economic developments on a regional basis as a way of solving our urban problems.

Making cities livable – Many U.S. cities are trying to build on this walkable, bike-able, and livable (if not yet swimmable) downtown concept (http://www.fta.dot.gov/about/13747.html).As important as business is to the health of cities, downtowns must be more than commercial centers. The sense of place has to be there, and it has to draw people for all sorts of reasons. If there is a strong natural element—a river, a harbor, or a hill—communities are building a sense of place around that iconic and often natural feature. One can then add to it by incorporating quiet green parks, busy sidewalks with buskers and street art, active farmers' markets, urban gardens, and other places that offer a sense of community and a reason to get out and interact with your neighbors.

As usual saving iconic places is an ongoing challenge in most cities. Once there were plans to build high-rise buildings right on the waterfront in Baltimore, limiting the view of the water. Some were stopped. There were also plans to put an interstate right through several historic communities and through one of my favorite places, Federal Hill Park. One resident, less than five feet tall, got up on a soap box and inspired her community to fight. People rallied to the call and stopped the destruction of their neighborhoods. The woman, Barbara Mikulski, went on to serve on the Baltimore City Council, in the U.S. House of Representatives, and then become the longest-serving woman in the Senate. All cities need citizens to participate in the planning and zoning process, not to limit development but to ensure that social and environmental concerns are part of the equation when decisions are made.

To reduce traffic and pollution, cities are also trying to become more walkable. One way our local community is trying to accomplish that is by constructing multiple-use buildings with retail on the bottom floor and apartments and offices on the upper floors (PlanHoward 2030). The goal is for people to be able to live, work, shop, exercise, dine, and relax without getting into a car. This seems to make the most sense where there is sufficient population density to support all the stores and services people need within walking distance. This trend to drive less may be real. According to the Federal Highway Administration, vehicle miles traveled per capita in the U.S. have actually decreased for the past eight years (since 2006). We are now driving about as much as we did in 1996. Due in part to a combination of baby boomers retiring and to less enthusiasm for cars among millennials, this positive trend can, if it continues, significantly reduce traffic congestion, improve air and water quality, and slow global warming.

Other encouraging trends include urban agriculture and community garden plots (http://afsic.nal.usda.gov/farms-and-community/urban-agriculture). City-dwellers are increasingly supporting local farmers markets, and the demand for produce is outstripping supply in most areas. It is one of the healthiest trends I've seen. People who may not have easy access to grocery stores can get fresh food, learn where it comes from, and get to know and support local farmers. Regular visitors, and there are many, get to know more people in their community who frequent these places. Urban farmers' markets have become a destination for shopping and for seeing people. We are making cities livable again.

We can do more to improve city life, but what's been done over the past few years is very encouraging. To help your city enhance its livability, contact your local sustainability or planning office, or community focused non-profit, and find out what you and your neighborhood can do. I have found that you can be of help in rebuilding your city by articulating and advocating for more integrated and sustainable thinking at every level of government and in every business and organization. It can't just be about single issues such as housing, or commerce, or social services, or education, or the environment. It has got to be about them all and how they can all be enhanced. None of us has the whole picture in mind, but all of us can help create a vision that our organizations can work toward. Many small steps bring big returns. Lots of projects need doing, and it is rewarding to see how the more creative and energetic communities are transforming themselves into fun, safe, and rewarding places to live and work.

CHAPTER 11

Alaska

In every walk with nature one receives far more than he seeks.
— John Muir

Primrose Point, 2013 — I sat down on lichen-covered rocks surrounded by six million acres of wilderness and was engulfed by the quietude of this vast, unspoiled land. This was the taiga, north of Denali, a natural landscape of rocks, shrubs, and sparse trees extending for miles in all directions. Around me was a blanket of foot-high, berry-laden plants falling away and merging into the variable green hues of valleys and hills. In the distance, stunted black spruce dotted the landscape all the way up to the tree line at 2,500 feet. Tundra continued from there, reaching up to the snow line marked by glaciers, snowfields, and the shattered granitic rocks on the tallest peaks. This was wilderness. I knew it innately, without seeing wolves, bears, moose, or caribou. Yes, I had seen their paw prints, scat, and tree damage, but just by sitting there in the undisturbed stunted vegetation my body knew I was in their home. One need not see a wolf to feel its presence.

A single, man-made path was the only easy way into this spot. There was no other evidence of man's intrusion on the land, on the mountain, or even in the skies above me. No sound—well, wait a minute. I cupped my ears with curved hands and heard a brook babbling. It was over there, hundreds of yards away, in a dense, shrub-and-tree-covered ravine. The sound traveled on the wind, increasing and decreasing in volume as the wavering air came and went, sporadically cooling my brow while filling my ears with the sound of falling water.

The air was dry and bore scents of blueberry, lingonberry, and crowberry. It was August, and the season would soon change with the fire-weed. The green shrubby blanket will turn scarlet, the cottonwood, aspen, and birch trees yellow, and Denali's snowy cap will reach downward with each passing week from the mountain peaks, across the tundra, and into the taiga. I wished I could stay and watch the coming and going of fall, but I was not prepared to spend a long, cold winter in this place of extremes. The twenty-hour days of summer will all-to-quickly change to twenty-hour nights. The moderate temperatures and cool breezes will drop to temperatures forty, fifty, and sixty degrees below zero. Winds, greater than hurricane force, will bring the howl of the North to a cabin door. No, I was not prepared for that. It takes a special soul to stay here year-round. I experienced this small piece of wilderness in the summer and after returning home will contemplate what it must mean to live so close to the Arctic Circle in such a rich and challenging land.

Yes, I came north to see, touch, and gain a deeper appreciation of Alaska. To feel the presence of wilderness is something that will always be with me, connecting me to these far reaches of our country. It is a feeling that we need to savor and protect. We have to save some undisturbed part of our country so that future generations can experience it as well. This feeling inspires me to engage in the debates on the future of the land, the wildlife, and the resources, all across America.

The Alaskan Conundrum — The great Alaskan conundrum is that its beauty and wilderness will attract so many people that our collective impact will damage its beauty and destroy its wilderness. With all of its majestic mountains, braided rivers, glacier-carved fjords, and wide open spaces, Alaska attracts the imagination of humans living "outside" in the lower forty-eight. Ever since its purchase by William Henry Seward in 1867, the gold rush of 1890, and statehood in 1959, it has been part of our collective consciousness. I can still remember what a big deal it was to add the forty-ninth star to the flag. It is one of our favorite places even for those who have not gone there yet. We consider it our wilderness, the last earth-bound frontier.

Alaska attracts over a million visitors each year. Some come to vacation, some for work, and others to stay. Some want to see if they can live off the land, providing for their families just by hunting, fishing, and trapping. Some want to live in a place beyond societal rules and regulations. They picture Alaska as a place where they can live without being told what to do.

This was once true. There were so few people that they had little impact on one another or on the land. As their numbers grew, they started to affect local ecological systems and had to learn how to deal with one another. I've met a few of the rugged individualists who make a living in Alaska. They moved there for a variety of reasons, and I respect their hard work in eking out a living in places where living can be a day-to-day thing. Unfortunately, there are now so many of these homesteaders that even living a very basic, subsistence-level existence is threatening the wilderness.

Then there are the tourists who come, largely between June and September, on cruise ships, rail, or by bus. From their ships or hotels, they go off on daily excursions. Other tourists want to experience the real Alaska, and there are more and more opportunities to get off the beaten path and explore the wilderness. Each trip reduces the wilderness, results in more habituation of the wildlife, impacts the country.

I include Alaska in this book because it offers good examples of the struggles societies face between unfettered use and preservation. Even in Alaska, as unpopulated and wide open as a place can be (one person per square mile), it is not easy to address the competing objectives of tourism, protecting the wilderness, respecting native people's rights, and sustainably using natural resources. As its population has increased, the balanced management of fish, mammals, trees, oil, minerals, and people has become a major struggle in defining American values.

It is a frontier that we are trying to manage better than we have done on other, earlier frontiers. Let's take a look at how we have done in the past and what we face in trying to manage this conundrum that is America's last great frontier.

Humans and Wildlife — Asian migrants have occupied different parts of

Alaska since at least 12,000 years ago. They came by land bridge (Beringia) and by sea in search of food. These first people lived off the sea and the land, moving around as needed when resources were over-exploited or when new migrants moved in. They lived by killing whales, walrus, seals, otters, and fish in the seas, on the ice, and in the rivers. They also ate mammoths, musk oxen, moose, caribou, bison, squirrels, ptarmigan, and bear. When the food ran out, they starved or moved on. The system worked when there was more game than people, and they were probably the cause, in part, of the extermination of mastodons, mammoths, and other Ice Age mega-fauna. They did not, and probably could not, know how to manage their food resources sustainably.

Russians occupied the coast of Alaska shortly after Tsar Peter the Great sent a Danish captain, Vitus Bering, to explore it in 1741. The overland journey from Moscow was long and treacherous, but the tsar wanted to establish the eastern extent of his dominion and didn't want to stop at the continent's edge. The Russians created and dominated a lucrative fur trade with China and in their wild, unfettered pursuit of furs decimated the otter and seal populations. By 1867, the Russians had depleted the fur supply from these frigid waters between continents and sold this "resource depleted" barren land of Alaska to the United States for $7.2 million to pay for their war in the Crimea. Secretary of State William Henry Seward, who engineered the transaction, was widely ridiculed for buying a worthless icebox, and Alaska became known as "Seward's Folly." Concerned more with reconstruction of the South after the Civil War, Americans paid little attention to the Alaskan territory and didn't really know what to do with this cold land sparsely inhabited by Russians and native people of Asian descent, few of whom spoke English.

Today the descendants of those hardy Asian immigrants self-identify as Inuits (Inupiat and Yupik), Athabascans, Tlingits, Haidans, Eyak, Tsimshian, Aleuts, and others. Some have Russian, European, and American ancestry as well. Although many have adopted some modern conveniences and modern ways, some still live in tribal villages and feed and clothe their families on what they can garner from the land

and the sea. But living as their ancestors did has become increasingly difficult as more and more people come into "the country."

Hunting has been gradually restricted over the years. There was a time you could shoot anything you saw, but that resulted in a scarcity of food, and starvation. The shaggy musk oxen, contemporaries of the Pleistocene mammoths, were regionally wiped out in the 1980s but have been reintroduced and are doing better today. During the first decades of the twentieth century, Charles Sheldon, a hunter and naturalist, was concerned that other big game, especially the Dall sheep, was endangered by commercial hunters supplying the booming gold mining camps with food. Sheldon campaigned to create a National Park to preserve these relatives of Big Horn sheep around what is now Denali. It was a classic case of development of one resource (gold mining) resulting in unexpected damage to other resources (sheep). Sheldon succeeded, and a national park was created in 1917 to protect a whole host of natural resources. Hunting is largely restricted in this and other national parks and is closely regulated in National Preserves and Forests.

This protected area was greatly expanded by Congress in 1980 when President Jimmy Carter signed legislation setting aside 100 million acres in Alaska as national parks, preserves, and wildlife refuges. Creating parks to protect animals was not welcome news to a lot of settlers and visiting big game hunters who were angry that they could not hunt anywhere they wanted. Slowly some of these folks are realizing that with Alaska's growing population there would be nothing left to hunt if some lands were not protected and managed.

Even with these protective steps, a large number of species in Alaska are still listed by the Fish and Wildlife Service as endangered or threatened. The list includes: polar bears, northern sea otters, and the wood bison. Species listed by the National Marine Fisheries Service as endangered or threatened in Alaska include: the Steller sea lion; leatherback, loggerhead, and green sea turtles; and bowhead, fin, humpback, and sperm whales. According to the Endangered Species Act of 1973, "It is unlawful for any person subject to the jurisdiction of the U.S. to harm, pursue, hunt, shoot, wound, kill, trap, capture, or collect listed species within the U.S., its territorial waters, or on the high seas." Furthermore, to meet the goals of the Endangered Species Act, we now realize we must protect habitats as well. In Alaska, we are attempting to preserve all the remaining wildlife species of this last frontier, so we are managing large amounts of protected habitat. Land preservation and protection of endangered species go hand-in-hand. It will be fascinating to see if any of the endangered or threatened species rebound in Alaska with our efforts to protect their habitats. It is a delicate balance to allow so much human access to Alaska and at the same time to preserve the wildlife.

Gold — In the late 1890s, a series of widely publicized, gold discoveries in Alaska and Canada attracted 100,000 people ready to risk their lives in places like Juneau, Dawson City, Eagle, Nome, Fairbanks, Skagway, and the Klondike. About 40,000 made it to the gold fields, and only 4,000 actually found gold. Canada and the U.S. allowed the prospectors to file claims anywhere on federally owned lands. Those who did strike it rich collectively took home millions of ounces of gold. They left behind a series of small towns, abandoned cabins, stories of getting rich quick, and their mine tailings and trash dumps. Their debris can still be seen at Lake Bennett and elsewhere along the treacherous trails to the illusive placer deposits and mother lodes.

A few intrepid explorers stayed behind after the boom and bust of the frontier mining towns. They lived off the land and never lost their lust for gold or their affinity for the wide open spaces. In fact, mining gold, lead, zinc, silver, and coal continues to be important in Alaska today. Over the past 115 years more than 40 million ounces of gold have been extracted. More than 100 active placer gold mining operations produce about 50,000 ounces per year. With a price in 2013 dollars of $1,500 per ounce, that adds up to a lot of revenue.

In contrast to the early placer deposits found at or near the surface, it is more difficult to get permission to extract ore from the larger, more challenging, and deeper, hard-rock deposits in Alaska. That is partly because most of the land today has been divided up between the state and federal government agencies and the native corporations. Furthermore, the process for extracting ore from hard rock deposits is now more carefully regulated to limit damage to other resources. One of the largest known copper-gold deposits in the world was discovered in the 1980s on state-owned lands near Bristol Bay in southwest Alaska. It is estimated to contain 94 million ounces of gold, plus large amounts of copper and molybdenum. There is a great deal of pressure within the state today to develop this deposit, because the price of copper has tripled in the past decade due to its importance in communication devices.

There is also a great deal of resistance to developing this deposit. "If built, Pebble Mine could become the largest open-pit mine in North America," claims the National Parks Conservation Association, which is monitoring it because it is only fourteen miles from Lake Clark National Park. "It could also become a catalyst for industrialization of 1,000 square miles of mining claims staked since 2003 along the west side of the park, all of which are precariously located in the watershed of Bristol Bay, one of the last remaining intact wild sockeye salmon fisheries on Earth." (For more information visit http://www.adfg.alaska.gov/index.cfm?adfg=com mercialbyareabristolbay.main.)

So the questions we must address are: is development more important than preservation of this pristine area, and, which resource is more important, copper or salmon? If the answer is "both" and the go-ahead is given to develop a huge new open pit mine here in the wilderness, how will it be monitored? How can the people of Alaska ensure the salmon, water, surrounding lands, local communities, and air are not harmed? Alaskans know the value of their fish and wilderness resources and want to protect them. In contrast to simply filing a claim in the late nineteenth century, gaining permission to extract the ore from this major new discovery will be a lengthy process. It will also be difficult to ensure that mine development does not have negative impacts on the other resources in the area. It has been twenty-five years since discovery of this vast resource, and they have yet to get permission to mine it.

Oil — Oil use on the North Slope is not new. For thousands of years, Iñupiat people there have freely used naturally occurring, oil-saturated peat as fuel for heat and light. The potential of this area was thought to be so great that in 1921 President Harding set aside 23 million acres on the North Slope as the National Petroleum Reserve–Alaska (NPR-A). The U.S. Geological Survey mapped the geology of this area during the 1920s. The "discovery well" for North America's largest oil field was drilled nearby by Atlantic Richfield (now BP) at Prudhoe Bay in 1968. To exploit this Arctic Circle resource, a major pipeline and shipping network was needed to get the oil to market. Conservationists strongly opposed its development because it was considered to be a high risk operation that crosses several seismically active areas and very sensitive wilderness ecosystems. But following the run-up in oil prices during the 1973 oil crisis, the 800-mile pipeline to Valdez was approved and completed in 1977. But the battle is far from over since there are more known reserves in Alaska.

Today the federal government still owns 157 million acres of Alaska, the state owns 101 million, and the native corporations own 44 million. Only 1 percent of the land is privately owned. This makes all Americans interested parties in the future of Alaska. Our voices and our votes will help determine how the federal land is used and how well it will be preserved. The attraction of the government owning so much of the land is that they can in theory manage it with the interests of all parties and the longer term view in mind.

An example of this is the Alaskan National Wildlife Refuge (ANWR) which at 19,286,722 acres is the largest wildlife refuge in the country. It lies on the North Slope of Alaska, just east of BP's Prudhoe Bay Oil Field, and is managed by the U.S. Fish and Wildlife Service. This is the summer calving grounds for 169,000 caribou and home to some of the most diverse and spectacular wildlife in the arctic, including 42 species of fish, 37 species of land mammals, eight species of marine mammals, and more than 200 species of migratory and resident birds. It is also believed to contain significant oil resources. To date drilling has not been approved by Congress because ANWR's potential reserves are estimated to be too scattered and too small to affect world prices, politics, and supplies, and its development could negatively impact the native villag-

The Alyeska Pipeline

After the 1968 oil field discovery at Prudhoe Bay the next challenge was getting the oil to market. The major hurdle oil companies faced in building a pipeline was getting approval and clear title to the land through which it would pass. Over the years tribes had filed numerous claims trying to regain access and ownership of their ancestral hunting grounds. Land rights claims, resource development, and conservation issues came to a head in the late sixties and early seventies. With so much potential revenue at stake, the tribes, oil companies, the state, and the federal government all wanted to negotiate a deal. With passage of the Alaska Native Claims Settlement Act (ANCSA) in 1971, 44 million acres and $963 million were divided among regional, urban, and village tribal corporations. In one of the more generous deals for American native peoples our government ever made, 100,000 Native Americans became stockholders in one of twelve major and many small native corporations. It brought education, resources, and opportunities to participate in the commercial world (if they chose to), to the native people of Alaska. It also let the oil flow.

I worked for the company that did the environmental assessment for the 800-mile Alyeska pipeline. We employed a host of top professionals across a range of disciplines. The scientists spent long hours attempting to assess the impact on the caribou and arctic ecosystems. Engineers tried to come up with designs that would least affect the migration patterns of wildlife. The pipeline was designed to be earthquake-resistant, and it has withstood numerous seismic events. There have been several significant oil leaks resulting from sabotage, maintenance failures, and gunshot holes. In retrospect, the pipeline on land has performed well. But that is only part of the transportation system. The *Exxon Valdez's* offshore oil spill in 1989 was the most significant failure of this long and complex oil delivery network (see Chapter 4).

es and caribou, polar bear, musk oxen, and bird habitats. Oil industry interest in developing this area also appears to be on the backburner. At some point that could change, so ANWR will continue to be an important struggle to follow in the halls of Congress. Its future and the future of all federal lands should be determined by facts and reason.

As the production of oil from the North Slope has decreased over the past several decades, major plans have been developed to utilize the vast natural gas deposits there. These plans include building another 800-mile natural gas pipeline from the North Slope to the Kenai Peninsula (http://www.arcticgas.gov/Alaska-Natural-Gas-Pipeline-Project-History). The gas will then be liquefied and shipped to Asian markets. Some of it could be used to fuel Alaska.

Homesteaders — Alaska's public lands are under a lot of pressure. The opportunity to live self-sufficiently has attracted a wide range of people, including some who could be described as rugged individualists. Many of them came here to live off the land and feel they should have the right to hunt, fish, timber, and trap on the vast public domain. I heard one estimate that about 100,000 people in Alaska still supplement their livelihoods by hunting caribou and other game. As more people come to Alaska, the challenges will grow. All parties will have to figure out how to get along and not destroy the land and wildlife they came to enjoy.

One example of the government trying to meet the various demands of homesteaders is the manner in which the land around Denali has been divided up and managed. The land is preserved under several different programs. Some of it is designated as a national park, some as a national preserve, and some as a state park. There is also a large wilderness area that has been designated within Denali National Park. Wilderness areas and national parks are focused on preservation and don't usually allow the exploitation of resources. National preserves are like national parks, but they also have congressional approval for carefully managed hunting, trapping, and oil and gas exploration and extraction. So where homesteaders can hunt and trap is now well documented.

Farmers' Market in Anchorage

Toward the end of my stay in the 49th state, I visited the large, Saturday morning farmers' market on the corner of 15th and Cordova streets in downtown Anchorage. Crowded and with live music, it has a festive atmosphere. I was surprised and disappointed to find only one stand of fruit and vegetables. I had heard about how large vegetables grew in the land of the midnight sun and had seen gigantic flowers and plants in gardens along the sidewalks. But I saw no large local produce in the market.

All the other stands offered baked goods, meats, flowers, crafts, and artwork that Alaskans made to supplement their incomes. Many vendors here live off the tourist trade, a four-month hustle, to earn enough cash to keep them going the rest of the year. Some of the craftspeople told me I should be careful about what I bought and who I bought it from—it was important to buy only crafts made by Alaskans. I then learned that there were several levels to that statement. Some craftsmen had moved to Alaska just for the summer, some had come earlier in their lives, some were born here, and some were truly indigenous. It was confusing to decide the right thing to do. I was happy to support them all.

I had encountered a similar challenge at some of the ports on the way to Anchorage, where I learned that many of the shops facing the wharves were owned by the cruise lines and did little to benefit the locals. To find stores owned by real Alaskans, I was instructed to go off the main streets. As I wandered the rows of booths at the market, one drew my attention. It was run by a moose calf rescue group. Evidently there is a need to rescue calves orphaned by hunters. To raise money for their cause they were holding a raffle. In what seemed to me a sad irony, first prize was a hunting rifle. I guess it could be used to hunt moose, leading to more orphaned calves —a prime example of the complex and conflicting perspectives in Alaska. There are many more.

In addition to restricting hunting and trapping, Denali National Park adopted a policy in the early 1980s of "bus only" traffic on its single access road to keep human intrusion to a minimum. That has resulted in much less damage to the park and far greater likelihood of seeing wildlife. Mount McKinley in Denali National Park is one of the most memorable places to visit in the U.S.

Tourism — This brings us to the timeless conundrum that accompanies finding the most beautiful place in the world: if you share it with others, it will be overrun with tourists. Alaska is beautiful and many people want to visit or live there. It had 210,000 residents at the time of statehood in 1959 and now has a year-round population of 730,000. It also hosts over 1.5 million summertime visitors and workers each year. That is not a lot for the size of the country but it must be carefully managed.

Fortunately, one can see a great deal of its beauty by cruise boat, train, air, and by float trip. The National Park System and the tour companies have developed a well-managed way of getting as many people as possible to be enamored with the concept of the Alaskan Frontier without leaving much of a footprint. Even though this is an efficient system for getting tourists in and out, there are a whole host of unsustainable practices employed by the cruise and tour companies and the towns along the way. One would think that Alaska and these businesses would want to be seen as leaders in protecting the environment of their state since so many tourists are coming to see nature at its finest. Maintaining Alaska's wilderness, abundant fisheries, and wonderful parks in order to continue to encourage tourists will take a lot of work.

Tourism is always a two-edged sword. It brings funds into Alaska which then increases the pressure for more development and more environmental damage. On the positive side Alaskan tourism can really educate the public in the Lower Forty-Eight about our last wild frontier because exposure to Alaska is also exposure to the issues *faced* by Alaska. Once you come here, those issues are no longer just theoretical. We become emotionally involved and we realize that we do have a say through our representatives as to Alaska's future. People may always be drawn to Alaska to get away from modern society, to live self-sufficiently, or to get rich quick, but tourism builds an increasing constituency for the preservation of unique parks and vast areas of wilderness for all of us to enjoy.

The Future — The future of Alaska and its wilderness are far from certain. Significant changes will occur with the waning of the oil royalties that now constitute 90 percent of the state's revenue. The fishing, mining, and timber industries, which are also important, only contribute 2 percent of the state's coffers. Currently Alaska has no state income or sales tax, so Alaskans are looking for the next boom before they run out of oil. They will have to decide where to go from here; how much growth they want; how much growth can be sustained without irreparable damage to their resources; what resources should be developed; and how to protect the other resources they have. Many of these questions about the future are being assessed at the University of Alaska. For more information visit http://www.iser.uaa.alaska.edu/Projects/investak/.

The costs of growth – Unfortunately, if current trends continue, the state will have to build more infrastructure in order to meet the needs of a growing population. They will have to add more regulations to limit the detrimental aspects of growth on residents, wildlife, and the wilderness. This is ironic, since many Alaskans came here to escape regulations and will fight attempts to limit their freedom to do whatever they like. The survivalists and rugged individualists who live off the land deserve seats at the table as the future of Alaska is discussed. There must also be seats for conservationists, preservationists, wildlife scientists, native peoples, and the business community. So much is at stake. It is reminiscent of the challenges we've faced in the Lower Forty-Eight. I hope that as Alaskans move into the future we can all learn from the failures and the successes of the haphazard settlement of the rest of the country.

Meeting energy demand – The oil revenue generated from Prudhoe Bay, which has been fueling growth in the state, has been decreasing since 1988 and may only last another decade. There is a lot of debate today on how best to meet the increasing energy demands of a growing Alaskan population in a post–Prudhoe Bay economy. There are already plans for a major new hydroelectric plant and an 800-mile natural gas pipeline. The dam is proposed for the beautiful Susitna Valley in south central Alaska (http://www.susitna-watanahydro.org/). The proposal includes a 735-foot-high dam that will create a very large lake and affect the flow of water downstream. That is a major concern since the Susitna is also an important salmon breeding ground. It would be the second tallest dam in the U.S. Damming the river is opposed on many fronts (http://susitnarivercoalition.org/).

The main alternative to a hydroelectric dam is natural gas, which is currently meeting the needs of Alaskans. More gas could be obtained from either the Cook Inlet or the North Slope fields. The North Slope gas would require a spur off the proposed 800-mile gas pipeline to the Kenai peninsula. Burning natural gas is not as clean as running a hydroelectric plant, so there are environmental, social, and economic issues to be weighed. Some people want to do both big projects. Some do not want to do either. Both projects bring a lot of short term construction jobs to Alaskans. Both projects bring a lot of long term environmental impacts.

Questions about growth – Other key questions facing Alaska are how much commercialization should be allowed on Alaskan State Park lands and how much development will take place on the native corporate lands. These are both unknowns that will take years to sort out. There has often been talk of building a whole new capital city, and in the 1970s there was talk about building a Teflon-domed Denali City. I can only assume that as Alaskans debate these issues, they will probably end up with an array of perspectives similar to those that arise all across America. They will engage in the same debates while trying to figure out the balance that meets the needs of their people today and in the future. Let's hope that the future of the federal and state lands is decided with all parties at the table and with the interests of the whole country in mind. Our job in the Lower Forty-Eight is to stay on top of the issues, voice our beliefs to our elected officials, and engage others in the fight to preserve the best of Alaska for future generations to enjoy.

We can learn much from the struggles in Alaska. To preserve our favorite places, no matter where they are, requires learning how to balance competing needs and staying on top of the key issues. Alaska contains great natural resources beneath the tundra and taiga, and offshore. Our society may need them at some point. We will have to consciously decide if and when we need them, and how we are going to utilize them, while minimizing the impact on our last land-based frontier.

CHAPTER 12

Oceans

It is a curious situation that the sea, from which life first arose, should now be threatened by the activities of one form of that life.
—Rachel Carson

Kitty Hawk, North Carolina, 1992 — Doug and I woke early. The silence of the vacation house was only broken by the soft sounds of sleep. Tiptoeing out the back door we left the rest of the family to their dreams and drove through the dark to an inlet on the Outer Banks of North Carolina. There we met up with Captain Bob and the four other men in our deep sea fishing party. We were heading out to the Gulf Stream on a charter boat intent on catching *big fish* but neither of us was quite sure what that meant. Doug and I were freshwater fishermen, used to catching one to two pound bass and trout. We had little experience fishing offshore. But we were planning on bringing home dinner.

No one spoke as each of us secured a spot on board and braced ourselves against the rocking of the boat. Cups of coffee securely in hand, huddled together in our hooded raingear, we headed east at quite a clip, and quietly watched as the sun emerged out of a calm sea. On the way to the Gulf Stream, Captain Bob found a spot with a large mass of floating seaweed. He slowed and stopped the boat at its edge. It appeared to me that we were in the middle of nowhere when he cut the engines. I wondered why he had stopped—was it the grass or did he see something on his depth finder. All he said was "there are fish down there." He handed out fishing gear and provided live bait for our hooks. He made it easy to be a fisherman.

The seaweed patch proved to be a good spot. As we lowered our lines, fish took the bait and ran with them. It was wild for a few minutes. Each of us pulled in a couple of three-to-five-pound dolphin—the fish variety of dolphin, not the mammal. They are a prized sports fish because of their ability to put up a good fight, go for long runs, and jump out of the water. They are also excellent eating, sold as mahi-mahi in fine restaurants. A mature dolphin has a very high forehead rising steeply from the low-placed mouth. They are beautiful, with skin of ever changing blue, green, yellow, and white hues. I wondered how they change their coloring so quickly.

After this taste of catching dolphin, we felt pretty good about our fishing skills, limited as they were. We were all excited and having fun, judging by the light conversation and laughter. We could have fished here all day. But then Bob told us to bring in our lines. Time to get serious and go trolling for bigger fish.

The waters of the Gulf Stream are known to harbor thousand-pound fish—marlin, sailfish, and tuna. Doug and the other anglers wanted to catch the "big one." As for me, I enjoy casting and trying to outwit and catch lots of fish as opposed to the boredom of trolling and trying to beat the odds against finding the big one. But Captain Bob said we were going trolling, and he was a man of few words. He was also the only one on board with local knowledge and was being paid to find fish. You had to trust him, he was a weathered waterman with an air of confidence that he knew what he was doing.

Now, there's nothing much for customers to do while trolling. The captain puts out multiple lines from the riggings in the superstructure of the boat and just motors around while we wait. You would think the engine would scare the fish away but trolling often works quite well. When a fish does take the bait from one of these lines, the captain takes the rod down from its perch and hands it to one of the paying clients so he can personally engage in the battle to land a big one. The trick is to be one of the first in line to get handed the rod because you never know how many fish might get hooked that day. The custom on charter boats, at least on this boat, was to draw straws to determine the order for reeling in the next fish hooked.

The captain got together six straws of different lengths. We all drew a straw. It was my bad fortune to draw the shortest—last place. This meant that we had to catch six large fish before I would see any action. Doug chuckled at my misfortune. He had drawn fourth place and began gloating about our respective draws, but I could tell that he too was concerned that we had just blown a day of our vacation and 150 bucks each. Everyone gave me their condolences but no one offered to trade places. It was indeed unlikely that my investment would pay off. What made matters worse was that I didn't like trolling and often felt seasick on the open ocean. So I took Dramamine to ride out what looked to be a long day of rocking back and forth in a boat. There was nothing to watch except the horizon in all directions. After about half an hour of no bites and rolling seas, I got drowsy. So I went into the cabin and laid down on some nets and life preservers. . . .

The next thing I knew, people were calling my name. I woke up to a lot of commotion on deck. It took me a minute to remember where I was and what was happening. I stumbled out of the cabin and found my turn had come! I had no idea how long I'd slept but they had hooked the sixth fish, and it was mine. Somehow they had already caught and landed five others while I was sleeping. I had missed it all. The fish now on the line needed quick attention or it might get off the hook. The others cheered and coached me into action.

I climbed up on what looked like a birthing chair in the middle of the stern. It had stirrups into which I put my feet, and they thrust the rod into my hand with the butt down near my groin. I immediately started reeling in the slack line, then it got taut. My mind quickly cleared. I was on one end of a line with what I instantly knew was the largest fish I'd ever hooked on the other!

The sensation of reeling in a very large fish is very hard to convey. All contact at first is through the line. You don't know what you've got, but you can feel the raw power of some living, thinking, and still unseen creature at the other end of a hundred feet of line. It was him against me, and he was fighting for his life. I was fighting for my dinner.

The reel was a monster, a Russian-like version of the light tackle that I was used to. I used my whole clenched fist to turn the reel. Every time I pulled in a few feet, the line would go whistling out as the fish on the other end made a run or a dive. The mechanical drag on the reel was set just right. If it had been tighter the line would have broken as soon as he took off on a hundred-foot run. At the same time, I was able to reel him in closer to the boat when he was not running hard in the other direction. When he got tired, I made progress. When he got mad and took off, he made progress. We seesawed back and forth for control.

I was in awe of such a fish! I kept trying to catch a glimpse of him but he kept himself hidden in the depths. What is it? One moment he was way out behind the ship. The next, he was racing us, and winning! The chair spun around on its swivel so I was always facing the fish. The worst thing that could happen now was if the line tangled and broke. The boat was perfectly designed for this type of one-on-one combat. Everyone stayed out of the way but eagerly watched to see what was on the line.

On one run the fish came to the surface as he passed the boat, his blunt forehead cutting through the water like an attack sub. Our mouths fell open. He was one tough fighter and could easily outrun us. He was a bull-nosed dolphin and a beautiful one at that. When he finally jumped, we could see how big he was. I was assured he was the biggest of the day by far.

After about half an hour of reeling in line and then listening to it stream back out, my friend and I slowly tired. At last I was able to bring him to the side of the boat, where Captain Bob brought him over the gunnel with a gaff hook. He was gorgeous, quickly changing from blue to green to yellow. I couldn't take my eyes off him. All of us stared at this beautiful creature. We dropped him in the hold, where he dwarfed the other fish. I now got to see that the others had also caught dolphin, larger than the earlier ones but a class below the great bull dolphin that had just come aboard.

Captain Bob called it a day and turned for home. At the dock my catch was measured and met the trophy classification. Doug and I headed back to the beach house and carried the bull dolphin down to the beach where the family was sunbathing. The fish was longer than the two youngest members of the family. We then cut him into steaks and cleaned our smaller catches. The total catch was enough to feed the twelve of us for the rest of the week. I ate fish for breakfast, lunch, and dinner.

Fish Stocks, 2013 — That was as close an interaction with raw nature as I've had on the ocean. Oceans represent the great unknown, and I was clearly out of my comfort zone that far from shore. They cover 70 percent of the earth's surface and, in the Marianas Trench, extend to nearly seven miles deep. The Census of Marine Life lists over 15,000 species of fish. Yes, whenever you go fishing you never really know what you are going to catch. When you do hook a fish it all comes down to a battle of wits between you, a displaced land mammal, and a marine creature in its own habitat.

There is something deeply primeval about fishing and man's long relationship with the sea. We have fed our families for millennia on its riches, and we have lost many of our ancestors to its whims. Fishermen and sailors have a sacred bond that ties them to the sea. We want the oceans in our lives, we want to be able to catch wild fish from the great aqueous commons of the earth, and we need the oceans to stay healthy and abundant for future generations. This is a tall order. We have to find ways to conserve their vast resources while at the same time exploiting them to feed the world's growing population. That will be one of the greatest challenges of this century.

Unfortunately, the once "unlimited resources" in our oceans have met their match. In the commercial fishing areas between North America and the British Isles, cod have declined 90 percent in the last twenty years. In fact, our global demand for all seafood has now *outstripped global supply*. What's worse, around 85 percent of global fish stocks are fully exploited, over-exploited, or depleted. We are at the point where every square mile of ocean around the entire planet is now "managed" to fully exploit the fish.

It is not just declining water quality and fish health that has brought us to this point of over-exploitation. Our harvesting technology has outpaced the planet's ability to replace what we take out. We have built larger fleets, open-ocean factory ships, transparent lines and nets, huge drift nets, bottom trawlers and electronic fish finders, and with all that we have overfished our planetary fishing hole. The global capacity for catching fish is now nearly double the sustainable supply. Fishermen desperate to make a living are now going after smaller and smaller species down the food chain.

The *tragedy of the commons* (see Glossary) has wiped out our once plentiful fish stocks. We allowed this free-for-all to decimate the most valuable, free resource on the planet. As with the vast timber resources of North America we have let the free market run wild, and its success is destroying the food that we badly need. What is so disappointing is that fish, like trees, can be a totally renewable resource if managed well. Our current overharvesting has to change. We have to find a way to manage our global fish stocks sustainably. One way to do this, without putting moratoria on fishing, is to assign fishermen to specific areas so they have more of an interest in managing their fishery in a sustainable manner. Another option is fish farming, or aquaculture.

To meet the increasing demand for fish, aquaculture has been growing and now provides 33 percent of the supply. That number is expected to continue to grow. Of course, environmental challenges arise when we try raising fish in farms. The first one is what we feed them. In some situations we chop up unwanted fish and feed that to the farm fish. This can result in bioaccumulation of any chemicals they have been absorbed into the tissue of the food fish. In other cases, we have fed contaminated grains (soybeans and corn) to fish in fish farms. An even bigger challenge is getting rid of waste products from the farmed fish. Fish farms are often offshore enclosures where all the wastes from fish grown in high density settings fall to the sea floor. This contaminates the area and depletes its oxygen. We need to be mindful when we try to raise fish in farms.

There is something wrong and doomsday-ish about the fact that we have so damaged natural fisheries in all of our vast oceans and now have to create new environments in order to grow our food. Why is it easier to create farms to raise fish than to manage the fish in their own natural and highly productive habitats?

Ocean Dumping — If the high point of my fishing trip off the Outer Banks was battling the dolphin, the low point was the trash that was mixed in with the seaweed at our first stop. We were miles from shore, yet here were several plastic bottles, a BIC lighter, and a plastic toy doll floating in the sea. It was not the first time I had seen human trash so far out in the ocean, but seeing it reminded me of the vast collection of plastic that lies in the northern Pacific hundreds of miles from shore. Trash has accumulated at the becalmed heart of the North Pacific Gyre, a giant clockwise circuit of currents that revolves between East Asia and North America. That plastic garbage patch covers an area the size of Texas. Similar accumulations of plastic and other trash have formed in all five of the major subtropical oceanic gyres, including the North Atlantic (Figure 7). What are we doing to our planet?

As plastic breaks up with wave action, it forms pieces small enough to be swallowed by fish and fowl. Many dead fish have been caught with plastic stuck in their throats and stomachs. Larger pieces of plastic and lost nets become *ghost snares* snagging fish for an eternity. In addition to the great loss of fish, scientists estimate that every year at least a million seabirds and a hundred thousand marine mammals and sea turtles die when they entangle themselves in debris or ingest it. Each piece of plastic we discard kills other living things. It should make us all stop and think about our use and abuse of plastic.

We have known about this problem of ocean dumping for a long time. In 1972, Congress enacted the Marine Protection, Research, and Sanctuaries Act, MPRSA, also known as the Ocean Dumping Act. The law was designed to prohibit dumping material into the ocean that could unreasonably degrade or endanger human health or the marine environment. This act implements the requirements of the London Convention, which is the international treaty governing ocean dumping, so we have been aware of the problem for a long time. We have taken steps, but the problem and the plastic persist.

What Fish Should I Eat?

Many are perplexed about what they can do to help our oceans, about whether they should even be eating fish, and if so, about what fish to buy. I am, too. After a week of eating the mahi mahi I caught on the charter boat, I started thinking about how much mercury, PCBs, dioxins, and pesticide residues I had consumed. So I checked with the Food and Drug Administration (FDA) and the Environmental Protection Agency (EPA) and learned that accumulated mercury is the main health concern with ocean-going fish. The major sources of PCBs, dioxin, and pesticides in our diet actually come from vegetables, meats, dairy products, and eggs.

Coal-fired power plants and incinerators deposit mercury on all of our land and in all of our seas. The mercury on land is flushed into streams and ultimately into oceans via stormwater runoff. Bacteria turn it into methyl-mercury. Fish absorb methyl-mercury as they feed, and therefore more accumulates in the larger and older fish. If you eat a lot of fish it can accumulate over time in your bloodstream. The typical levels of accumulated mercury are not considered a health risk for most adults, but methyl-mercury can be harmful to young children and the unborn. Pregnant women and young children are advised to avoid the bigger fish that may have high accumulations of mercury in their fat: marlin, orange roughy, tilefish, swordfish, shark, king mackerel, and Ahi Tuna.

But none of us should give up on eating fish. The FDA encourages everyone to eat at least 12 ounces of fish weekly because fish provide high quality protein and other essential nutrients, are low in saturated fat, and contain omega-3 fatty acids. A well-balanced diet that includes a variety of fish and shellfish can contribute to heart health and proper growth and development in children. Weekly consumption may also reduce the risk of stroke, depression, Alzheimer's disease, and other chronic conditions. The low-mercury fish you should be eating include shrimp, canned light tuna, salmon, pollock, oysters, flounder, and catfish.

Even with this law on the books, reports of fouled beaches were recurring news items in the 1980s. I recall the East Coast beaches being shut down numerous times when medical syringes washed up on the New Jersey and Delaware shores. We learned that New York City had been getting rid of its garbage, including medical waste, by sending garbage barges out into the ocean and dumping them offshore. Evidently it was not *offshore* enough! Congress responded by passing the Ocean Dumping Reform Act in 1988. Nevertheless, according to a recent EPA report, the U.S. still releases more than 850 *billion gallons* of untreated sewage and stormwater runoff into the oceans every year. Some countries are much worse.

"Floatables" in the oceans come from many sources; only a small part comes from people intentionally throwing trash directly into the sea or on land. Most of it comes from stormwater runoff carrying the stuff that spills out of our trash, falls off of our back porches, or flies out of our car windows. This morning after two days of heavy rain, I saw several hundred pieces of trash floating on our lake, including numerous plastic containers on their way to the ocean. Where did it all come from? My neighbors are responsible, thoughtful people, but we are all inadvertently contributing when we leave anything outside and uncontained where the elements can start it on its journey to the sea.

We have taken some steps to reduce what we dump into the oceans. Recycling and trash trucks are more self-contained today. There are now requirements in many areas that boats stop dumping their waste into the water. Some communities have installed booms at the mouths of rivers designed to collect trash coming downriver. These are last ditch attempts to prevent plastic floatables from getting into our oceans. Unfortunately, all of our rivers need booms, but booms are expensive to maintain and not as effective in storm conditions.

Today the main things officially dumped into U.S. waters are dredge spoils and fish remains. And yet much of our coastline and even Alaska's 33,000-mile "pristine" outer shoreline, which is largely uninhabited, is still littered with trash.

Of course rivers dump a lot more than just floating plastics into the sea. Even though most western countries treat and manage their sewage streams, a lot of nitrogen and phosphorus passes through. Farmers and gardeners try to apply just the right amount of fertilizer to their land, but some of it washes downstream when a storm passes by shortly after it has been spread. Though many farms have a nutrient management plan to control the sewage lagoons on their livestock operations, some of that ends up in the oceans as well. Then there are developing countries, who do not have any of these controls in place yet. That is why there is an extensive "dead zone" at the mouth of nearly every major river on the earth.

The National Center for Coastal Ocean Science claims that dead zones worldwide have increased exponentially and that, despite conservation efforts, more than 150,000 square miles of ocean are devastated. *Billions* of fish now die annually in these areas. Certain algae found in dead zones produce powerful toxins that cause illness and death in animals and humans and when airborne can cause asthma-like effects. Blue-green algae is so toxic that even recreational contact, such as swimming, can be harmful. The problem is getting worse. The algae bloom of 2012 in Puget Sound, Washington, was described as "unprecedented."

In addition to floatables and fertilizers, all other chemical residues of our society—pesticides, gasoline, fuel oil, grease, cleaning solvents, cosmetics, and medicines, etc.—also end up in our seas. Most enter our oceans right where they are the most prolific, on the edges of continents. In fact, 99 percent of the worldwide annual seafood catch comes from coastal waters within two hundred nautical miles of the coastline. These narrow coastal fringes are the most productive and the most vulnerable parts of our oceans and they are where we dump most of our waste. Chemicals waiting to be picked up by the smaller life forms (phytoplankton and zooplankton) are then passed on and upward through the food chain to . . . us. When I think about it, I wonder if I really want to eat dolphin or any catch from the sea. Just the fact that there are so many warnings of how often one should eat fish makes me pause and reflect. Fortunately, the research to date indicates that the contaminant levels in fish are generally below what has been proven to be toxic to humans. That doesn't make me feel much better. Most of us who eat fish accumulate these toxins in our blood, in our organs, and in our fat tissues.

The FDA and EPA set national guidelines on how much fish we should be consuming. Each state has its own fish consumption guidelines based on local sources of pollution. They will tell you how often you should eat fish from various rivers, lakes, or estuaries. The guidelines have gotten tighter during my lifetime. Normally they are couched in terms of limiting consumption of fish to a specific number of meals per month. For example the advisory in Maryland used to say don't eat striped bass more than once a week. Unfortunately, now it says not to eat it more than once a month. That's not a healthy trend. It just doesn't seem right that we have allowed our waters to become so contaminated that we have to keep track of how often we consume fish. We have crossed the line. It's time to change our behavior and clean up the oceans. We have to get mercury and other toxic chemicals out of our air, water, and food.

An indicator of what we are doing to our oceans can be seen by taking a good look at our reefs. Roughly one-third of the world's coral reef systems have already been destroyed by pollution and climate change. Reefs serve as invaluable habitat and nurseries for a wide variety of fish and sea life. We cannot afford to lose more reefs. What happens to all of these species when the reefs are all gone?

What Can We Do? — If we don't do more we'll have a bigger problem on our hands than just the loss of a fishery or two. It is possible that at some point we could have a major collapse of the oceanic ecosystem. The first thing to do is to find a way to continuously educate yourself and to track the issues. The National Oceanic and Atmospheric Administration (NOAA, at http://www.noaa.gov/) is a great source for information, as is the Smithsonian Ocean Portal (http://ocean.si.edu/). Of course many of the major non-governmental organizations can keep you on top of the main issues in their newsletters (e.g., the Nature Conservancy). Some of them have been very effective. The Defenders of Wildlife have helped create marine sanctuaries and curtail the very deleterious practice of large-scale driftnet fishing. The trashing of our oceans should make us angry enough to take some action on their behalf. What else can we do?

Reduce ocean dumping – We must, all of us, understand that the oceans are indeed in peril and it is a direct result of our everyday behavior—behavior that we could easily change. We have to stop generating so much waste, and stop dumping it into rivers and oceans. We have to change our throw-away culture to one based on "reduce, reuse, and recycle," so that we end up with less trash dumped into the environment.

We should start by not buying non-degradable, throw-away materials such as plastic bottles and packaging, replacing them as often as possible with readily degradable materials and reusable containers. Good advice when shopping in most grocery stores is to just shop around the edges. This is because that is where the fresh vegetables, fruits, and meats are usually located. These basic foods are less processed and can be obtained with less packaging. Processed foods have wasted more energy, water, and other materials in their manufacturing.

We must slow the runoff from our backyards. Capturing our storm-water in rain gardens before it becomes runoff will reduce how much trash is carried downstream to the sea.

We have to encourage local governments to enhance the water treatment facilities that dump "treated" but not clean water into our rivers and coastlines. We should also make sure that all of the chemicals we choose to buy are readily bio-degradable and not ones that contribute to the poisoning of our seas. We should *never* dump extra medicine, grease, cleaning solvents, or any chemicals down toilets, sinks or drains. We should always keep in mind that those medicines or chemicals that we do choose to consume will eventually end up in the ocean, too. The once pristine oceans cannot continue to be our waste disposal system for materials that do not degrade rapidly.

Reduce emissions from fossil fuel power plants – To get contaminants out of our food supply will require stopping the emission of mercury and other chemicals into the atmosphere where they will eventually reach the ocean. We also must stop acidifying our oceans by halting carbon emissions from coal fired power plants, cars, and waste incinerators. Increasing acidity has already destroyed numerous reefs and weakened the shell structures of many forms of marine life. We can send the message to the power companies by reducing our energy use at home and at the office and switching electricity suppliers to those who support wind and solar energy.

Fisheries management and sustainable seafood – We need to push our representatives and the global nonprofits to improve national and international treaties that govern all the oceans. We can all chose to eat more sustainably, thereby encouraging the marketplace to make the right decisions as well. The Monterey Bay Aquarium *SeafoodWatch Card* is a great pocket guide that you can carry with you or share with others to help spread the word about what to eat and what to avoid.

Support the efforts of non-profits – There are many local and national non-profits that help get the word out, and they can certainly use your support. You can find them by looking at Charity Navigator or Guidestar. Some NGOs (e.g., Grist, ENSIA) provide their members with information and opportunities to take action. Others, like Earth Justice, are more aggressive watchdogs that often use litigation to accomplish their goals. Some, like the Natural Resource Defense Council (NRDC), offer the carrot-and-stick approach. They like to work with industry and government agencies but are not hesitant to sue if necessary. There are also ocean specific organizations such as the Ocean Conservancy and OCEANA. The Ocean Conservancy began operations in 1972 and focuses on the coasts of the U.S. They work closely with fishermen, residents, and governments to preserve natural and manmade features and to restore the offshore fisheries. Oceana was established by the Pew Charitable Foundation and others in 2001 and now, with 500,000 members, is one of the largest international organizations focused solely on ocean conservation.

Don't give up on these issues. They are important enough to get angry about and to turn that anger to action.

CHAPTER 13

The Planet

The human race, without intending anything of the sort, has undertaken a
gigantic uncontrolled experiment on the earth. In time, I think, this will appear
as the most important aspect of twentieth century history.
— J. R. McNeill

Droughts and Storms — In 2012, I traveled to the hottest climate in
America, Death Valley, California. It is a place of extremes. Situated
within the Mojave Desert, it is the *lowest, hottest, and driest area* in all
of North America. The lowest part of Death Valley is 282 feet below sea
level. Just to the west one can see Mount Whitney, the tallest mountain
in the contiguous U.S. The average high temperature in July is 116°
Fahrenheit and the record is 134° Fahrenheit, the hottest measurement
ever made on earth.

I went during the cooler months when I knew the temperatures
would be more moderate than in the summer. Spring is a good time to
visit if you want to hike the canyons, see the flora and fauna, and not
be burnt to a crisp. After all, this is a place where many people have
died from thirst and exposure. There are stories from the time of the
California gold rush when 49ers got off the main trail and wandered for
weeks in Death Valley, often fatally. It is also the home of muleskinners
and the twenty-mule teams that carried heavy wagonloads of borax out
of the mines and across the baked desert floor to be shipped back east.
It is no paradise but is nonetheless well worth seeing to experience a
desert climate.

When the weather is good, there are beautiful views of bare mountains that border the slowly subsiding valley floor. Yes, this is an active,

fault bounded, rift valley where the continent is trying to pull apart. I could almost feel the valley floor falling out from beneath my feet. There are great hikes up the narrow but bone-dry secondary river valleys that cut way back into the mountainous walls on both sides of the main valley. When it does rain, flash floods rush down these side canyons and feed sediment onto the alluvial fans that stretch out into the sinking basin.

It became quite clear to me why they called this desolate area Death Valley—at these temperatures not much can live. Scrawny roadrunners were the most interesting fauna we saw. There are no trees for shade and few clouds this time of year. The streams that scoured out the steep marble canyons were all dried up. The average annual rainfall is 2.25 inches. What water falls here does not drain out to the sea but quickly evaporates, leaving borax and other mineral salts behind. In fact, if it were connected to the ocean, the seawater would actually drain into the valley because of its lower elevation.

Sometimes the weather is challenging in Death Valley. When I returned to our campsite one night after hiking all day, the wind had come up and a sandstorm had blown in with all its fury. My blue tent was already gone, ripped from the rocky soil and blown into a brittle, mesquite copse by a dry river bed. The sand assaulted my face and got into my eyes, nose, ears, and mouth. All I wanted to do was to escape this dry sand blizzard, to find shelter from the gale.

Extreme temperature differentials between the valley floor and mountain ridges, and the storms off the Pacific produce these wicked sandstorms. This type of airborne sand can penetrate clothing, tents, and cars, leaving a layer of dust on and in everything. It is a most inhospitable place to live. I kept thinking how the climate models predict that we will be in for more droughts and more desert conditions as the climate warms. The earth could become a cruel place when the climate changes, vegetation dries up, and the winds rage.

Many places that used to be farmed on our planet are deserts today (Montgomery, 2007). I have visited areas here in the U.S., in the Middle East, and in Africa where the everyday practices of our ancestors brought on desertification. Old buildings (caravanserai) reflecting once prosperous cities are now buried beneath migrating sands. The sandstorm in Death Valley brought to mind images of those ruins of past civilizations. How many cities might we lose if our climate continues to warm? Here in the American Southwest, we are expecting higher temperatures and less rainfall. Drought could become the normal state of things in large parts of the nation and in many other places on the planet as well. Just this summer, Death Valley set a new historic record for high temperatures. What is to come?

As a young boy on a farm, I lived through a major drought in the 1950s. It is hard to watch as one's crops stop growing, wither on the vine, and blow away. That was a long time ago, but I clearly remember how desperate we were for water for our crops, our animals, and for ourselves. We had a thirty-foot-deep, hand-dug, stone-lined well that went dry as the groundwater table dropped over the course of the summer. It was the first time it had ever happened to us. The closest creek, Bob's Run, also went dry. In the midst of the drought, my father somehow acquired a thousand-gallon water tank that we strapped to the back of our one-ton flatbed truck. We then drove ten miles to fill it from a still flowing spring. We didn't know how long the spring would last, or even the quality of the water, but we were immensely grateful to get what it offered. Dad then drove around the farm to water our livestock and gardens. Life is not easy in a drought. It makes you consider your priorities. It makes you appreciate rain.

In addition to areas that will see more drought in the future, the climate models suggest that parts of the planet will experience wetter conditions and larger storms than normal. I keep thinking back to the past ten years. When Katrina hit Louisiana in the late summer of 2005, I remember seeing footage of 200,000 American men, women, and children leaving New Orleans. I have a hard time accepting even the concept of refugees escaping an American city, one we were supposed to be safe in, one the Corps of Engineers spent a great deal of money to protect from storms. Katrina dominated the news not just for weeks but for months. It was the costliest hurricane in history with $81 billion dollars in damage.

After Katrina the news media moved on to other stories, the collective consciousness moved on, and we have not done enough to prevent more catastrophes, the big storms of the future, from coming and wreaking havoc all over again. This is the dirty little secret of New Orleans. We failed to learn our lesson. It will happen again.

Next came Hurricane Irene and Tropical Storm Lee striking the East Coast. In this area of the country, average rain fall is a little over 3 inches a month. During the month of August 2011, parts of the Mid-Atlantic region got 22 inches in one month, 8 inches in one day, and 4 inches in one hour. That broke the records. Flooding was big news for a few days, but again the news moved on.

Hurricane Sandy hit New York City in October, 2012 and once again we witnessed nature's destructive capability. The storm was bad, damaging hundreds of thousands of homes and businesses. At a cost of $60 billion, it was the second most damaging storm in history, behind Katrina. All this destruction resulted from a storm surge that was only fourteen feet high, not the twenty-foot storm surge that hit New Orleans during Katrina. Again we saw the suffering and the damage, before the news moved on once more.

Then, in September 2013, a "1,000-year storm event" occurred in Colorado. Nineteen thousand homes were damaged in widespread flooding. This storm, like Hurricane Sandy, apparently resulted from higher than normal ocean water temperatures that increased evaporation and filled the atmosphere with much more moisture than normal. This very unusual tropical air mass stalled over Colorado, dumping 17 inches of rain, 9 inches in a single day. And these are not the only stories. According to the 2013 National Climate Assessment report, most parts of the U.S. have seen an increase in extreme precipitation events. We might not be able to link any one storm to global warming, but neither can they be separated. Sea levels are rising, ocean temperatures are warming, and the air is holding more water vapor. Therefore all weather events are related to and part of global climate change.

The U.S. has been spending about $100 billion per year over the past few years to *repair* the damage and build greater resiliency into our cities. But not enough is being done to *prevent* bigger storms in the future. To rebuild but not prevent future disasters seems extremely short-sighted and irresponsible. Why do we think we can protect cities all over the map from increasingly larger storms when we don't know where they will strike, how often they will occur, and how hard they will hit? It would be cheaper and more protective of human life and property if we did something to prevent them in the first place. We will discuss these options later in this chapter but there are some obvious steps to take first: shutter the worst coal-fired plants, put a tax on carbon, and invest in alternatives.

When it comes down to it, we lost these recent battles with Mother Nature because we were using the wrong strategy. We thought we could make our cities resilient. We chose to be defiant, claiming we could take on whatever nature had in store for us. We took no steps to prevent the war but chose instead to fight the storms, and we lost, badly. That is hubris, and guess what? We will lose again. We have to shift our focus to slowing the rise in sea level and halting the projected increase in the frequency and magnitude of storms. If indeed bigger storms are an outcome of global climate change, we have the responsibility to our fellow man to reduce the likelihood of the next disaster. Global climate change is the biggest, *preventable*, planetary challenge that will affect us all, no matter where we live. That is our common enemy.

The UN Scientific Expert Group on Climate Change & Sustainable Development suggests that we have three basic options:

1) Mitigate global warming to avoid the unmanageable,

2) Adapt to manage the unavoidable, or

3) Suffer.

Various jurisdictions are handling these options in different ways. Mayor Michael Bloomberg launched a $20 billion climate adaptation effort for New York City. At the other end, North Carolina's state legislature has prohibited local authorities from even considering sea level rise in their urban/coastal planning.

Of all of our daily activities, those with the greatest negative impact on our way of life are the things we do that contribute to global climate change. It's time we think what we're doing. If you have any doubt that our behaviors can impact the climate, read the accompanying "A Species to be Feared."

Human Impacts — All the places that are important to us, the mountains, lakes, rivers, and beaches that we love and want to preserve, have one thing in common. They are all on this planet we call home. Anything that affects the entire planet will have an impact on each of our favorite places. Global changes have local impacts. If each of us has a favorite place we would like to protect, then we must be aware of the planet-wide impacts of our daily activities. Let's put this into perspective.

The twentieth century was full of major economic, energy, health, political, social and environmental disruptions. International insecurity may have been the biggest driver throughout most of the century, but historian J. R. McNeill believes that the twentieth century's greatest legacy will prove to be the environmental disruptions we caused. McNeill points out that the full, long-term effect of chlorofluorocarbons, plastics, nuclear waste, medicines, the overuse of antibiotics, genetically modified foods and drugs, contaminated food and water supplies, habitat loss, and the warming of the earth are at this point still unknown. It is likely that some of these items will come back to haunt us in the future. We will have to be increasingly vigilant to manage the long-term impact of the technologies we've unleashed. McNeill also points out in *Something New Under the Sun* that "many of our ecological buffers—open land, unused water, unpolluted spaces—that helped societies weather difficult times in the past are now gone." One thing that should be clear is that without these buffers many of our current practices are unsustainable.

Humans have demonstrated their great talent for making many parts of this planet habitable. We have also demonstrated the terribly destructive power to make large, once fertile areas of our planet *uninhabitable*. And we have done it over and over again. Earlier civilizations grew rich off the land where there were vast, free resources. That unregulated growth worked well until the population outstripped the resources.

A Species to Be Feared

As a boy, I scoffed at the idea that I could have any effect at all on the planet. It is so large and diverse that we can feel insignificant relative to its size, its complexity, and the sheer beauty of the life it has fostered. Volcanoes and meteorites may disrupt life on earth, but how could anything as small as a boy have any effect on such a big place? I have since learned that the impact of 7,000,000,000 boys, girls, men, and women is significant.

• We have caught most of the fish from what we thought were endless supplies in the earth's great oceans.

• We have hunted the earth's mammals and birds and consumed their habitat to the point where many are now extinct, regionally extirpated, or endangered.

• We have cultivated most of the earth's arable land, using much of its fresh water to turn deserts into productive farms—so long as the dwindling supplies of fresh water in aquifers last.

• We have filled the atmosphere with a wide range of manmade chemicals that can now be found at dizzying heights and which travel all around the globe.

• We have changed the chemistry and the acidity of vast oceans, innumerable lakes, millions of miles of streams, and even underground waters.

• We have destroyed past civilizations and are destroying current ones because we have mismanaged our natural resources (water, fuel, food, and mineral wealth) resulting in droughts, famines, social unrest, revolutions, and wars.

• We have raised the temperature of the oceans, the land surfaces, and the atmosphere by pumping continuous streams of methane, carbon dioxide, and other greenhouse gases into the air.

Yes, it is hard to believe, but the data are clear. What we humans do does matter. We are a species to be feared. We must be careful about what we do.

According to Jared Diamond in his book *Collapse*, once man got out of balance with nature, those civilizations fell to ruin. Much of the Middle East, where civilization was born, has been destroyed (multiple times) by the uncontrolled growth of those civilizations. The so called Fertile Crescent is no longer so fertile. The cycle repeats itself because we seem to have difficulty learning from past mistakes. The question is whether we can learn from them today. Can we find common ground with one another in the management of our natural resources for a better future for all of us? Making human impacts positive and not negative is the challenge of the twenty-first century.

What is different today from, say, a thousand years ago, is that we now understand many of the processes that eventually destroyed whole ecosystems and civilizations. Over the past fifty years people of the world have come together, taken action, and actually reduced the harm we do to the environment. Individuals all over the world are trying to learn how to live more in balance with each other and with nature. It is clear that men and women world-wide care about their health, the health of their communities, and the health of their children. But do we care enough? There is still so much to do.

Global Climate Disruption — The biggest impact man has had on our planet is the disruption of our global climate. Warming oceans, lands, and atmosphere are melting icecaps, raising the sea level, and creating more extreme weather. As we have seen, these changes are already having significant impacts on our way of life.

No one knows *how bad things will get* as the planet continues to heat up. If we continue to dump greenhouse gases into the atmosphere, the models predict average temperatures rising one to two degrees and sea levels rising two to six feet in this century. These may appear to be small variations for the planet, but they are huge changes for us and our civilization. All we know is that with just one degree of temperature increase and less than one foot of sea level rise to date, the effects have been significant. It is economically and socially imperative that we slow or reverse the warming trend.

On the question of what can we do if anything to prevent continued warming, I believe that the American people and others have shown that there are a lot of things we can do. We can lower energy usage, reduce greenhouse gases, and move to cleaner and more sustainable energy sources. We are moving in the right direction, but progress is too slow. Our government could, if they decided to, accelerate our transition to cleaner energy with a clear vision, incentives, and subsidies. We have made progress already by installing 14 gigawatts of solar capacity and 60 gigawatts of wind power. This seems like a lot, but it pales beside the *four thousand* gigawatts used in the U.S. alone. So the problem is much bigger. Either we have to make a much greater effort to move toward alternatives, or we have to move on multiple fronts to clean up the other energy resources on which we still depend. The solution is probably some of both because of economics, best available technology, vested interests, and practicality.

A large part of the problem in the U.S. is that we don't have a price on carbon emissions. As a result there is less marketplace incentive to find solutions to the pollution produced by using fossil fuels. This is one of the biggest market failures in human history, since it gives a false price signal in terms of the "bargain" that fossil fuels would appear to be as opposed to renewables. We must correct that.

The larger questions on the global front are whether China and India will decrease their dependence on fossil fuels and what might they use to replace them. Both countries are still building cheap, coal-fired plants despite the impact on their citizens' health. The air quality has gotten so bad in many Chinese cities that the government has started to take a number of emergency measures to reduce the pollution. China has also developed major plans to build solar and nuclear plants. They could also use natural gas. Recently, the World Bank and the U.S. Export Import Bank have decided to sharply restrict funding for new coal-fired plants in developing nations. This represents a significant turning point. We will have to wait and see if those nations can reduce their reliance on coal. Perhaps we can encourage them to move to cleaner alternatives. For example, they would more likely shift toward renewable energy if the U.S. stopped exporting cheap coal into the world markets. We should also demonstrate how to enact a successful transition from coal to alternative sources of power. So, yes, there is a lot we can do to slow down climate change. We should be the leader in moving away from coal and developing and deploying the technologies of the future.

Energy Resources — As we all realize by now, one of the biggest causes of global climate change is the use and abuse of fossil fuels. At the same time we must recognize that the wealth of our country is largely due to our access to cheap energy. At first, *free wind energy* sailed us across the ocean to this energy-rich land. Then an apparently *unlimited supply of wood* fueled the country's growth. Wood heated our homes and fed our furnaces. Then we harnessed water power behind hundreds of thousands of dams across America. This was followed by our discovery and development of fossil fuels, a very rich and easily transported form of energy. These abundant sources of energy have allowed us to build a wealthy nation and a high quality of life. We should not lose sight of the importance of our cheap energy resources. At the same time we have to realize that our current use of fossil fuels is threatening our health, economy, and security. We therefore have to figure out how to dramatically clean up fossil fuels or significantly reduce our use of them.

Today we are fortunate to have multiple energy options. We have the luxury, to some extent, of supporting those that are less damaging to us and our way of life. President Obama said we should pursue them all. It's fine to let the marketplace do what it does best, but as responsible citizens and stewards of the future we should make certain that *all* the costs to society are included when we decide what energy sources we should be using. We must include health, climate change, and national security concerns into the real cost of fuel. There is an important role for federally funded research, incentives, and regulation when it comes to supporting our energy future. In order to determine which resources to support, we must understand their impacts and the role they could play in an increasingly competitive and crowded future.

Coal – The U.S. has greater energy resources (coal, gas, and oil) than any other country on earth. Our reserves of coal are five times greater than our reserves of oil or gas. We are a coal-rich nation—not something we should forget. Coal is widespread across America and has provided as much as half of our electricity generation in the past. It was our dominant fuel from 1885, following the age of wood, until 1950, when petroleum surpassed it. Unfortunately, we have not yet found an economical way to utilize our vast coal resources without polluting our land, water, and air. Someday we might.

Due to coal's inherent pollution problems and the current abundance of cheaper natural gas, coal use has been on the decline in the U.S. Today it meets about 36 percent of our electrical needs, sliding from over 53 percent a decade ago. So the coal industry is under pressure to clean up and keep their costs down. They have added scrubbers and precipitators to reduce the particulates and some of the sulfur emission from smoke stacks but they have a long way to go. Emerging technologies are improvements over their current processes, but they are more expensive. They will probably not be deployed unless regulations on carbon drive the coal firms in this direction. Future efforts to utilize coal more cleanly could include carbon sequestration and storage plants, the extraction of coal bed methane, and in situ conversion of coal to liquids.

For now we have to do whatever we can to reduce our reliance on conventional coal even further. Going *beyond coal* is a policy and political imperative at this point in our history. Not mining this coal today is not a bad thing. We could save it for a time when we either have figured out the technology to use coal safely or when we have no other choice— a *strategic coal reserve* if you will. In the meantime, we should not be exporting this product to other countries. Burning coal anywhere on earth still hurts us and everyone else. *Furthermore, stopping our coal exports will raise the cost of coal internationally and help other countries shift to cleaner, alternative energy resources.* This is a very important step in the global shift to cleaner fuels. If we do not stop exporting coal to China our fight against global climate change and polluted air will probably fail. With China's increasing demand for it, coal will surpass petroleum and become the world's dominant fuel source by 2020.

With the new EPA requirements to reduce emissions, many of the older, coal-fired plants in the U.S. are being decommissioned and taken off line. This is significant since these plants were some of the worst polluters and the lessened effects on health and costs should far outweigh any economic losses from closing them. Evidently the worst fifty coal-fired plants contribute about 12 percent of the total greenhouse gases that the U.S. is dumping into the atmosphere. Shuttering them would be a major step forward. The new rules will also affect the dozens of new coal plants currently on the drawing boards, which may never be brought on line at all because of the involvement of so many people who turned their anger with coal mining, shipping, and burning into action. The cost of new plants keeps rising as coal companies realize they will finally have to incorporate new technologies to mitigate the deleterious effects of burning coal. The future of the coal industry depends on its ability to demonstrate a much cleaner process for using the energy stored in coal than they have been able to achieve in the past.

Petroleum – Petroleum fuels our transportation, petrochemical, and heating oil industries. It has been produced from various subsurface reservoirs across the U.S. and overseas. Over the past fifty years the U.S. has become so thirsty for petroleum that we have enriched unfriendly and undemocratic nations and engaged in wars to ensure we can get as much as we want. Even with more production slated from U.S. fields, the negative repercussions of this era of overseas petroleum exploitation will be felt around the world for decades to come.

The most important national security issue with being so dependent on oil is that its price and availability are currently controlled by others. In the 1970s, OPEC drove the price up dramatically. That created economic havoc in the U.S., so we started a major alternative energy effort that could have freed us from depending on imported oil. OPEC did not want that to happen so they dropped the price of oil down to $20/bbl in the 1980s and 1990s. Our short-sighted response was to end much of our investment in alternatives including synfuels [synthetic fuels from coal and natural gas]. It was not a good decision on our part because it gave the power back to OPEC to raise the price again whenever it chose. In fact, over the last decade the price has risen back up to $110/bbl, once more causing economic havoc around the world and reinvigorating our interest in alternatives.

This time, however, the price may not go back down. We appear to be at "peak oil," meaning conventional oil supplies will decrease from here on. Conventional global oil production has been decreasing at about 4 percent per year in recent years. To meet the demand for liquid fuels in the future, we will probably be developing oil shale and oil sand deposits and possibly creating liquids from coal and natural gas. These will be more expensive. In either case, liquid fuels are predicted to be more expensive in the future and more scarce.

Liquid fuels are valuable because they are easy to transport and are used by many forms of transportation. They also have a vast array of other uses—medicinal, material (plastics), and chemical. Petroleum will continue to be necessary for many of our transportation applications for many years to come, at least as a bridge fuel. There will be ongoing pressure to develop high-risk petroleum fields in the Gulf Coast, East Coast, and Alaska, as well as the U.S. oil shales and the vast oil sands of Canada. We must ensure that these areas are not developed without serious safeguards. Although better than coal, petroleum is still a major source of air and water pollution. Figure 8 illustrates that pipeline spills occur all across the U.S. In the air emissions arena, even though we have made progress, cars still emit nitrogen and sulfur oxide compounds that pollute the air, land, rivers, and oceans. So until the technology gets dramatically better and the supplies more reliable, we should continue to reduce our use of and dependency on petroleum for environmental, economic, and national security reasons. The quickest way to do that is to buy more efficient cars and trucks and to drive less.

Natural Gas – Natural gas is the most energy intensive and cleanest burning of the fossil fuel sources. There are also large proven reserves across the U.S. and offshore (Figure 9). Recent drilling and hydro-fracking has enlarged the available supply and driven down the price. Most projections (e.g., from the Energy Information Administration) suggest that natural gas will make up the greater part of new electrical generating capacity in this country over the foreseeable future. This is a good thing relative to burning oil or coal for generating power, but it still produces about half the pollution of a coal-fired plant. Without a carbon tax to cover the external costs of burning this fossil fuel, natural gas outcompetes many of the alternative energy options. We need a way to make sure natural gas prices include the costs of their pollution and that industry is incentivized to clean up their processes even further.

Our country has been moving toward natural gas dramatically in the past few years due to its "low cost." However it should not be used ahead of our ability to produce and use it safely and cleanly. I have drilled natural gas wells and used *hydro-fracking* as a way to stimulate the flow of water, oil, and gas out of tight geologic formations. Where appropriate this technology can dramatically increase the volume of oil and or gas recovered from a well. Recovering more of the oil and gas that is locked in the rocks is a good thing if we can do it without damage to us or other resources. But drilling is not a clean or low-risk operation. The scale of hydraulic fracturing today is far greater than in the past and has a greater impact. It requires much more water, the fracking fluids are potentially toxic, and there are significant treatment and disposal problems with the recovered water. The risks may be manageable but this is yet to be demonstrated by the industry. EPA is conducting a thorough review of the fracking process and a report is expected within the next year or two. If fracking is allowed to proceed, serious oversight will be required to ensure that damage is minimized and that funds are available for reparations.

To provide adequate oversight, state governments must have budgets, training, and monitoring mechanisms in place. Independent state agencies will have to carefully monitor water use and disposal as well as the impact of development on forests, roads, rivers, and the air. When an enforcement program is not adequate, we are encouraging a race to the bottom. Some domestic and community water supplies have been damaged from large drilling and fracking operations. To pay for all of this, escrow accounts should be funded from permit fees and revenues paid by the drilling firms. The accounts must be large enough to repair the damage caused by drilling, production, and shipping operations, now and in the future.

In addition to greenhouse gases escaping during drilling (methane) and combustion (carbon dioxide), there is a large concern over ongoing *fugitive gases,* largely methane, from old wells and aging collection and distribution pipelines. There are more than 500,000 wells producing gas, many more that have been abandoned, and over 300,000 miles of pipeline distribution networks all over the country. Many of these wells, pipelines, and local distribution lines continually leak methane into aquifers, the soil, and the atmosphere. I have measured fugitive gases in oil and gas fields all across the country. Who is responsible for monitoring and fixing this leaky infrastructure? It is a major problem here and a much greater problem overseas where there is less oversight and professionalism. These issues can be addressed but will not be unless adequate funding and regulations are available to ensure it is done well.

Some operators have illegally dumped polluted fracking fluids and formation brines into healthy fishing streams, killing the fish and contaminating human water supplies. Those firms should be shut down, fined, jailed, and banned from the industry. There is no room for irresponsible firms when dealing with the potential for so much damage. Waters produced during the drilling and fracking process have to be filtered so it is drinkable before being released back into the environment.

A third issue is the stormwater runoff from poorly constructed and maintained drilling sites and the many, many miles of gas pipeline paths cut through forests. These scars continue to cause erosion and pollution in our streams and rivers. Where will the money come from to monitor and repair these problems of the past that continue into the future? We will need more responsible and transparent processes, individuals, corporations, and state enforcement agencies if we are to restore trust in the industry and allow further development of gas resources. Almost any way you look at our energy supply, natural gas will be a significant part of our future. We should therefore establish appropriate regulations that reduce these problems and incorporate the external costs as soon as possible.

Nuclear energy – Nuclear power was supposed to be the clean energy of the future. It could have replaced many of the fossil fuel plants in this country and dramatically reduced greenhouse gas emissions. But investment in new plants stopped after the 1979 Three Mile Island cooling malfunction that caused part of the reactor core to melt. That event scared us even though no one was injured from the minimal radiation that escaped into the atmosphere. The future of new reactors in the U.S. is still uncertain today following the 2011 Tohoku 9.0 Earthquake and the fifty-foot-high tsunami that caused the Fukushima Daiichi nuclear plant meltdown in Japan. Although no deaths from radiation exposure have been documented, the ongoing problems in Japan renew questions about our ability to locate, operate, and monitor these plants in a safe manner.

We do need to recognize that nuclear power is responsible for a significant portion (20 percent) of the electricity generated in the U.S. today. The 100 commercial reactors in the U.S. will not be easily replaced with equally clean energy when we mothball currently operating but aging plants sometime in the future. Japan is facing that challenge right now. They have announced that they will no longer be able to meet their Kyoto greenhouse gas emissions commitments now that they are switching from nuclear back to fossil fuels. Was this the right decision? It might be—in those tectonically and seismically active islands.

The nuclear industry reports that in addition to the plans for fusion reactors (many years away) the new wave of fission reactors will be smaller and safer than those currently deployed. Evidently adequate supplies of fuel are available and the technical challenges for waste disposal at Yucca Mountain have been resolved (Muller, 2012). How quickly the new reactors will be accepted depends upon how soon the nuclear industry successfully demonstrates the new technology and how soon it regains the trust of the American people. There is still a great deal of fear associated with radiation and nuclear power. When analyzed, though, the industry's forty-year track record has been far better than that of coal or oil, with fewer attributable deaths and illnesses.

There are now over 430 commercial nuclear power reactors operating in 31 countries. About 70 more are under construction. They provide over 11 percent of the world's electricity without emitting carbon dioxide. Fifty-six countries operate about 240 research reactors, and another 180 nuclear reactors power some 150 ships and submarines. Nevertheless, the nuclear industry has been hamstrung in some areas because it has experienced two major accidents (Chernobyl and Fukushima Daiichi) in the past 40 years. In addition to rebuilding trust, the industry must deal with insurance, cost, and lead time to gain permission and then build each new unit. As challenging as those hurdles will be, nuclear power will continue to be part of our future. It also could be a big part of the solution for China and India. It could help them get off coal.

Renewables – The alternatives to fossil fuel and nuclear are not easy, quick—or perfect. Solar, wind, geothermal, hydroelectric, landfill gas, and biomass deserve the same scrutiny as any other energy source. Let's focus on solar arrays and wind turbines, which appear to offer significant promise and potential for growth. We call them clean because they do not produce emissions when operating, but carbon is released and chemicals are used in the manufacture and delivery of the systems. It is estimated that this amount of carbon spread over the lifetime of the unit equates to 0.1 pounds of carbon dioxide equivalent per kilowatt-hour. That is an order of magnitude less than the lifecycle emission rates for natural gas and other fossil fuels. Solar panels and wind turbines also use raw materials that come from mines all around the world, but, after fifty years of research and development, these alternatives appear to be much cleaner options for powering our future. They appear even more attractive when you take into account their lower risks to human health, national security, and the environment.

The steady progress and wide adoption of wind and solar speaks volumes. Rising from essentially nothing to 3 percent of our domestic energy pool in the last decade is a huge accomplishment and a vote of confidence. It is due in part to the dramatic decrease in costs for solar and wind systems as production scaled up and competition increased. It is also the result of county, state, and federal incentives and mandates. The realization that, after all of the effort and growth in these industries, solar and wind only meet 3 percent of our needs illustrates how big that need is. Alternatives have a long way to go to become a really meaningful part of our energy supply.

Although solar generation capacity reached 14 gigawatts by the end of 2013, a fivefold increase from 2010, even with that dramatic amount of growth it remains at less than 1 percent of the country's energy mix. The Energy Information Administration predicts that it could rise to 4 percent by 2040. That is significant but if that is all it does, it is a very small part of the solution to climate change. As the price of solar cells comes down, labor becomes the major cost of installation. In developing countries with cheap labor, like China and India, solar might grow more quickly.

So why can't it be larger in the U.S.? Of the 90 million single-family homes in the U.S., only 250,000 have installed solar units. There are also many businesses, warehouses, and higher density living units with available roof space. So we appear to have room for much more rooftop growth. Space is a challenge, though, especially for the larger, utility-scale systems we'll need to meet the demands of electrical grids. Conventional photovoltaic (PV) arrays require from 3.5 to 10 acres per megawatt, while estimates for concentrating solar thermal plants (CSPs) fall between 4 and 16.5 acres per megawatt. The Department of Energy's National Renewable Energy Laboratory (NREL) calculates an average of 8 acres per megawatt, or 32 acres per 1,000 homes. Do you have that much land in your neighborhood to dedicate in perpetuity to meet your energy needs? To meet 100 percent of our electrical energy needs solely with solar panels would take up 0.1 percent of our land area. This might not sound like a lot in the desert, but it might be hard to come by in congested areas; not all rooftops are suitable. This is actually less than the land requirements for wind, hydroelectric, and ethanol, but more than for nuclear, gas, or coal.

Let's look at what is happening in the solar marketplace. The good news is that prices for solar have dropped 40 percent from 2008 to 2013 and are predicted to drop another 40 percent by 2017. Many businesses are offering solar systems via leases with little to no upfront costs to the homeowner. This has made it very easy to say yes, and the leasing market is expected to grow rapidly over the next few years. These are very encouraging trends.

There are challenges to the wider use of solar, though. The tremendous growth in solar has been dependent on incentives, mandates, and the availability of net metering. Utilities and conservative think tanks like the Heritage Foundation are trying to roll back incentives and net metering. This could certainly slow or stop the growth of emerging technologies. On the other hand, they might get a boost if utilities found a way to make money from solar, for they have the muscle to really push its development. They will also have to spend a lot to improve the electrical grid if there is going to be a large amount of distributed solar power. Of course creating a smart grid would have major advantages in managing all of our energy sources in a much more efficient manner.

Some jurisdictions are tired of waiting for utilities to create a smart grid and achieve a better balance of sustainable energy sources. The citizens of Boulder, Colorado, are trying to take over their local distribution system. Visit their website to see how they propose to do it and what the benefits would be if they succeed (www.boulderenergyfuture.com).

In some parts of the country, wind and solar are becoming more cost-competitive with fossil fuels, especially if we factor in the health costs of fossil fuel. Yet, even if the most optimistic projections are realized, by 2030 each of them will probably only be providing the world with about 15 percent of its electrical needs. The market is enormous, so meeting the need will take time, and we will continue to require and use a mix of energy sources. Fortunately, there are multiple options these days, though they must all improve and find ways to optimize their performance, and reduce their negative impacts. If we can level the playing field with a carbon tax (?) and stiffer regulations, each of these industries will have strong incentives to develop better, cheaper, and cleaner technologies that meet our energy needs in a more sustainable manner. The National Renewable Energy Laboratory projects the possible mix of energy sources out to 2050. Figure 10 illustrates one rational scenario showing that renewables may indeed become significant but even by 2050 they cannot meet the demand by themselves.

Many individuals and some organizations (Sierra Club, 350.org, Solar Energy Research Institute, Union of Concerned Scientists, etc.) claim that if we supported the construction of solar power plants as much as we support oil, gas, and coal power, we could drive the price down and become the leaders in the world in moving to clean energy (http://www.ucsusa.org/clean_energy/smart-energy-solutions/increase-renewables/ramping-up-renewable-energy-sources.html). They suggest that by engaging our best minds in a major effort we could refine and perfect the technology and be in a position to sell it to other countries. That strategy could have major positive global benefits. It is a promising and direct path toward reducing the rate of global climate change, and another instance in which joint federal/private cooperative research could pay off. This is an area that is very important to our future but one that is not receiving adequate attention and support from Congress. It needs funding and a comprehensive energy bill that includes a tax on carbon.

International Efforts — Since energy emissions and climate disruptions are planet-wide problems, let's look at how we are dealing with them on that level. The international community was slow to mobilize on this very complex issue. The data connecting carbon emissions and temperature had been quite clear in the 1960s, but global warming did not attract significant international political attention until the late 1980s. The Intergovernmental Panel on Climate Change (IPCC) was formed in 1988 as the internationally accepted authority on climate change.

I recall how exciting it was to think that the whole world might actually come together to tackle a threat to us all, but instead of taking immediate action on such a daunting problem, the process was delayed. Some people wanted more certainty, others, especially the oil-exporting countries, wanted no agreement that would reduce the value of their resources. So, as a global society, we decided to finance a great deal of research into how things are changing and what we can do to adapt to those changes. We have now spent decades and billions of dollars researching the details of climate change and have created an even more robust understanding of the processes. We've also squandered a great deal of time. During this interim we have seen extensive validation of the earth's warming, just as climate models predicted. The scientific community has thoroughly scrutinized the data and is united in accepting man's significant role in climate change. The only good news in all of this to me is that if man is causing the changes, then—if it is not already too late—man should be able to slow the warming. We may still be able to keep the earth's climate in the sweet zone for human existence.

Reducing emissions from the fossil fuels that we depend upon today will be difficult and complex. Sure, some fuels are less polluting than others, so we could be switching to them. There are also emerging technologies that would make each of these fuels less polluting but also more expensive. We will therefore need an economic or regulatory driver to change the mix. This is where, at least for the moment, we are stuck. Some people question whether the U.S. should take steps unilaterally, fearing that it might make us less secure, less competitive, and weaken our economy. They don't believe it makes sense unless China and India agreed to join us and are therefore opposing any proposed changes. What many do not realize is that incorporating the *real* costs into each of the options will help us pick the overall best and cheapest option and make us economically stronger and more secure than we are today.

But concern about unilateral action is widespread. Since climate change is the result of carbon emissions from all countries, it is a good subject for an international agreement. The pursuit of a world treaty, however, has proven to be a challenge for twenty-five years and counting. As we saw in the chapters on forests, campaigns for cultural change typically take fifty years to accomplish very much and require a great deal of collaboration, information, and alignment of interests. Most countries did come together in the Montreal Protocol on chemicals producing the ozone hole (CFCs). That treaty had the support of industry and has resulted in the shrinking of the ozone hole and the reduction in skin cancer. It also had very little negative impact on participants.

In contrast, slowing climate change requires significant action by many of the nearly two hundred parties to the United Nations Framework Convention on Climate Change (UNFCCC). That is virtually impossible, especially when fossil-fuel exporting countries have so little incentive to agree to anything that implies a major move away from fossil fuels. An international treaty on this subject is also problematical to the largest companies in the world and to the U.S. because we are among the biggest culprits when it comes to generating greenhouse gases. The international community has had a difficult time coming up with a solution that would work for huge multinationals and for China, India, the developing world, and the U.S.

Initially, in the 1997 Kyoto Protocol, the UNFCCC focused on a paradigm that required just the industrialized countries to cut their emissions of greenhouse gases. Today this makes no sense, since China is now the number one emitter and India is ranked third. The paradigm has been shifting since the 2009 Copenhagen climate change conference and now we are focused on finding a solution that is applicable to all countries. There are hopes that might happen by 2015. If not, we will keep trying. It will happen someday. I hope it will not be too late.

In the meantime the U.S. has begun building an international coalition to tackle short-lived climate pollutants like methane, black carbon, and hydrofluorocarbons (HFCs) through the U.S.-initiated "Climate and Clean Air Coalition" (CCAC). In two years, the coalition has grown from six partners to more than seventy. There efforts will not require a treaty and is spurring action on several initiatives. Best of all, even though the UN is a partner, the CCAC is truly a "coalition of the willing" that is decidedly *not* part of the UN or beholden to the difficult UNFCCC process. See http://www.unep.org/ccac/.

National Efforts — Even if we could agree on a strategy at the international level, it still would have to be approved by Congress. The Sen-

Push-back on Global Climate Change Action

Several million people work for the fossil fuel industry in this country and they don't want to accept the data if it means they may lose their jobs at some point in their careers. Fear often generates anger. There has been significant and vociferous push-back at every step of the way to a national policy on climate change. Anger on both sides often ends in stalemate, in gridlock, in disinformation campaigns (Oreskes, 2010). That is partly why it has taken decades to implement common sense solutions to our problems. It is why it has taken us fifty years to get our environmental and health regulations in place. It is why it took us fifty years to get lead out of our gasoline, even though by then we all had lead in our blood and in the soil. We have to get past the anger to where we can accept the facts and act. Many people prefer the status quo because they are doing well in it. Societal change is therefore often constrained by the tenacious power of successful corporations. They don't want to change and will continue maximizing current wealth while ignoring the long-term impacts on human health and the environment. We have to figure out a vision they can buy into as well. The more progressive corporate leaders are coming on board.

When everyone realizes that climate change is a threat to national security, and that taking action creates greater economic opportunity, the possibilities for real action become much better. We must emphasize, and publicize, all the health, disaster relief, and national security costs and include them in the price of fossil fuels. If we can do that, corporations will realize that they can lower their costs and their risks by moving away from them. The key analysis of the economics of climate change was *The Economics of Climate Change: The Stern Review* (2007). Nicholas Stern concluded that "the benefits of strong, early action considerably outweigh the costs," and that our inability to deal with global climate change "is the greatest and widest-ranging market failure ever seen."

ate has to ratify all treaties by a two-thirds majority, and that body has indicated that it will not ratify a treaty without first seeing agreement on a path toward carbon reduction to support an international treaty. Their viewpoint makes sense, but agreement on a path has so far been elusive.

Domestically this issue has been a hot potato. George H. W. Bush signed the 1992 Earth Summit (Rio de Janeiro) accord and the Senate ratified it. That was a high point. Unfortunately it was a voluntary agreement just to look at each country's emissions. Many nations have now done that, and the good news is that most have taken unilateral action to reduce their emissions. Unfortunately, George W. Bush pulled the U.S. out of the climate change treaty process ten years later. That was a low point. Then the House of Representatives passed the "Waxman-Markey Bill," the American Clean Energy and Security Act of 2009, a *cap-and-trade* approach to reducing greenhouse gases. This market-based approach to controlling pollution provided economic incentives to achieve reductions. That would have established an emissions trading plan similar to the European Union Emission Trading Scheme. It appears to be the strategy China is pursuing as well. Waxman-Markey passed with bipartisan support and many of the top leaders in Congress on both sides promoted it as the path to a cleaner energy future. Then the tides turned and the Senate, under pressure from the fossil-fuel industry, decided it was too busy to pass an energy bill that year. It has not gotten that far again. Some people think this was a failure of people who supported the bill not building the necessary grassroots support at the critical time to advance it.

Some of the largest corporations, including Exxon Mobil are now supporting a *carbon tax*—another way to reduce emissions. It would incentivize the fossil-fuel companies to reduce their carbon emissions, and it could work. We should continue to press Congress and industry to come up with a plan and enact it. Most of the biggest companies in America are projecting a future where carbon is taxed. It is just a question when. A clear sign that this tax will result in greater use of natural gas (relative to the higher carbon-emitting fuels) is that Exxon Mobil has been purchasing natural gas reserves in recent years and is now the largest supplier of natural gas in the U.S.

Without leadership or support from Congress, the Obama Administration has acted on its own in pursuing a "stealth climate policy." In 2012, it raised the Corporate Average Fuel Economy (CAFE) standards. The new standard will increase fuel economy for cars and light-duty trucks from the low twenties to the equivalent of 54.5 mpg by Model Year 2025, which will greatly reduce air pollution, greenhouse gases, and the nitrogen that pollutes our soil and water and effectively cut consumers' fuel consumption in half. It also provides the stimulus to industry to find technical fixes to the carbon pollution challenges we face here and abroad.

The administration is also enforcing restrictions on mercury and toxic air pollution that should lead to the closing of between 68 and 231 of the nation's oldest and dirtiest coal-fired power plants. Obama also issued an executive order in 2009 requiring all federal agencies to reduce their environmental impacts by 2020. The goals include reducing fleet gasoline use by 30 percent, boosting water efficiency by 26 percent, and implementing sustainability requirements for 95 percent of all federal contracts. Since the government is the country's single biggest purchaser of goods and services, this last item is expected to have significant ripple effects throughout the economy for years to come by creating better and more sustainable goods and services. The U.S. is making progress toward lowering our emissions (see the U.S. State Department's 6th Climate Action Report at http://www.state.gov/e/oes/climate/ccreport2014/) and have begun to decouple GDP and emissions growth curves.

Nevertheless, we need even clearer direction from our government and also a clear message from consumers. With governmental coordination and leadership, fossil-fuel firms will have an opportunity to adjust and participate in our move toward cleaner fuels with fewer stranded assets. Consumers could also send a message by, for example, buying electricity from cleaner fuel sources. The global marketplace will listen to what we demand. I always ask if there is a more efficient or more sustainable option when making any purchase. *The choices we make with all of our purchases will send the clearest signal to the marketplace.*

We should not think our efforts in the marketplace are not being heard. Almost all major corporations have serious efforts underway to lower their greenhouse emissions. Some of this just makes sense to them, and many do want to be seen as good corporate citizens. In fact, a recent report revealed that 49 out of 100 major corporations are well on their way to meeting their emission goals (see *Assessing Corporate Emissions Performance through the Lens of Climate Science*). These goals were based on what it would take across the board to meet the reductions necessary for avoiding a two-degree Celsius increase in global temperatures.

Local Efforts — In addition to federal and corporate actions, there are even more encouraging signs on the local level. Counties, cities, and states are making a good deal of progress on their own. The U.S. Conference of Mayors Climate Protection Agreement follows the Kyoto Protocols, which set a carbon emission reduction goal of 7 percent below 1990 levels. It has been signed by more than 1,000 cities, towns, and counties all over the country, representing over 87 percent of the U.S. population. Many signatories have exceeded those goals already. This is most encouraging, but we have to do even more.

What Should America Do? — Everyone wants to know what we should be doing as a nation to fix the problems facing the planet. I think there are four basic actions we can take.

First, we have to stop rolling the dice with our future. One of the greatest gifts we've been given is the scientific method. It is the process we've followed to create amazing technologies and solutions to our biggest problems. Congress should fund basic research on the topics discussed in this book and agree to use the findings to make decisions about our future. Much of the funding needed for essential research in this country has dried up in the budget battles of the past few years. That has put the future financial security of our country at risk. We face very difficult challenges and need the best data and our best minds focused on finding the best solutions.

Second, we have to slow and probably stop population growth. The expanding population competes for resources and keeps adding more greenhouse gases to the atmosphere. The planet and its resources are finite. If we don't stop the growth of our species before we reach the earth's carrying capacity, Mother Nature will. It is just a question of how our population growth levels off. The best approach, and one that is already achieving success in many countries, is to educate girls all around the planet and let them make their own decisions about their lives.

Third, move toward a cleaner and more sustainable energy regime. Accelerate the retirement of older and more polluting technologies and stimulate more rapid diffusion of the cleaner ones. Help developing countries adopt cleaner technologies.

Fourth, move to more sustainable thinking in business, government, and in our homes. Reward leaders whose horizons extend farther than the next election, regime change, or quarterly reporting period. Encourage a less wasteful and more sustainable ethos among all with whom we share this planet. Consumers and investors can encourage firms to adopt a longer term view by only supporting firms with a more sustainable vision (see Hawken, et al., *Natural Capitalism*).

What Each of Us Can Do — We have to lead the charge by considering the impact of their actions and slowly changing their behavior. Many Americans are stepping up to the fossil-fuel challenge, trying to make a difference by reducing their energy use and switching to alternative sources of energy. It reminds me of the stories my parents told of the individual and community efforts so widespread in this country during WWII. Many families today are buying hybrid cars, insulating their houses, and starting "victory gardens" in backyards and even front yards. People all over the world are re-engaging with their families and communities and seeking ways to reduce their footprints. We all don't have to agree on everything, but we each have to take action. Creating a healthier future will require action from us all:

We, the people, must show the way by first changing our own ways and the operational processes of the organizations we can influence. We do this by assessing our impacts and dealing with them one at a time.

Secondly we must demand more sustainable products, processes, and policies from the governments and the marketplaces of the world. We do this with our votes, our purchases, and our conversations.

Tremendous change has taken place over the last fifty years. Just think of all the progress we've made in cleaning up our air and water. Now we have more to do. We must continue to fuel the flames of knowledge, communication, and action. These steps may seem quite rational, but too many people feel they are too busy, or have higher priorities, or just do not know what to do. Here are a few ways to get started.

Assess your impact – If you would like to get a sense of what your global impact might be, I invite you to Google *carbon calculator* (and *nitrogen calculator*) and calculate your impact. Your carbon footprint is how much carbon dioxide you are dumping into the atmosphere. Your nitrogen footprint tells you how much nitrogen you dump into your local watershed. Decide how to best lower these impacts and take action. When I did this, I discovered that air travel was the major contributor to my carbon footprint. I thought reducing it would be a problem for me because I travel around the country and overseas. As it turned out, with a little more planning I reduced my impact by taking fewer trips, but making them of longer duration.

Reduce your energy use – Conduct an *energy audit* of your home and office. I spent $400. Now I understand you can get them for $100 or for free with many local incentives available today. The auditor informed me that I had a leak—an open pathway from my attic down to my utility closet where I was losing a great deal of my heat in the winter. That was a simple and inexpensive fix. Closing that leak, adding insulation in the attic, and upgrading my HVAC resulted in a 35 percent drop in energy use and in my utility bill, and a much more comfortable home.

Reducing our use of energy is the most obvious action and one from which we will all benefit immediately. Investments in energy efficiency and productivity offer a higher (and tax free) return than almost anything else we can do, and the return will go on forever. There is no reason to wait for anyone else to do this. We can do it today. The cash-strapped federal government clearly recognized as much and hired "performance-based contractors" to lower the energy use at some three hundred buildings around the country. At no cost to the taxpayer, the government will save billions on energy bills and reduce their energy use simply by making these buildings more energy-efficient. The National Association of Manufacturers (NAM) has evaluated the federal program and has called it an unqualified success (www.nam.org). My county has hired a performance-based contractor to do the same thing on all of its buildings. Similar programs have also been a big boost to private industries competing on these projects, resulting in a whole range of new technologies and services these firms are marketing to others. Since residential and commercial buildings account for 40 percent of the energy consumed in the U.S., there is a great deal of potential for significant reductions and savings in homes and businesses across the country and the world.

You can reduce your use of fossil fuels by signing up with a new electricity provider that supports the development of *wind energy* (or solar) for your home. This turned out to be cheaper than buying electricity generated by fossil fuels from my distributor. It was easy to do (I signed up on-line in about ten minutes), and it is sending a signal to the marketplace to build more wind (or solar) capacity. I also convinced scores of my friends to sign up as well. They appreciated learning how they could save money and support the development of alternative energy. In retrospect these steps were no-brainers, I just had to get up and make them happen. It is also time to buy a hybrid.

Each of us can also reduce air and water pollution with simple things like driving less and buying the more fuel-efficient cars as they become available. But can Americans change our free-wheeling love of driving and the love of big, gas-guzzling cars to save America's forests and improve our health? I would like to think so. The recent trend of young adults away from automobile ownership for economic and environmental reasons may be a good sign for the future. In fact our petroleum use has been decreasing for the past few years. Simple changes in behavior are the quickest and cheapest ways to fix many of our environmental, social, and economic problems. Besides, I find that by driving less, I have more time to enjoy my life.

Build coalitions to make changes on the state and local levels – There are probably several *non-profits* already in your area pursuing similar agendas. The biggest challenge is to get us all working together. Not all of us can be the first, but we all can be part of the legions we'll need to create a more sustainable society. Once we act, politicians will follow. Talk to them, go en masse with your associates, convince them that you are serious and represent a significant portion of the community. Find people on the inside in companies and governments that you can support.

Decades of social and market research have revealed that local actions can be very powerful. Everett Rogers's work on the "diffusion of innovations" is particularly germane to the adoption of new ideas and behaviors. The key is getting the "innovators" and "early adopters" engaged in mobilizing the "early majority," which can hit a tipping point and thereby make change inevitable. When 5 percent adopt a new idea, it becomes embedded and won't go away. When 20 percent adopt, the idea becomes unstoppable.

In addition to local non-profits there is a lot of good work being done by national and international groups. There are 1.5 million NGOs in the U.S. The most influential environmental organizations in the U.S., according to Andrew Rowell (*The Green Backlash*) are the so-called Group of Ten:

- Defenders of Wildlife,
- Environmental Defense Fund,
- National Audubon Society,
- National Wildlife Federation,
- Natural Resources Defense Council,
- Friends of the Earth,

- Izaak Walton League,
- Sierra Club,
- The Wilderness Society, and
- World Wildlife Fund

These and other groups can keep you abreast of the major issues, and your support will help them accomplish goals at a level where few of us can have impact. They provide information and lobby to get legislation and treaties passed on a national and global scale.

Don't be discouraged when you get push-back. You will. These are very complicated issues with complex solutions. Many individuals (and political leaders) think mostly about *short-term goals* and profits because they are successful and comfortable with the status quo. They are not sure that it is in their short-term economic or political interest to change. They don't see the value of taking the steps to find a safer balance, a more sustainable way to live on this planet. I have found that many people who do push back on some issues are still taking some of the right steps forward. Try to find out what they are doing and encourage them to take a few more steps. They may not agree with everything that you believe in, but I'll bet they believe in some of them.

Few realize it, but the reluctance to change a wasteful behavior is the violence of the twenty-first century. We are damaging everyone on the planet and all future generations by not adopting more sustainable practices in our homes, our workplaces, our communities, and our countries. In the big picture, what appear to be insignificant everyday inactions become dangerous when multiplied by seven billion people doing the same thing. To ensure a better present and a better future, we must all start taking steps and encouraging others to take them as well. If we don't, life on this planet will be much more difficult for all of us on the planet today and for our children in the future.

CHAPTER 14

Last Thoughts

To see the earth as it truly is, small and blue and beautiful in that eternal silence
here it floats is to see ourselves as riders on the earth together, brothers on that right
loveliness in the eternal cold — brothers who now know they are truly brothers.
—Archibald MacLeish, written upon seeing the
first picture of the Earth from space, 1968

I think back on the interstate that I fought against when I was a boy.
I was angry and felt I had few means to resist that foreign invasion—an
invasion to the only world I knew, our farm. In coming to terms with
that loss, I learned how people feel when they lose something they love.
The pain is very real. It is always best to take steps ahead of time to
prevent those losses.

Since that time, I have also learned that interstate highways offer
us a lot more than just getting around faster. They let us expand our
horizons. They help us understand how we are all connected and how
society and nature all fit together. By getting outside and visiting more
of our country, we certainly develop a much greater appreciation for
other people and other places. We discover places, people, and ideas
that become important to our own growth into responsible members of
a larger society.

It is as members of this larger society that we have the greatest opportunity to change things. To do this, we first must understand how
things work, and then we need to see how they could work better. This
is our homework—to understand the present and to envision a better
tomorrow. Then comes the hard part—building a movement that will
achieve our dreams. I believe this is where most of us fail. We don't

make the effort, we don't shoulder the responsibility to take action, to lead the way, to set the example, to become the champion. We need more champions—in families, in communities, in organizations, in companies, in government. We need you to be a champion.

The realization that we need to act is why we are starting to see the most successful businesses, governments, and organizations adopting sustainability planning as a best management practice. They know that to succeed in the future they will have to find ways to balance economic, social, and environmental issues in all of their decisions and actions. Most of the Fortune 100 firms now have sustainability plans, directors, and annual reports. Their progress is tracked in their Annual Reports and by the Dow Jones Sustainability Index. That strategy has paid off for them. Nationwide we are seeing widespread adoption of systematic processes for balancing competing but equally necessary agendas (see Savitz, The Triple Bottom Line). There are numerous groups dedicated to this goal (e.g., the International Society of Sustainable Professionals).

The federal government has also begun pursuing rational sustainable initiatives over the past decade. Presidents Bush and Obama have each issued executive orders directing all departments of the federal government to have department-wide sustainability plans. The Department of Defense has been a real leader in this regard, realizing the necessity of efficient and sustainable operations in all the theaters in which they operate. The CIA is constantly assessing the potential impacts of global climate change on the future security of our nation and the sustainability of water, fuel, and other natural resources around the globe.

States, cities, and counties are also pursuing sustainability initiatives. Many are ad hoc efforts, but an increasing number of localities have adopted specific goals and plans. They have implemented programs that are lowering energy bills, creating alternative sources of energy, reducing waste sent to landfills, reducing water usage, and evaluating the life-cycle costs of their purchases. It all comes down to common sense business decisions in the planning for the future.

Unfortunately, some individuals and organizations disagree with this approach and are pushing back on these best management practices. A nearby county fired their sustainability staff and gave up on their sustainability initiatives when a new county council took over. One councilperson claimed that sustainability was a communist plot and cited a UN document that had been written to describe development options in third world countries. Contrast that intransigence with our county. By pursuing a whole range of sustainability objectives, we were able to save millions of dollars in energy costs, while reducing our carbon footprint and building our economy. Systematic change has been very good for us.

I wonder why some people act as if there is no problem when their actions damage others and the environment where we live. Don't they have favorite places they want to protect? Have they not seen how human folly has destroyed so many places and even whole civilizations in the past? Are they not aware of the pandemics, the blights, the famines, the droughts, and the social collapses that our ancestors endured because of the overuse and mismanagement of their natural resources? Do they not realize how fragile our existence is on this thin veneer of life on the surface of our Earth? These are realities that threaten our existence. Well-planned course corrections are not to be feared; in most successful businesses they are the normal process for achieving a goal.

If you think that calling life on this planet "fragile" is an overstated literary metaphor, I suggest taking a ride on the interstate. Many roads are cut right through ridges, hills, and mountains. When we pass through these cross-sections of the planet, we can see how thin the veneer of life really is. The trees and grasses and houses of our living world literally sit on only a few inches or feet of organic enriched soil, and then there is the inorganic rock that makes up the other 99.9 percent of our planet. That lifeless rock continues downward from crust to mantle to molten core and then out the other side. Life is but a small fragment of reality on this rock hurtling through space—it is improbable that we will find another one quite like it close enough to make any real difference to us. Life is fragile, and we are threatening it from every side. We will have to work to stay in balance with the rest of nature or we are going to lose a wide variety of life support systems currently provided by nature for free. These services will not be easy, or cheap, and they may not even be possible to replace.

As I sit along the banks of the Potomac, Mississippi, or Columbia rivers, watching the majestic flow of the water, I realize that these mighty rivers will flow for many years beyond the age of man. The era of our attempt at dominion over nature will end, and man will lose. The earth will do its best to recover; it will be changed, but it will go on, and life will go on as well. In the long run, human impacts will be felt the most by humans. The good things we do will benefit us, and the bad things we do will cause human suffering. The suffering might come quickly, or it might come slowly. Like the frog in the proverbial pan on the stove, we may never know that we are being slowly cooked, that the quality of our lives is being degraded, and that our security is being eroded.

The environmental movement is all about restoring the health of our communities, managing the wise use of our natural resources, and improving our lives on the planet. Yes, many people are rightly concerned about what we are doing to other species. At the same time, when the attention is focused on a spotted owl, there are some who say that environmental extremists are more concerned about an owl than about humans. I wonder if there were ever any coalminers who spoke that way about a canary?

A broader view of environmentalism takes in both camps. We must get back in balance with nature to save not just humans but the other species and resources on which we are dependent. That is why many of our environmental laws and regulations are written "to protect human health and the environment." By achieving that goal we are strengthening our security and improving our lives.

My efforts to push, drag, or inspire myself and others back into balance with nature come from fear. I am afraid that when I am on my last legs I will be watching my children and grandchildren struggling. To see them struggling in a world that we all could have prevented would be my version of hell. I don't want that to happen.

My hope is that everyone alive today will work together to restore the places we love and in the process learn about the other great places in America. Children can inspire their parents. People in the workplace can make their organizations more sustainable. People working at home can make their communities more sustainable. I hope that the Baby Boomers will rekindle some of the spirit that drove them into the streets fifty years ago to demand a better future for our society. A lot was accomplished during their normal working years. Now many of them are embarking on encore careers. I hope they will devote the rest of their lives, energy, and wealth toward this cause, the cause Paul Hawken (Blessed Unrest) claims is the greatest social movement of all time.

Some of us were fortunate enough to have found a special place to visit when we were young; some of us found these places later in our lives. If you have not yet found one, then go outside today and fall in love with nature for the first time. Sometimes the place we love is small or it may be as vast as a watershed, as long as a mighty river, it may be as widespread as a way of life that is slowly slipping through our fingers. I believe our best strategy for the future is to ignite that love affair in every one of us, so that there will be seven billion places on this planet (Earth's current population) that someone is taking the time to restore and protect. Some will not be saved—it is simply too late, we have waited too long. But that is no reason not to save the places we can.

Johann Wolfgang von Goethe recognized that some magical quality befalls us when we take action. It has a life of its own. We may prepare all of our lives for something great to happen, but if we don't act, it seldom does. If you are concerned on what to do first, go back to the places you love and take the people you love with you. Do what it takes to save those places for future generations. As you focus on the places you love think about the bigger picture. We have to lead and demand that the government and the markets follow. They must provide us with better and more sustainable products, policies, and performance. We don't have to be perfect to make a difference, but we do have to act.

So go change something about your life. It is all up to you. After all, the struggle for America is not just a battle between people and ideologies, it is the struggle in our hearts and minds that is manifested in the choices we make every day.

A Tribute to
Stewards of the Past

We owe a great deal to past (and present) visionaries who spoke of a special place that centered them and made them who they were. We have them to thank for the preservation of many wonderful places and for their ability to move us all toward living in balance with nature.

Edward Abbey (1927–1989) was one of America's most dedicated environmentalists. Born in Pennsylvania, he is best known for his passionate defense of the deserts of America's Southwest. After working for the National Park Service in what is now Arches National Park in Utah, Abbey wrote Desert Solitaire, one of the seminal works of the environmental movement. His later book, *The Monkey Wrench Gang,* gained notoriety as an inspiration for radical environmental action.

Wendell Berry (1934–) is a prolific and thoughtful American novelist, poet, environmental activist, cultural critic, and farmer. He grounds much of his work with stories about his home state of Kentucky. His parents' families had farmed in Henry County, Kentucky, for five generations. He believes strongly in the importance of maintaining a connection to the land and developing a sense of place for centering modern man. In the 1970s and early 1980s, he was a contributor and the editor of the Rodale Press, including its publication, *Organic Gardening and Farming.* He is an outspoken activist on the Farm Bill, coal-fired plants, and war.

David Brower (1912–2000) of Berkeley, California, has been associated with wilderness preservation since he began mountain climbing as a young man. He scaled many of the peaks in the Sierras and was appointed the Sierra Club's first executive director in 1952; over the next seventeen years, membership grew from 2,000 to 77,000, and they won numerous environmental victories. When his confrontational style got him fired, he went on to found the Friends of the Earth, the Earth Island Institute, and the League of Conservation Voters.

Rachel Carson (1907–1964) was an American aquatic biologist in the U.S. Bureau of Fisheries. She later became a conservationist and a full-time nature writer and published a series of books which are credited with advancing the global environmental movement: *Under the Sea Wind* (1941), *The Sea Around Us* (1951; won the U.S. National Book Award), *The Edge of the Sea* (1955), and *Silent Spring* (1962). All were bestsellers. *Silent Spring* was viciously attacked by the chemical industry, but her work was supported by others and led to a reversal in national pesticide policy and the banning of DDT. She grew up in Pennsylvania, lived in Maryland, and vacationed in New England.

Verplanck Colvin (1847–1920) was a lawyer, author, illustrator, and topographical engineer who spent summers from 1866 to 1869 exploring the Adirondacks and later published articles about his travels. He was contracted to survey the area, and his love and knowledge of upstate New York led to the creation of New York's Forest Preserve and the Adirondack Park. Claiming that deforestation of the park would damage the highly valuable Erie Canal, he not only surveyed the area he thought should be preserved but argued for years that the Adirondacks should be saved as a park. During his explorations he discovered the source of the Hudson River (Lake Tear-of-the-Clouds) and climbed many of its peaks, including Mount Marcy.

Ralph Waldo Emerson (1803–1882) of Concord, Massachusetts, was not only America's foremost philosopher but the father of the Transcendental Movement, which led many to alter the way they thought of themselves and the world. He claimed that by observing all the changes in nature we should realize that we can change ourselves and transcend the situation into which we were born. He was an ardent individualist and neighbor and mentor to Henry David Thoreau.

James Hansen (1941–) from Denison, Iowa, received a PhD in astrophysics and has now been at the forefront of global warming research for close to thirty years. His work as head of NASA's Goddard Institute for Space Studies has resulted in some of the most substantial proof of the dangers of global warming. He has testified before Congress, taken on the George W. Bush administration's censorship of science, and has been one of the most vocal scientists opposing the propaganda campaigns of those who deny the reality of global warming.

Ferdinand Hayden (1829–1927) was a geologist, paleontologist, and medical doctor from Massachusetts. Encouraged to go west by James Hall, State Geologist of New York, he led many expeditions through the Rocky Mountains and mapped the Yellowstone area as head of the U.S. Geological Survey projects in the territories. His reports inspired the creation of Yellowstone National Park and interest in the West. Hayden Valley in Yellowstone is named for him, as is Hayden, Colorado.

Aldo Leopold (1887–1948). Initially from Iowa where he was an outdoorsman from an early age, Leopold attended Yale Forestry School, served as a forester in the Southwest, and accepted a position at the University of Wisconsin–Madison. He was the nation's foremost expert on wildlife management. He developed a wilderness ecological ethic that replaced the concept of dominion over nature and rejected the utilitarianism of conservationists such as Gifford Pinchot and Theodore Roosevelt. Leopold founded the Wilderness Society with Bob Marshall and others. After buying eighty acres in Sand County, Wisconsin, which was once a forested region but had been logged, swept by repeated fires, overgrazed by dairy cattle, and left barren, he put his theories into practice and later wrote *A Sand County Almanac* (1949).

Stephen Mather (1867–1930) was from California and became a successful businessman in New York and Chicago (he created the slogan "Twenty Mule Team Borax" for his product). He retired in his forties to pursue his passion and love of nature and in 1916 led a publicity campaign to create an agency to manage our national parks. He then served as the first director of the National Park Service within the Department of the Interior from 1917 to 1929. A friend of John Muir and a member of the Sierra Club, he was instrumental in improving access to the parks by road and rail. During his tenure he molded the NPS into one of the most respected arms of the government.

Benton McKaye (1879–1975) was raised in Connecticut and studied forestry at Harvard. He worked for various federal agencies and was one of the founders of the Wilderness Society. He envisioned and is considered the originator of the Appalachian Trail (AT), an idea he presented in a 1921 article entitled "An Appalachian Trail: A Project in Regional Planning," published in the *Journal of the American Institute of Architects*.

John Muir (1838–1914). In 1849, the Muir family emigrated to the United States from Scotland. Until he entered the University of Wisconsin in 1861, Muir worked from dawn to dusk on his family farm near Portage, roaming the fields and woods whenever he was allowed a short period away from the plow. Muir later wrote that his strenuous years in Wisconsin's outdoors prepared him for his later wilderness ramblings. He then wandered, eventually settling in California, where he worked for many years trying to save as much of the Sierras as he could. He was a founder of the Sierra Club and served as its president or twenty years. His writings are credited with the creation of the National Park System.

Rev. William Murray (1840–1904), also known as Adirondack Murray, was the author of *Adventures in the Wilderness; or, Camp-Life in the Adirondacks*, which popularized those mountains. Due to the popularity of his book, his public speaking and his extensive writing, he became known as the "Father of the Outdoor Movement." He promoted New York's north woods as a place to improve your health and spirit by spending time in the wilderness.

Gaylord Nelson (1916–2005) was from Wisconsin but is best remembered for his call for an Environmental Teach-In that became the first Earth Day in 1970. After returning from service in the Pacific during World War II, Nelson began a career as a politician and environmental activist that was to last the rest of his life. As governor of Wisconsin, he created an Outdoor Recreation Acquisition Program that saved about one million acres of park land. He was instrumental in the development of a national trails system (including the Appalachian Trail), and helped pass the Wilderness Act, the Clean Air Act, the Clean Water Act, and other landmark environmental legislation. He was a staunch supporter of environmentalism, conservation, civil rights, and small business issues and was an early critic of the Vietnam War. He advocated for and passed the first bill requiring the disclosure of side effects in labeling on a pharmaceutical drug.

Gifford Pinchot (1865–1946) grew up in Connecticut and went to Yale, studied forestry in Europe, worked at the Biltmore Estate in North Carolina, and became the first head of the United States Forest Service from 1905 until his firing in 1910. He created the concept of scientific management of forests to optimize their value. As a conservationist he was sometimes at odds with the preservationists like Muir, but he was able to work closely with President Theodore Roosevelt to set aside tens of millions of acres and have them classified as national forests. He later advised Franklin D. Roosevelt as well, in the major tree plantings that took place during the Depression.

John Wesley Powell (1834–1902) grew up in the Midwest, spending much of his free time outside collecting samples and becoming a teacher of natural science. He lost most of his right arm at Shiloh but returned to duty. After the war he studied natural science and geology and led several expeditions down the Colorado River. He later became the head of the U.S. Geological Survey. His expeditions in the West convinced him that its lack of wter and rainfall made it unsuitable for agriculture, but his ideas were dismissed until the terrible Dust Bowl of the 1930s.

Franklin D. Roosevelt (1882–1945). As president he set up the Civilian Conservation Corps and the Tree Army headed by General Douglas MacArthur. They employed millions of men, planted millions of trees and built hundreds of trails and shelters during the Great Depression.

Theodore Roosevelt (1858–1915) was brought up in New York City. After losing his wife, he took off to explore the West. He became quite the outdoorsman and as U.S. president worked closely with fellow outdoorsman, Gifford Pinchot, to set aside tens of millions of acres of land as national forests.

Henry David Thoreau (1817–1862) lived in Concord, Massachusetts, and wrote extensively about traveling or living in the woods. He captured the essence of future environmental movements in his books, *A Week on the Concord and Merrimack Rivers* (1849), *Walden* (1854), and *The Maine Woods* (1864). Though never perceived as successful during his forty-five-year struggle living an "authentic life," he became much more widely appreciated many years later when the likes of Leo Tolstoy, Mahatma Ghandi, and Martin Luther King Jr. celebrated his writings, especially *Civil Disobedience* (1849).

Izaak Walton (1594–1683) lived in Stratford, England, and is often considered to be the father of conservation. In 1653 he published one of the first works on the topic, *The Compleat Angler,* a celebration of the art and spirit of fishing in prose and verse in which two new companions, an angler and a falconer, each share the joys of their sport. The Izaak Walton League of America is one of the oldest conservation groups in the country.

Howard Zahniser (1906–1964) of Pennsylvania, was the environmental activist most responsible for the creation and passage of the Wilderness Act of 1964. In 1956, while working with the Wilderness Society, he drafted what would become the Wilderness Act. It required the last eight years of his life, multiple rewrites, eighteen public hearings, and personally lobbying nearly every congressman. Sadly, he died of heart failure a few months prior to President Lyndon Johnson signing it into law, but thanks to his hard work, over one hundred million acres of land are permanently protected.

References

Assessing Corporate Emissions Performance through the Lens of Climate Science: December 2013. A Collaborative Study between Climate Counts and the Center for Sustainable Organizations. Available at www.climatecounts. org.

Abbey, Edward. *The Monkey Wrench Gang*. Lippincott, Williams & Wilkins, 1975.

Ahern, M. M., et al. "The association between mountaintop mining and birth defects among live births in central Appalachia, 1996–2003." *Environmental Research, 111* (2011): 838–46.

Ambrose, Stephen E., *Undaunted Courage*. New York: Simon & Schuster, 1996.

Barry, John M. *Rising Tide: The Great Mississippi Flood of 1927 and How It Changed America*. New York: Simon & Schuster, 1997.

Barth, John. *The Sot-Weed Factor*. New York: Doubleday, 1960.

Basso, Bruno, Anthony D. Kendall, and David W. Hyndman. "The Future of Agriculture Over the Ogallala Aquifer: Solutions to Grow Crops More Efficiently with Limited Water." *Earth's Future*, Volume 1, No. 1 (December 2013): 39–41.

Berry, Thomas. *The Dream of the Earth*. Sierra Club Books, 1988.

Berry, Wendell. *That Distant Land: The Collected Stories*. Washington, D.C.: Shoemaker and Hoard, 2004.

Boone, G. M. *A Wassataquoik History*. Presque Isle, Maine: Northeast Publishing Company, 2011.

Carson, Rachael. *The Edge of the Sea*. Boston: Houghton Mifflin, 1955.

———. *Silent Spring*. Boston: Houghton Mifflin, 1962.

Coleman, Eliot. *The New Organic Grower: A Master's Manual of Tools and Techniques for the Home and Market Gardener.* Revised and Expanded Edition. White River Junction, Vt.: Chelsea Green, 1995.

Cronin, William B. *The Disappearing Islands of the Chesapeake*. Baltimore: Johns Hopkins University Press, 2005.

Crosby, Alfred W. Jr. *The Columbian Exchange: Biological and Cultural Consequences of 1492, 30th Anniversary Edition*. Westport, Conn: Praeger Publishers, 2003.

Diamond, Jared. *Collapse: How Societies Choose to Fail or Succeed*, Revised Edition. New York: Penguin, 2011.

Dorothy, Olivia. "Restoring America's River." In *Outdoor America*, No. 2, 2013.

Egan, Timothy. *The Big Burn: Teddy Roosevelt and the Fire that Saved America*. Boston: Houghton Mifflin Harcourt, 2009.

———. *The Worst Hard Time: The Untold Story of Those Who Survived the Great American Dust Bowl*. Boston: Houghton Mifflin, 2006.

Epstein, Paul R., Jonathan J. Buonocore, Kevin Eckerle, Michael Hendryx, Benjamin M. Stout III, Richard Heinberg, Richard W. Clapp, Beverly May, Nancy L. Reinhart, Melissa M. Ahern, Samir K. Doshi, Leslie Glustrom. "Full Cost Accounting for the Life Cycle of Coal. *Annals of the New York Academy of Sciences*, vol. 1219, February 2011, Ecological Economics Reviews, pp. 73–98.

Friedman, Thomas L. *Hot, Flat, and Crowded: Why We Need a Green Revolution—And How It Can Renew America*. New York: Farrar, Straus and Giroux, 2008.

Greenlee, John and Saxon Holt. *The American Meadow Garden: Creating a Natural Alternative to the Traditional Lawn*. Portland, Ore.: Timber Press, 2009.

Hardin, Garrett. "Tragedy of the Commons." *Science,* vol. 162, no. 3859 (December 13, 1968): 1243–48.

Hawken, Paul. *Blessed Unrest*. New York: Viking Press, 2007.

Hawken, Paul, Amory Lovins, and L. Hunter Lovins. *Natural Capitalism: Creating the Next Industrial Revolution*. Boston: Little, Brown and Sons, 1999.

Jenkins, McKay. *What's Gotten into Us? Staying Healthy in a Toxic World*. New York: Random House, 2011.

Kaplan, Rachel and Stephen Kaplan. *The Experience of Nature: A Psychological Perspective*. New York: Cambridge University Press, 1989.

Kaplan, Rachel, Stephen Kaplan, Robert L. Ryan. *With People in Mind: Design and Management of Everyday Nature*. Washington, D.C.: Island Press, 1998.

Kingsolver, Barbara. *Animal, Vegetable, Miracle: A Year of Food Life*. New York: HarperCollins, 2007.

Longfellow, Henry Wadsworth. *The Village Blacksmith*, 1840.

———. *The Song of Hiawatha*. Boston, 1855.

Louv, Richard. *Last Child in the Woods: Saving Our Children from Nature-Deficit Disorder*. Chapel Hill, N.C.: Algonquin Books of Chapel Hill, 2008.

———. *The Nature Principle: Human Restoration and the End of Nature-Deficit Disorder*. Chapel Hill, N.C.: Algonquin Books of Chapel Hill, 2011.

MacLean, Norman. *A River Runs Through it.* Chicago: University of Chicago Press, 1976.

McGill, Frederick T. Jr., and Virginia F. McGill. *Something Like a Star.* Star Island Corporation, 1989.

McNeill, J. R. *Something New Under the Sun: An Environmental History of the Twentieth-century World.* New York: W. W. Norton & Company, 2000.

Michener, James. *Centennial.* New York: Random House, 1974.

Miller, Richard G. and Steven R. Sorrell. "The Future of Oil Supply." *Philosophical Transactions of the Royal Society A,* January 13, 2014, vol. 372, no. 2006.

Monbiot, George. *Feral: Searching for Enchantment on the Frontiers of Rewilding.* New York: Penguin Books, 2013.

Montgomery, David R. *Dirt: The Erosion of Civilizations.* Berkeley: University of California Press, 2007.

Muller, Richard A. *Energy for Future Presidents: The Science Behind the Headlines.* New York: W. W Norton & Company, 2012.

Murray, Richard C. *Tree Biology Notebook: An Introduction to the Science and Ecology of Trees.* Silver Spring, Md.: STL Pub., 2011.

Murray, William H. H. *Adventures in the Wilderness: or Camp-Life in the Adirondacks in 1869.*

Oreskes, Naomi and Erik M. M. Conway. *Merchants of Doubt: How a Handful of Scientists Obscured the Truth on Issues from Tobacco Smoke to Global Warming.* New York: Bloomsbury Press, 2010.

Pimentel, David, Rodolfo Zuniga, and Doug Morrison. "Update on the Environmental and Economic Costs Associated with Alien-invasive Species in the United States." *Ecological Economics* 52 (2005): 273–88.

PlanHoward 2030, 2013, Department of Planning and Zoning Howard County Maryland. www.planhoward.org.

Pollan, Michael. *The Omnivore's Dilemma: The Natural History of Four Meals.* New York: Penguin Press, 2006.

Preston, Richard. *The Wild Trees.* New York: Random House, 2008.

Prochaska, J. O., and Norcross, J. C. *Systems of Psychotherapy: A Transtheoretical Analysis,* Sixth Edition. Pacific Grove, Calif.: Brooks-Cole, 2006.

Raffa, K. F., B. H. Aukema, B. J. Bentz, A. L. Carroll, J. A. Hicke, M. G. Turner, and W. H. Romme. "Cross-scale Drivers of Natural Disturbances Prone to Anthropogenic Amplification: The Dynamics of Bark Beetle Eruptions. *BioScience* 58 (2008): 501–17.

Raffa, K. F., E. N. Powell, and P. A. Townsend. "Temperature-driven Range

Expansion of an Irruptive Insect Heightened by Weakly Coevolved Plant Defenses." *Proceedings of the National Academy of Sciences,* 110 (2013): 2193–98.

Rogers, Everett M. *Diffusion of Innovations.* New York: Simon and Schuster, 2003.

Rowell, Andrew. *Green Backlash: Global Subversion of the Environmental Movement.* New York: Routledge, 1996.

Rutkow, Eric. *American Canopy.* New York: Scribner, 2012.

Savitz, Andrew W. *The Triple Bottom Line.* San Francisco: Wiley, 2006.

Schueler, Thomas. *The Clipping Point: Turf Cover Estimates for the Chesapeake Bay Watershed and Management Implications.* Chesapeake Stormwater Network, Technical Bulletin No. 8. 2010.

Sharp, Henry K. *The Patapsco River Valley: Cradle of the Industrial Revolution in Maryland.* Baltimore: Maryland Historical Society, 2001.

Sherwonit, Bill. *Denali: A Literary Anthology.* Seattle: The Mountaineers Books, 2000.

Steinbeck, John. *Grapes of Wrath, 1939.*

Stern, Nicholas. *The Economics of Climate Change: The Stern Review.* Academic Press, 2007.

Tallamy, Doug. *Bringing Nature Home: How You Can Sustain Wildlife with Native Plants.* Portland OR: Timber Press, 2007.

Tillman, Ned. *The Chesapeake Watershed: A Sense of Place and a Call to Action.* Baltimore: Chesapeake Book Company, 2009.

Twain, Mark, *Adventures of Huckleberry* Finn, 1884.

Worster, Donald. *A River Running West: The Life of John Wesley Powell.* New York: Oxford University Press, 2002.

Yeoman, Barry. "Rebel Towns." *The Nation,* January 16, 2013.

Glossary

Acid Mine Drainage – When coal or mine tailings are exposed to air and water, the metal sulfides (e.g., pyrite) within the rock oxidizes and generates low pH or acidic waters. These waters can leach metals (nickel, copper, lead, arsenic, etc.) out of other rocks and can contaminate water supplies.

Acid Rain – Acid rain is the result of emissions of sulfur dioxide and nitrogen oxide (from coal and oil fired power plants and car exhaust) that react with the water molecules in the atmosphere to produce acids. It can damage plants, aquatic animals, and infrastructure.

Cap and Trade – An environmental policy tool that places a mandatory cap on emissions while giving polluters flexibility in how they comply. It is designed to reward innovation, efficiency, and early action and provides strict environmental accountability without inhibiting economic growth. The Acid Rain Program was very successful in reducing the amount of sulfur that was released into the atmosphere.

Carbon Tax – A tax imposed on releases of carbon dioxide (CO_2), which is emitted largely through the combustion of fossil fuels from electricity production, heating, and transportation. The tax will start low and rise over time to encourage producers to reduce the amount of carbon they produce.

Carrying Capacity – The maximum number of organisms of a particular species that can be supported indefinitely by an ecosystem. Some scientists believe that the human population has exceeded the earth's ability to support it.

Climate Change – can be a natural event but it has accelerated with the rising concentrations of man-made greenhouse gases that have entered our atmosphere. Changes in patterns of precipitation and rising sea levels will have much greater impact on humankind than the higher temperatures alone.

Commons – the cultural and natural resources available to a group.

These may include natural elements such as air, water, pastureland, and a livable environment—or man-made features such as highways or the Internet. These resources are held in common, not owned privately.

Fly Ash – Waste product from coal combustion.

Global Climate Change – according to NASA, "global climate change" is the more scientifically accurate and holistic term for describing all the impacts of global warming.

Global Warming – is the correct term for referring to the increasing temperatures at the earth's surface that correlate with the increasing amount of CO_2 that man has pumped into the atmosphere.

Greenhouse Gases – Gases produced from the burning of fossil fuels and forests that contribute to the warming of the atmosphere (the greenhouse effect). These gases include carbon dioxide, carbon monoxide, methane, nitrous oxide, sulfur hexafluoride, water, ozone and others.

Hydrofracturing or Fracking – A process of enhancing oil, gas, or water production from a well. It involves pumping large volumes of liquid, chemicals, and sand down the hole until the rock formations crack open. The sand tends to hold the fractures open so that more liquid can be extracted.

Locavore – Someone who buys food from locally grown sources.

Mountaintop Removal – A mining method that removes the tops of mountains in order to more easily extract the coal seams.

Rain Garden – A garden designed to capture rain flowing off impervious surfaces and allow it to filter down into the ground, where it can recharge groundwater tables. Usually the bottom of the depression is filled with more permeable soils and plants that have a deep root structure and which absorb higher volumes of water.

Stormwater Runoff – Rainwater that falls on impervious surfaces and does not filter into the ground. It usually follows gravity and washes downhill into streams or stormwater drains carrying pollution from our yards and roads.

Tragedy of the Commons – When the use of the commons is not regulated and one or more parties over-exploits the common resources in a non-sustainable manner. This causes the collapse of the resource (Hardin, 1968).

Trophic Cascade – These occur when predators in a food chain suppress the abundance of or alter the behavior of their prey, thereby releasing the next lower trophic level from predation. A food chain can also be disrupted by removal of a predator.

Watershed – That area of land in which all the rain that falls on it drains into a single body of water.